CAPTAIN J. A. BROOKS

TEXAS RANGER

Captain James Abijah Brooks.

Courtesy Beverly Brewton and Brooks Family, Pasadena, Texas.

CAPTAIN J. A. BROOKS

TEXAS RANGER

PAUL N. SPELLMAN

Number 3 in the Frances B. Vick Series

UNT PRESS

University of North Texas Press
Denton, Texas

10 9 8 7 6 5 4 3 2 1

Permissions:
University of North Texas Press
P.O. Box 311336
Denton, TX 76203-1336

The paper used in this book meets the minimum requirements of the American National Standard for Permanence of Paper for Printed Library Materials, z39.48.1984. Binding materials have been chosen for durability.

Library of Congress Cataloging-in-Publication Data

Spellman, Paul N.
Captain J.A. Brooks, Texas Ranger / Paul N. Spellman.
p. cm. -- (Frances B. Vick series ; no. 3)
Includes bibliographical references and index.
ISBN-13: 978-1-57441-227-7 (cloth : alk. paper)
ISBN-10: 1-57441-227-2 (cloth : alk. paper)
1. Brooks, James Abijah, 1855-1944. 2. Texas Rangers--Biography. I. Title.
HV7911.B76S74 2007
363.2092--dc22
[B]

2006032376

Captain J. A. Brooks, Texas Ranger is
Number 3 in the Frances B. Vick Series

Cover illustration by Mark Leifrig

Contents

List of Illustrations

Acknowledgments

One of the pleasures and privileges of doing historical research is communicating and working with other professionals in the fields: librarians, archivists, and authors. First among these persons for Texas history is the staff at the Texas State Library Archives in Austin. Donaly Brice is a steadfast fount of wisdom and a good friend who is always ready to help find those miniscule bits and pieces that an author overlooks or cannot find.

In Paris, Bourbon County, Kentucky, Mrs. Kenney Roseberry at the John Fox, Jr., Genealogical Library helped me a great deal getting started on the Brooks family heritage there. Sharon Taylor in the Bourbon County clerk's office was also more than helpful and I appreciate her extra effort on my behalf. Bill Penn of Paris provided important details on the movement of troops in Bourbon County during the Civil War.

In Texas, Mrs. Lourdes Cantu and Ernesto Vecchio in Falfurrias, Rodney Crouch at the Southwest regional offices of the National Archives in Ft. Worth, Mickel Yantz at the Cherokee Heritage Center in Tahlequah, Oklahoma, Tom Robinson at the Brownsville Public Library, Jerry Hoke at the Wharton County Junior College library, and Antonio Martinez at the Kerrville Library proved most helpful to me along the way. I am indebted to Bill Stein at the Nesbitt Memorial Library in Columbus who generously contributed time and information on the Reese-Townsend "feud." My friend and colleague Dr. Andres Tijerina at Austin Community College helped me sort through items related to South Texas ranching and the Garza War, and is always supportive of my endeavors; so too Harold Weiss and Robert Utley made valuable contributions.

The staffs at the Center for American History (Barker Texas History Center) in Austin and the Ft. Bend County George Memorial Library genealogy archives in Richmond, and the reference librarians at the Texas Room of the downtown Houston Public Library, gave me aid as I looked for Captain Brooks. Fred Romanski at the National Archives in College Park, Maryland, helped me sort through the presidential pardon papers located there. And I should mention the aid of reference librarians at the Clayton Genealogical Library in Houston, and those at public libraries and historical societies in Cooke, Collin, Sabine, Ector, and Denton counties, Texas. My visits with the reference staff at the library in Alice proved especially lucrative.

The friendly folks at the Heritage Museum and Texas Ranger Room in Falfurrias gave me a personal tour through their collection of Brooks memorabilia, and graciously allowed me to take photographs of the several items pertaining to this book. When I went looking for the burial site of Virginia Willborn Brooks, the staff at the Holmgren Mortuary in Alice pulled a wonderful old map of the Alice City Cemetery–hand drawn on now dilapidated cotton fabric, where we located the captain's wife's grave.

In the summer of 2004 I introduced myself to Beverly Brewton, the captain's granddaughter, in Falfurrias, and have had several wonderful visits with her and her daughter Suzanne Montgomery, who resides in Pasadena, Texas, where Mrs. Brewton has since moved. They have in their keeping the captain's memoirs and files, photographs, newspaper clippings that he kept, letters and personal notes, his last will and testament from 1939, and the presidential pardon signed by President Cleveland in 1887. They have been so generous to allow me to rummage through all of the papers and use many of the photographs for this biography, and I happily dedicate this book to them.

Ever grateful for the support of my family–Matt and Paula, Kathleen, and the extended kin, colleagues, and friends who encourage me along the way–I am humbled once more to think how much they give to me while I work on these projects.

INTRODUCTION

Captain Brooks stood at the edge of the slightly rolling hills that spread across to the horizon, his eyes fixed on the vibrant colors of the autumn sunset. A slight rustle of wind pressed gently against the field grass. Brooks let his mind wander to earlier that same day, when a wonderful opportunity had been handed him. To be captain of such a company of men was a fond dream, a wish now granted after only a relatively few years in the service. At age thirty-three, the command came to him long before many would have expected it, although those with whom he had served never doubted that his tenacity, his courage, and his bent to organization would be rewarded in this way.

His life of barely three decades had already been a full and adventurous, if not completely satisfying, one. Born far away from where he now stood, the young officer allowed his memory to retrace some of the events that he had witnessed, new lands to which he had traveled, battles fought and won. He had been a restless one all his life, never content to stay in one place or one job. But every time he moved on he seemed to find a new challenge and, having met each one, emerged better and stronger for it. He had left some family behind but always found near or distant cousins at the next stop of his life's journey.

And the newly commissioned captain looked into his future as he stared at the reddening sun. A fascination with the law, both its interpretation and its enforcement, made him wonder if another career still awaited him. Law and order were solid principles to which he adhered, and his trek thus far only reinforced that commitment. Perhaps, when he finished this turn in law enforcement, a judge's bench would be next.

The quiet, contemplative moment passed, it was time for the captain–Captain Thomas Brooks of the Massachusetts Bay Colony foot soldiers–to get back to work.

★

Thomas Brooks, born in Suffolk, England, in 1610, and the great-great-great-great grandfather of James Abijah Brooks, lived out a life remarkably similar to the young man who followed 250 years later. The British colonist was promoted to captain of the foot soldiers' company at age thirty-three, the same age that J. A. Brooks became captain of the Texas Rangers in 1888. Six years later, Thomas sat on the colonial bench as Deputy to the General Court of Massachusetts, a position he held for much of the next two decades.[1] His descendant was a Texas county judge for twenty-eight years following his retirement from Ranger service. Both men were known for their dedication to the law and to the land they kept safe and secured.

This is the story of James Brooks, born and bred in Kentucky during the Civil War and Reconstruction years, restlessly moving to the American frontier as a young man and thence to Texas, a cattle driver, sheepherder, miner, and a Texas Ranger at age twenty-seven. His rise to the captaincy, for those days, bordered on meteoric. But his skills with a pistol and rifle, his leadership qualities evidenced over and over, and his perseverance–the Brooks family's motto on their English coat of arms–elevated him above others.

Captain Brooks served eighteen years in command of Company F of the Frontier Battalion and Company A of the restructured Ranger Force. And after two terms in the Texas state legislature, during which he helped secure the creation of a South Texas county that would then bear his name, "the Captain," as he always preferred to be called, served that county faithfully as judge until illness forced his retirement at the venerable age of eighty-four.

There has been some confusion over recent years regarding Brooks's first name, James. Almost every book and article written in the last several decades refers to him as *John* Abijah Brooks, although unmistakably his name is James, and his descendants never heard of his even being nicknamed John. The confusion seems to stem from two sources, one of which is the predominance of Brooks himself using his initials J. A. not only in his signature but in nearly every record in his own hand. Many of his colleagues and associates, all of whom called him "Captain," may not have even known his first name.

A prime example of this and a second source of confusion is W. W. Sterling's autobiography, which has been utilized as an important resource for Ranger history of Brooks's era. Sterling knew Brooks, respected him as a mentor and inspiration for his own career, always addressed him respectfully as "Captain," but calls him John throughout his book. Sterling's *Trails and Trials of a Texas Ranger* contains important eyewitness and personal interviews with Brooks, but as a resource for later Brooks biographical notes, left the captain's first name indelibly incorrect.

James Brooks's life was far from idyllic. Even though the "call of the frontier" was his excuse, his restlessness came from a troubled childhood that witnessed a terrible war fought literally in his own front yard, a war of division that took his father's life and left him and his large family nearly destitute. A teenager during the terrible days of Reconstruction in central Kentucky, James–Bud as his siblings called him–stumbled through an adolescence that left painful memories scribbled on notepads sixty-five years later.

Young Bud Brooks left behind a county famous for its whiskey distilleries but took that part of the county with him as a traveling companion for the rest of his life. In a candid conversation with author Dora Raymond in 1935, Brooks shared an anecdote about when he was "liquoring up one day in a Cotulla saloon," clearly forthright about his problem over the years.[2]

He eventually found his other lifelong companion, Virginia Willborn of Kerr County, Texas, but along the earlier journey left sweethearts and broken hearts wherever he went. Never a womanizer but hardly ever without a female companion–Florence and Ella and Mag and Ida and Martha and more–Brooks was faithful to his wife of thirty-seven years but hardly attentive. In his family years he doted on his son but practically ignored his daughter.

Before and most certainly during his service as a Texas Ranger, Brooks became renowned for his expert gun handling and sharp-shooting prowess. And Bill McBride, a foreman on the King Ranch, even remembered an elderly shooter: "When Captain Brooks was well past sixty years old, I saw him shoot five shots at a knot on an oak tree. He fanned the hammer of an old forty-five so fast that it sounded like an automatic and hit the target four times. It made him mad when the fifth shot was a little wide of the mark."[3]

At the same time, some may have thought him too quick with the trigger, and at least one incident nearly cost him a remarkable career that had barely begun. And that moment followed hard on the heels of another confrontation that came within a hair's breadth of ending his life. Brooks never backed down from a fight, but on some occasions may have stepped in too quickly.

But his dedication to the Texas Rangers, and the state he adopted as his own, never wavered. James Abijah Brooks of Kentucky became a son of the Lone Star State without reservation, committing his life to the orderly, safe progress of Texas until his dying day in 1944. His advancement through the Ranger organization, his election and reelection to the state legislature, and fourteen consecutive votes of confidence by the citizens of Brooks County to keep him on their judicial bench, speak to the loyalty of those who knew him and those to whom he kept his promises.

During many of the eighteen years of his Ranger captaincy, J. A. Brooks found himself surrounded by other equally dedicated leaders of men, as one of the legendary "Four Captains," whose collective leadership helped bring the Texas Rangers into the twentieth century. One of those men, the profoundly religious John Harris Rogers, grew up in the Ranger service alongside Brooks and the two became close friends with almost nothing in common. Rogers, the only one of the four commanders Texas-born, was Presbyterian-raised like Brooks but far more evangelistic, quiet, humble, and likely dedicated to a re-conversion of his colleague and friend who cared more for the campfire toast than a Sabbath prayer. Rogers and Brooks stood side by side at least twice in their illustrious careers when shots being fired could have brought both of them down, and one of those shoot-outs did in fact wound them both seriously.

Two other captains served during that turn-of-the-century era with Rogers and Brooks. William Jesse McDonald, three years older than Brooks, settled in Rusk County as a young man and became the second of the four, after Brooks, promoted to the captaincy. McDonald never saw a reporter or a photographer he didn't like, and his exploits, though not necessarily more exciting or dramatic than the others, nevertheless became the stuff of which legends and myths are made: Quotations claimed to be his became mottos for the Ranger Force itself. A U.S. marshal after his retirement from the Rangers, McDonald was the first of the four to die, of pneumonia in 1918.

John Reynolds Hughes completed the set. As quiet as Brooks and Rogers, and notoriously perseverant on the trail of a fugitive from justice, Hughes came to Texas from Illinois in 1880, joined the Rangers seven years later, and captained Company D. He retired in 1915 and outlived his compadre Brooks by three years.

These four men exemplified the tenacity and exceptional leadership that helped salvage a Ranger militia destined for the political scrap heap in the late 1890s for being too antiquated, and instead managed to re-tool the unique law enforcement agency and ready it for another century of service to Texas.

When Richard Harding Davis, a reporter and managing editor of *Harper's Weekly*, traveled out to "discover" the West in the early 1890s, he spent time with Captain Brooks and Company F and later wrote about the experience in *The West From a Car-Window.* "The West is still not reconstructed," he wrote. "There are still the Texas Rangers, and in them the man from the cities of the east will find the picturesqueness of the Wild West show and its happiest expression . . . The Rangers are a semi-militia, semi-military organization of long descent, and with the most brilliant record of border warfare."

"The Rangers' camps look much like those of gypsies," Davis continued, "with their one wagon to carry the horses' feed, the ponies grazing at the ends of the lariats, the big Mexican saddles hung over the nearest barb fence, and the blankets covering the ground and marking the hard beds of the night before." In a visit with Adjutant General William H. Mabry while at Brooks's camp, Davis admitted that even the Ranger boss had trouble talking the captain "into relating a few of his own adventures. The result was a significant and complete failure." Brooks, like Rogers and Hughes, refused to elaborate on what he considered to be just doing his job, Davis noting that "Captain Brooks' version of the same story the general had told me, with all the necessary detail, would be: 'Well, we got word they were hiding in a ranch down in Zapata County, and we went down there and took 'em–which they were afterwards hung.'"

Misplacing the events when he wrote later, Davis still made his point when he said: "The fact that [Brooks] had three fingers shot off as he 'took 'em' was a detail he scorned to remember, as he could shoot better without those members than the rest of his men who had only lost one or two." On that same day in camp Davis had been treated to a display of the captain's shooting prowess as the two fired rifles at a target: "To shoot a Winchester there are three movements," the journalist recalled. "Captain Brooks, as far as I could make out from the sound, used only one movement for his entire eight shots. When I had fired two shots into space, the captain had put his eight into the board."[4]

For all of his shooting prowess and reputation as a "fast draw," Brooks, like his friend Rogers, never dressed the part of the western gunman, preferring a conservative suit to the flamboyant cowboy outfit. "Brooks wasn't ever strung around with cartridge belts and six shooters hung out in plain view," a colleague remembered. "He always kept his coat on."[5] Said Brooks himself in a 1935 interview: "We only performed our work as best we saw it, and all this 'Hell in Boots' stuff is tommy-rot."[6]

Four decades later when Ranger Capt. William Warren Sterling wrote his autobiography, Captain Brooks stood clearly as "the man who inspired me to be a Texas Ranger." Sterling recognized the tenacity of the man that accompanied his sharp shooting skills even during Brooks's early years as a private out of Cotulla: "Brooks' steely blue eyes, square jaw and panther quick movements were the marks of a good man to let alone. After sizing him up, the array of local gunmen decided to take him at his face value. He quickly became a veteran."[7]

Walter Prescott Webb, in his formative study of the Rangers, compared Brooks to the redoubtable Leander McNelly of a generation earlier: "Brooks stood, in his way, equally well, although there was always a distinction in the border's regard for these two captains. By this, I mean that while the reputation of both McNelly and Brooks was that of strong, just, and fearless men, Brooks had not McNelly's reputation for insight into the hearts and minds of men."[8] In the 1930 biographies of *The New Encyclopedia of Texas*, it was said of the then seventy-five-year-old Judge Brooks: "In his public life he has held fast to his ideals, doing his duty as he sees it, and has had the courage to back his convictions in his every action."[9]

Recruited off the coal trains that chugged from Laredo to Cotulla to San Antonio in 1883, James Brooks joined Lt. Charles B. McKinney's Company F just in time to narrowly escape a budding La Salle County feud between McKinney and William O. Tompkins. In the six years before he was promoted to captain of that same company, Brooks withstood a harrowing gun battle during the fence-cutter wars in Brown County, the deadly Conner Fight along the Sabine, and a point-blank shoot-out in Indian Territory. Wrote Sterling: "Captain Brooks once told me that the memory of his dear old Presbyterian mother had sustained him in many battles."[10] And it took a presidential pardon to sustain him in the legal battle following the Indian Territory scrap.

In the next decade and a half, as captain, the Kentucky native participated in the controversial De La Cerda incident involving his trusted sergeant A. Y. Baker, the Catarino Garza Wars in the lower Rio Grande Valley, the El Paso prizefight in 1896, and kept the peace for most of a year in the oil boom town of Batson Prairie. He, like most Rangers of that era, suppressed his frustration over a state judicial system that more often than not acquitted or mistried the cases of the brigands tracked and captured, harnessing that aggravation and pointing to the next trail; Brooks only rarely mentioned it and instead concentrated on the job at hand. Most Ranger records and letters of commendation indicate his particular skills at tracking horse and cattle thieves in the Rio Grande Valley while in command of Company A.

In 1890 he paused long enough from his adventures to court and marry Virginia Willborn, kin to two famous Rangers and quite the frontier horsewoman, able to ride and shoot with the men according to family recollections. Their children, Corrinne and John Morgan, were raised in Alice and Falfurrias and mostly by their mother. Ever a law enforcement agent more than a husband or father, Brooks seemed to spend his family time, especially after Virginia's death in 1928, almost exclusively with his son, who in later years succeeded his father on the Brooks County bench.

The Brooks descendants recall "Pat's" (as his daughter called him) bouts with his whiskey, his long absences from home when young John Morgan kept food on their table by hunting in the rough South Texas country, and the derogatory comments aimed at his daughter when the captain was at home. His remarks about Corrinne's "ugly, fat arms" forced her in emotional despair to wear long-sleeved outfits all of her life: she never married, and mourned the loss of her mother for years ever after. At the same time, photographs of the judge around Alice and Falfurrias show him almost constantly with his son proudly by his side, and his granddaughter has fond memories of her visits to his Falfurrias home in the 1940s.[11]

In 1904 J. A. Brooks looked toward retirement, buying property near the small railroad town of Falfurrias and hooking up with wealthy rancher Ed C. Lasater. The two men would eventually work together to create a new county–Brooks County, in South Texas–despite raucous opposition from factions all around them. Brooks's two terms in the state legislature were spent exclusively working toward that objective, and the rewards of the new county's name and a judgeship launched his second career into the next three decades. Illness and age finally caught up with the old Ranger, whose retirement in 1939 left him only five more years to live. Even to those last days, though, many remembered him saying "I've still got one more good fight left in me."[12]

But Brooks's hardest fight was a lifelong struggle with the Kentucky companion that drove him and haunted him. His family long-remembered that each trip from home, every trek to the Austin legislative session, Brooks packed "a starched white shirt and a bottle of Kentucky bourbon whiskey."[13] Liquor chased him up the Chisholm Trail in 1879, and ran him south to San Antonio the next year. It shadowed him in Cotulla and Vernon and Alice, and in Falfurrias. It caused a rift with his children that finally brought a chastened confession too little, too late. It wore him down and may have finally killed him; indeed, it was his fatal flaw.

But the specter of alcoholism never kept him from completing the tasks of either career. Hardened on the trail, consumed by the challenge of bringing law and order to the wide-ranging state he had adopted, James A. Brooks garnered and kept a high and well-deserved respect from friend and foe and citizen alike throughout his life. He battled the ravages of whiskey as he battled every criminal, every fugitive, and came out victorious, if bloodied, on the other side.

A scholar recently wrote of Brooks: "Tall, lean, and tough, he was also modest, quiet-spoken, and courteous, and possessed of a high sense of duty fortified by determination, courage, and a mind that grasped both the larger mission and the immediate task. A masterful marksman, horseman, and outdoorsman, Brooks proved smart, energetic, and persistent, and displayed his usual qualities of leadership." Specifically regarding his efforts in the Batson oil boom days, "Brooks confronted a new challenge, met it decisively and creatively, pointed the way for Rangers to come, and confirmed his stature as one of the four great captains."[14]

This is the story of a man who endured a hard life in a hard country, calloused and courageous, flawed but never broken, as much an example of the frontiersman as any who rode the trail alongside him. He is the prototypical Texas Ranger of both legend and harsh reality, who to his last day believed he had one fight still left in him.

1

OLD KENTUCKY HOME

My father having gone to his final rest, my mother was left in the midst of that great struggle with six daughters and two little boys.

JOHN STRODE BROOKS STOOD AT THE CORNER POST OF HIS NEW property, surveying a portion of the 247 acres of Kentucky bluegrass he had recently purchased. A tributary of Houston Creek flowed easily along its rocky bed through the eastern acreage. A stand of maple trees promised maple syrup the next season, a rolling field just past the grove looked favorable for summer corn, and an apple orchard would complete the annual harvest.

The pike road that connected tiny Paris to the growing town of Lexington drew one line for his land, a small road that wound northward along the Fayette-Bourbon county border marked another. New neighbors included Aaron and Mary Smedley, John Giltner just across the pike road, Frank and Nancy Willmott, Joshua and Rachel Corbin to the north, and the James Baggs family on the southern boundary. The main house would go there, he pointed up the pike, and the slave quarters in the hollow not far from the corral and barns.

The main house would need plenty of bedrooms: his five girls could share part of the upstairs, and the child now on the way and expected in the fall would inherit the crib three-year-old Fannie had just vacated. Annie would turn sixteen soon; Jennie, Addie, and Sallie rounded out the bunch. Dr. Brooks's wife Mary Jane had her hands full even with Annie's help and the slave Old Mary at her side.

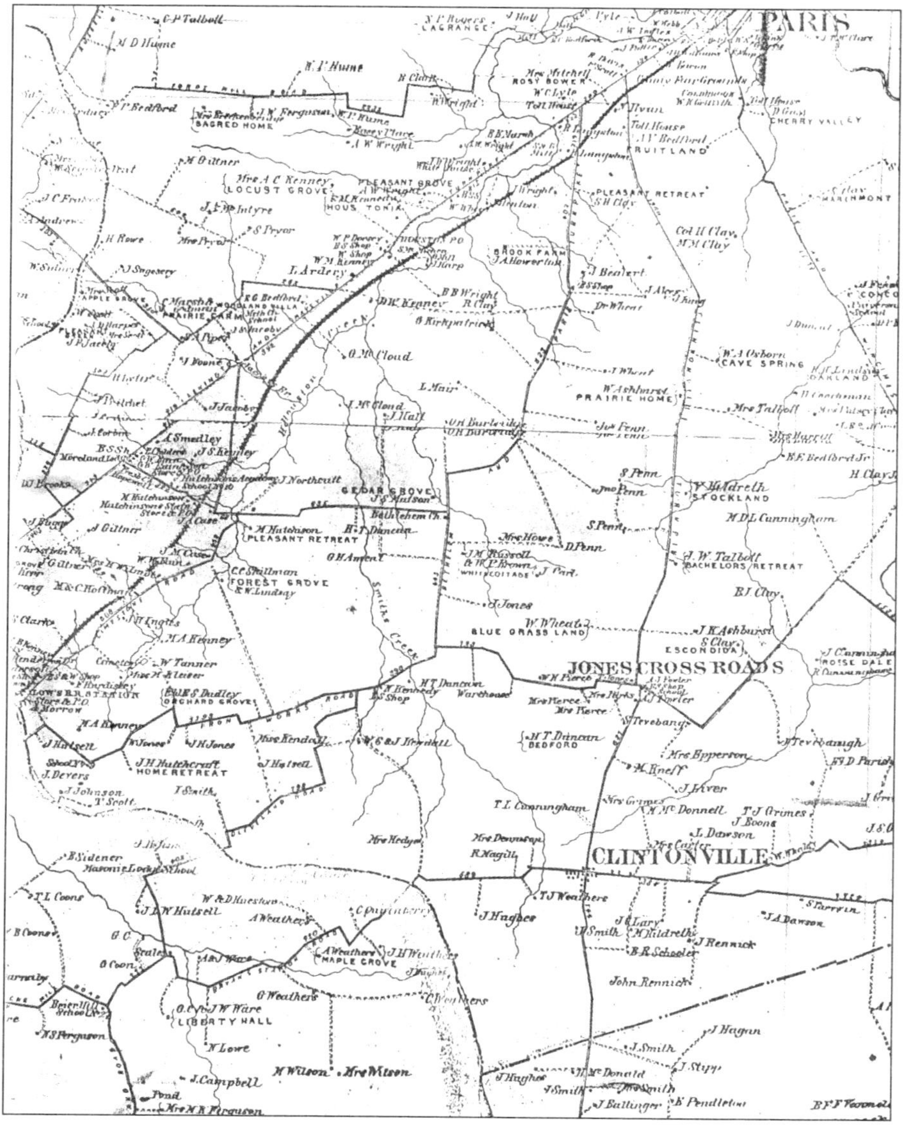

1861 Road and Trail map of Bourbon County, Kentucky. Dr. J. S. Brooks's estate is at far left center.

Courtesy John Fox, Jr., Genealogical Library, Paris, Kentucky.

The small village of Hutchinson stood less than a mile north on the pike road, where a smithy and a general store complemented the Presbyterian Church and two schools. A seven-mile carriage ride beyond took the family into Paris and over to Uncle Samuel Brooks's estate, and it was not much farther south into Lexington. The move over from Winchester in Clark County, the old homestead where John Brooks had grown up, would be well worth the effort: Bourbon County in 1855 needed another physician and Doc Brooks looked forward to opening his practice here.[1]

The doctor's sixth child and first son, James Abijah, was born on November 20, 1855, in the new home on the Lexington Pike Road. "Being the sixth child and the first boy to arrive in that family," Brooks recalled later, "I believe that I was a little bit spoiled. Later there was another girl (Lillie Belle) and then my little brother came named John Jr. I was christened James Abijah, but called Bud for short."[2]

Bud's first six years were filled with the delights of living in the rolling splendor of the Inner Bluegrass Region of central Kentucky. Eight slaves handled the chores around the estate, and "Old Ned" was generally assigned the duty of keeping up with the rambunctious eldest son. "There was [also] Old Mary and Little Mary, a boy [Adam] my age who was my playmate, Henry (Hen for short), Big Ben and his wife and daughter," Brooks remembered. "There was another Negro slave, Bad Charley, but he ran away and we were glad about that." Life was carefree, food was plentiful, and the joys of wandering the rolling hills or riding the thoroughbred horses kept young James outdoors even through the bitter winter months.

The family regularly attended the Hopewell Presbyterian Church in Hutchinson, and Dr. Brooks maintained a high degree of respectability throughout the community. The U.S. Census in 1860 recorded the eight-member family on the pike road near Morelands Post Office, the estate and property valued at $33,000, considerable for that area. Daughter Addie married Charles Throckmorton on October 24, 1861, and the eldest, Annie, married James Henry Kerr on January 16, 1862.[3] It was a joyous time for the Brooks family.

A 1938 interview with James Brooks reveals more of his childhood story. "When eight years of age, Jim would take old Red and Buck, two oxen, hitched to a sled and haul fodder in over snow-covered fields. In the spring, when the sap began to flow, he would press old Red and Buck into service again, bringing the sap in from the maple trees, where it then went through the various stages of cooking necessary for the finished product."[4]

That world changed forever with the coming of the Civil War. Kentucky wrestled with its decision whether to leave the Union, and President Lincoln fought to hold on to the border state. On December 10, 1861, a rebel government formed in Kentucky to join the Confederacy, but Union troops came in the spring and the Bluegrass State remained under tight control throughout the war.

Confederate General John Hunt Morgan's Raiders rolled through Kentucky in July and September of 1862, but the South's defeat at Perryville in October forced Gen. Braxton Bragg's troops back into Tennessee. Morgan made two more entries into the state, including the famous Christmas Raid of 1862, but the Union's Home Guard First and Second Kentucky Brigades kept Kentucky in the fold for the remainder of the war.[5]

And the tragedy of war came to the very doorstep of the Brooks estate. Dr. Brooks worked at the hospitals established in and around Lexington from the first days that some of the 4,900 casualties arrived from a battle fought around Richmond, Kentucky, in August 1862. As the Perryville wounded replaced those, and the Christmas Raid sent more ambulances their way, the exhausted physicians and their staffs worked around the clock and into the new year. The sixty-year-old Brooks rarely saw his home or family, and wore himself to the point of being hospitalized himself in the spring. On April 3, 1863, John Strode Brooks succumbed to the deadly pace that had been set before him months earlier by the war. He was buried in Lexington Cemetery the next day, his pregnant widow and the older children there to bid him goodbye.

"My father having gone to his final rest," James Brooks wrote years later, "my mother was left in the midst of that great struggle with six daughters and two little boys [John Clarence was born in October], and a number of Negro slaves to provide for. Harsh and wild was living in those trying days.

"Some days even parched corn was pretty good. Then when the old Negro slaves found a fat possum and could by foraging bring in a few yellow yams, we had a feast fit for a king.

"Our clothes were about gone when we found the old spinning wheel and loom our grandparents had brought to old Kentucky. I can see my old grandmother [Elizabeth Strode Kerr, Mary Jane's widowed mother and related through the Strodes and the Kerrs by marriage] sitting by the fireside carding thread into clothes. And the slaves in their homespun as the wolf was howling at our door."

Brooks recalled how the good times quickly disappeared and then the Yankees came to the Pike Road homestead. "We could always depend on the old Negro Mary, to my mind she was a Queen, now with her planning and canning our larders were soon full again, cellars too with apples and apple cider. We had livestock, too, sheep, horses, and cattle, and we hoped not to be molested, but being near the dead line, Masons and Dixons, our first great trouble was soon upon us.

"John Morgan was a rebel captain, a dare devil, too, who dared to cross into Ohio, a Union state. But he did not stay long and retreated back through Kentucky." This was most likely Morgan's raid in June 1864, which went up through Cynthiana and then was driven back south by Union Gen. Stephen G. Burbridge's Ohio and Kentucky troops. Morgan escaped but suffered nearly 1,000 casualties in his fighting retreat through the Bluegrass region. The Yankees chased the remnants of the rebel raiders right down the pike road from Paris and through Lexington.[6]

Here is how Brooks described it in his memoirs: "It was after Midnight [June 12, 1864], when among the Negroes there was a great commotion. Old Negro Ned came to my bed, watchful over me because he loved me, in my night gown he took me down towards the old turnpike. We then learned of Capt. Morgan's skedaddling. Back to bed he took me, but the excitement was too great, I could not sleep.

Just before sunrise the Yankees were there close on the heels of our Kentucky Rebel Captain. On the front gate post Ned sat me– 'twas my first view of the Union soldiers.

"A little later one of the Yankees left the line and said, 'Here is one damned little Rebel I will capture.' I fell from the post which left several bruises, and I have hated the blue coat ever since. As Ned took me back to hide behind the corral we saw the flames and smoke go up from [Jacoby's] bridge to the south, and we all knew that Capt. Morgan's retreat was a success, that the Union artillery could not cross the river and its quicksand bottom.

"The Union soldiers looking for a place to camp until such time they could resume their march, there being a large fish pond on our farm, and the Yankees learning that there was a well of cool freestone water in our yard, they established camp and the officers were guests for some days. Our larders were full and a large two story brick house for the officers' quarters, and Negro slaves to look after their wants, that tired and famished hoard of Union soldiers seemed content, but watchful. For they knew that the wily daredevil rebel Captain was not far away.

"I will say that every courtesy and consideration possible was extended to my mother and sisters, even though they had played havoc with our larders, pig stys [*sic*], ham roasts, ducks and geese. They foraged for miles around. When they were preparing to resume their march, it was anguish almost unbearable for us to watch one of those officers mounted on our favorite thoroughbred horse, his horse having gone lame.

"Well, there were the old oxen Buck and Red and two old brood mares left, which was some consolation, for with them the good old Negroes could continue to sow and reap such crops as were grown at that time." The slaves remained with the family after the war ended, and the young boy Adam who had grown up with Brooks later became a famous race horse jockey in Kentucky. "When the Yankees came through they killed and ate all of our sheep. But they couldn't eat the wool, so some of the slaves took the wool, carded it, spun it into thread, and wove the cloth for my first pair of long pants."

The war left the Brooks estate behind by the end of the summer of 1864, and by the following spring the contest had given way to the pangs of Reconstruction. James Kerr aided the widow Mary Jane Brooks in the efforts to file the estate records after her husband's death; in February 1864, the first of several extracts was filed dividing the homestead in sections and selling off a number of parcels in order to pay for the restoration of the family's war-ravaged possessions. The slaves were distributed among the heirs, and several of them stayed with their respective family members after they had been freed in 1865.[7]

The 1870 census shows the reduced homestead valued at $9,600. Still, Brooks remembered, "I will say that our family and many others that I knew were fully compensated for the destruction and havoc wrought [by the war]."

But Reconstruction proved harsh and dangerous still. "Then came Reconstruction days, with the advent of the carpetbaggers, the renegades, there was still something to fear. Then the Ku Klux Klan mounted on their fiery chargers, robed and masked in pure white, a sight to behold, for riding in the moonlight they struck terror to the minds of men."

In the midst of war and its ravages, young James managed to attend school at least part time, though he admitted it was never his choice compared to being outdoors hunting and fishing. "My schooling began during my seventh year [1862] in a little red brick schoolhouse [Hutchinson Academy] about a mile away from home. Miss Julia Davenport was my first teacher, God bless her, for to me that first day she was great, and her name through my long life never forgotten."

But much more interesting was his world outside the schoolhouse. "In my early teens I was a great lover of fishing and hunting, and our Christmas visits to my old grand mother's mountain home in the hills on the banks of the Kentucky River were always wonderful trips. I killed my first pheasant there, and bob whites and gray squirrels and other game were in abundance, all the sport that a boy in his teens could stand."

In fact, the desire for a shotgun of his own led James Brooks down an interesting path in a deal cut with his mother the year he turned fourteen. "The Christmas holidays were over and my good Presbyterian Mother said to me, 'My dear boy, I want you to read the Bible through this year: three chapters a day and five on Sunday, and a $65 shotgun is yours when you finish.' The trade was made and the next Christmas the double barreled shotgun was mine, for I read more than five chapters on Sundays as an excuse to stay at home."

James continued his schooling until he was seventeen, taking more responsibility for the family still there on the pike road. Everyone in the immediate clan survived the cholera epidemic in 1873, but many in Paris and across Bourbon County lost their lives. Sister Jennie married Matthew Kenney, a wealthy landowner and neighbor, in 1867, and Fannie, three years older than James and his closest sibling, married Will Morgan in 1874 and also left the household, leaving only Sallie and the two younger ones to watch over. "Hunting and fishing in those mountain streams was all that a boy could desire, with the chestnuts, walnut and hickory trees in spring bloom, the pawpaw, persimmon and other wild fruits in abundance: why should a boy's mind not be satisfied?

"But I longed for the wide open spaces," Brooks answered his own question. "Having heard tales of the great cattle hands and cattle trails of Texas, my mind was made up when I was twenty-one. At a Christmas meal with the gathered family, I bid all good-bye. Even my boyhood sweetheart could not hold me back." With only a single suitcase in hand, James Brooks boarded a train out of Lexington, made his way to Chicago and then south to Texas, arriving in the Lone Star State on January 1, 1877.

"I stepped off the train at a little backwoods town, McKinney. I had at last landed away out in the great west, renowned for its open spaces, where every young man could have a chance, and a square deal, too: Texas at that time was renowned for greatness far and wide.

"I stopped in Collin County to see a cousin in law, Joseph Darnall, and his family. Cousin Joe was not only a successful farmer but a renowned backwoods preacher of the Christian faith, a Campbellite. He was a graduate of the University of Virginia who had courted and married my cousin Mollie Thomas."

Mary Elizabeth "Mollie" Kerr Thomas's mother was sister to James's mother. Mollie's father, John W. Thomas, was a prominent tobacco farmer and justice of the peace in Bourbon County.

The Darnalls settled in Collin County after the Civil War, establishing the community of Cottage Hill northwest of McKinney, raising seven children of their own in addition to bringing in the homeless on many occasions, and organizing several Christian congregations and schools in that area. They brought two young ex-slaves to Texas with them, only to have the Ku Klux Klan appear at their door one night and escort the couple away to Dallas; the couple eventually fled to California.[8]

"I was again ushered into a hunter's paradise. The bobwhite and the prairie chicken were in abundance, and it was a great treat for my relatives to have a real hunter as their guest, for I brought in all the game needed by them and many of their neighbors."

The young boarder stayed with the Darnalls into the spring, attending the Corinth Presbyterian Church nearby where his cousin preached. There he met families, and men and women his own age, whom he would befriend for the next two years, including the Mason Webster family from Kentucky who lived on the Darnall spread, the Hubbards, and the large Fox family. He met Joe Case and his daughter Ida, Jim Knighton and John Ousley, and Ben Wills.

"Then the spring time came, and with it the round up of the vast cattle, the wide open spaces, a vast cattle range free to all, the 'Flats' as it was called at the time, miles of no fencing." Northwest Collin County west over into Denton County and north into Grayson, a rolling prairie, completes the southern tip of the Great Midwest grazing land. Spring-fed streams and ponds scatter across the grassy fields, and thousands of head of cattle roamed there in the winter months.

"Uncle" Willett, Bob, and Frank Hickman ran a successful cowboying company in Collin County not far from Pilot Point, especially famous for busting broncos and organizing cattle drives up to Kansas.

Fascinated by the new country he now called home, Jim Brooks sought out the cowboys of that area to learn the trade, seeking adventure and a paycheck.

"I rode out to Hickman's Prairie to try out my new horse, running with the coyote and the jack rabbit. I had heard of the Hickmans and their bucking bronco ways or reputation, and I rode up to where the crowd had gathered, greeted by 'Hello Stranger.'

"A daring young woman [Mag Hickman, Frank's daughter] had mounted, put her feet in the stirrups that had been tied together under that wild animal, and remarked, 'Turn him loose.' She seemed to sit easy and follow every move and motion of that raging beast. She returned victorious, guiding that humble steed with her big sombrero. I was thrilled, and could only wonder if the time would come when I too was a success as a cowboy."

The love-struck young man from Kentucky found himself entranced by both beast and beauty. "It was not long before I was bowing at Miss Hickman's feet, with my hat in the ring. And I was successful, too," Brooks remembered with a touch of sarcasm, "for a few months later I was selected as best man at her wedding, and the little girl friend she selected to be my partner at that marriage ceremony was just too wonderful for me to make any attempt at description." The girl friend was Ida Case who later married Dave Light over in Denton County. Said Brooks years later in a newspaper interview, "I don't know which I think is prettier, a fine race horse or a pretty girl in a hoop skirt dancing the Virginia Reel."[9]

Also part of the fare at Hickman's Prairie were the pony races, "where I first met Sam Bass, the noted outlaw," Brooks wrote. The young Kentuckian had a good mount and entered the race. "Bass was the only one wearing a black hat, but he had the fastest pony and he carried off the dough." Later that night as Brooks returned homeward, he spotted a campfire in the darkness that beckoned to the lonesome cowboy. "When I approached the camp, a lot of men grabbed their carbines and gave me the greatest scare of my life. Well, it was Sam Bass's camp. I had a fast horse myself and rode out of there."

Brooks worked at his cowboy skills through the summer and fall of 1877 while hunting and providing for, and living with, the Darnalls. He loved the country but longed to own his own spread. In Collin County, a large section of "School Land, Survey No. 14" went up for sale in the spring of 1878, and Brooks seized the opportunity. The 1878 tax records show J. A. Brooks as the owner of 116 acres on the headwaters of Wilson Creek, valued at $300, plus one horse, one wagon, forty-nine head of cattle, and four hogs. The total valuation of his property was listed as $820, and he paid $11.20 in taxes that year. "It was part of the old [John A.] Taylor farm. A spring on it was flowing pure clear water which fed that branch of Wilson Creek, and there was a fair little shack on it, too." The Hickmans purchased eighty acres of the School Land, Jefferson F. Fox owned 154 acres of farm land, and Jim Knighton claimed 166 acres, 90 cattle and 12 hogs. John Ousley was there as well: The young cowboys were making an attempt to settle down.

"I began to think of romance, and a housekeeper I began to think I needed." The young farmer courted two sisters by attending the choir practice at the Corinth Church, but after a short while the younger sister Florence got cold feet when Brooks pressed her toward the altar. "She refused and to this day I am glad of it: if she had accepted I would still be on that farm and missed all the excitement."

Soon the West beckoned again. Jeff Fox was the first to go, when he partnered with Benjamin Franklin Wills to buy a ranch in Wise County fifty miles away. Wills, twenty-seven, was originally from Kentucky himself, now married and a baby on the way, and Jeff Fox would also marry in Wise County.[10] When Jim Knighton decided to go work for Wills and Fox, Bud Brooks could not stay behind. He sold his property after only six months, "the state having opened a lot of the free grazing land for settlement, and the nesters moving in from other states to grow up with the west. It was time to move.

"I stayed at Fox and Wills' small ranch. They were traders, Knighton and myself herded their cattle the same as our own, for board and lodging, which was a blessing to us. But I was restless and dissatisfied. I had learned to ride the bucking bronco, and to rope the wild steer and tie him, too. In two years I had learned to be a fair cowboy. And when [William] Bartlett pitched camp in our range I was the first visitor he had."

Bartlett and his partners hailed from Kansas and were making their annual trek to Texas to hire cowboys and drive cattle back north to the railroad. "I soon learned that Mr. Bartlett was a native of Clay County, Missouri, and knew my relatives there [the Thomas Duncans].

"I knew the ropes of the cattle game by that time, and a trade was made: I was to render them all the assistance possible in getting their herd together. Then I was to throw in my small herd and make a trek over the old much talked about Chism [*sic*] Trail. 3,400 head of cattle were soon punched and delivered. The owner of the herd had employed Mr. [John R.] Brown, an experienced old trail driver, to manage the herd.

"The morning we left Brown called the boys together and assigned each one the duties that they were to perform on the drive. I wondered what would be my lot. Brown finally called to me, and said 'Kid, you and I will point the herd.' That was a proud day for me."

Brooks worked the point all the way to the Red River crossing, where flooding waters and a lightning storm caused panic and a stampede that left the herd scattered and the cowboys exhausted. Safe on the other side at last, "that effort on my part to overcome difficulties gave me courage, and I was beginning to feel my oats, and believed that I could cope with any emergency that might arise."

Along the treacherous trail that spring in 1879, young Brooks met up with some of the men who were or would soon become legends in the cattle industry: Charlie Cates, Glenn Halsell, Joe Crystal, Jerry Burnett of the Denton Creek 6666 Ranch, and C. V. Terrell, later chairman of the Texas Railroad Commission. John Hughes, later one of the legendary four Ranger captains, rode the trail during that period but neither he nor Brooks ever mentioned that they knew each other then.[11]

C. V. Terrell told a story on the young cowboy years later, about the time when Brooks rode into Decatur to purchase a load of supplies for the trail company. Stopping at the general store, Brooks downed a little too much whiskey and the Decatur city marshal marched over to arrest him. The grocer, "Uncle Charley" Cates, interceded and Brooks rode out of town. After a few miles the drunken cowboy fell asleep on his horse, awakening to see his mount lapping water from a settler's water barrel. The settler, a man named Neni Hobson, let Brooks sleep off the liquor overnight, and Hobson's wife fixed the boy a big breakfast the next morning. When Brooks offered to pay for the meal and lodging, the settler replied, "Not a cent. Just don't drink anymore." There is no indication Jim Brooks heeded the admonition.[12]

The remainder of the drive continued to challenge the young cowboy, more stampedes, later a parched herd's run for a watering hole, and finally to the Kansas line where the cattle were "loose herded" over the summer until the first frost. Bartlett, like many other cattlemen in the late 1870s, took his herds to Caldwell instead of Dodge City, and the cowboys spent their time, and much of their hard-earned dough, on the town's abundant entertainment. Southwest of the Kansas line was Fort Reno and the government Indian reservation, and it was there that Brooks spent some of his summer.

"It was my good fortune and pleasure to visit the tepees of many of the Native Americans during the few months of my stay in that country: I learned many things about human nature."

Some of the herd were bought by the government to give to the Indians, and Brooks helped get those cattle to the reservation.

"The cattle assigned to the families, as their names were called off, were cut out of the herd and driven a specified distance; then the warriors were turned loose with their ponies and their bow and arrows; then the skinning knife, and soon the hungry crowd was crooning and singing their old hunting songs. Then the pony races, the sport fit for a king," appreciated by the boy from the Bluegrass thoroughbred country.

"The hard strife on the trail and also the rough camp life was a little too much for me. My health almost failed. I was discouraged." Brooks went to the Boston & Billings Ranch about fifty miles from

Caldwell where he was nursed back to health in the fall of 1879. Miss Sara Billings thought the young cowboy had a future ranching in Kansas, and "she began arranging a meeting between me and Miss Ella Purdy. We were in a short time good friends. But still being in bad health, my physician advised that I return to Texas." With little fanfare and few goodbyes, Brooks boarded a train after Christmas: "I arrived in San Antonio January 1st, 1880."

Brooks was in Texas to stay.

2

A TEXAS RANGER

Capt. Scott encouraged me to be a real worthwhile Texas Ranger under all circumstances.

San Antonio was a bustling town in 1880, filled with every opportunity imaginable, and every temptation, for an impressionable twenty-four-year-old cowboy just stepping off the train. Whatever Jim Brooks hoped would happen for him there, however, never materialized. His later memoirs pointedly omit nearly all of the events of the next three years of his life, except the confessions of an old man that the most famous distilled product from his Bourbon County home now became his lifelong partner. In one recollection Brooks simply wrote: "I located in San Antonio, [and] after a number of trips looking over South Texas, and a few business adventures most of which failed, one took me to Cotulla, La Salle County, several times."

But another memoir, scribbled on a desk calendar when Brooks was in his eighties, gives more insight into one of those "failed ventures." After spending a few days in San Antonio, first at the old Southern Hotel, and then at "Miss Porter's boardinghouse," Brooks came back in contact with William Bartlett, the Kansas cattleman, and befriended Jerry Burnett's son Sam, who had established himself in the Wichita Falls area (and who lent his name to the town of Burkburnett years later), as well as the Maltsbergers, father and son, of La Salle County.[1]

"Having satisfied myself that it would be dangerous to my health to return to Kansas, I sold my small herd of cattle to Mr. Bartlett, who placed the money on lien for me. Ever being on the alert for a chance to make an honest dollar, he interested me in making a trip to San Diego, Duval County. I sized it up as rather a dilapidated, slow little place. But when Sebastian Bell [a well-known cattle driver in those parts] and his rough and ready cowboys made their appearance late that afternoon, the town was much alive."

In San Diego, Brooks made several inquiries as to work opportunities and there met Ed Buckley, a rancher with whom he soon partnered up and invested his meager savings. "Having purchased 3,100 Mexican mutton, and having received them, Buckley and I started on our way [to drive them] to San Antonio, hoping to make a fine profit on them."

The wild frontier of South Texas in 1880 approached his camp the first night on the trail with word that King Fisher and his boys were on a raid in the area. John King Fisher was an infamous cattle rancher and cattle thief, a lawman of sorts in his later years, and either the scourge of that region or a Robin Hood figure to some. Flamboyant and ruthless, he was often described as wearing a black Mexican sombrero, a gold-embroidered jacket with red sash, and two pearl-handled revolvers. A sign on a La Salle County trail read: "This is King Fisher's road. Take the other."[2]

In his memoir, Brooks wrote, "There was suppressed excitement in our camp, for King Fisher and the King boys were on a raid. We passed a sleepless night.

"On our way at sunrise we first reached the Nueces River, then the Frio at Dogtown (Tilden), arriving south of the Medina. My partner being well known in that sector, arranged for our camp in what was then free range, and left me and our old Mexican sheepherder to look after our herd. He soon returned with old man Hiram Clark who gave us a good profit on our mutton. I was surely a happy boy, barely two months as a herder of sheep. Well, I was satisfied with my part of the profit."

Brooks's career as a sheepherder, however, proved short-lived. "I often wonder how a young man who had made a successful cow hand could become so dull. My partner, being in love and the girl of his dreams being everything worthwhile, sent me adrift. I again was thrown on my own."

Although surely Jim Brooks would have heard of or even encountered the Texas Rangers in and around Collin County, his first mention of them comes about the same time he gave up on sheepherding: "While at San Diego I learned that Capt. Lee Hall had succeeded Capt. McNelly in command of Company F, Texas Rangers." Jesse Leigh "Lee" Hall served in command of the company in 1876; Leander McNelly died in 1877. T. L. Oglesby was actually in command during the time Brooks worked out of San Diego, but the passing decades only misplaced these Ranger legends by a little in his memory. "The people with whom I was doing business spoke of the Rangers, and I learned that Charlie McKinney and Bill Scott, later my captain in the Ranger service, were stationed at that place." Apparently the young Brooks went to talk with the Rangers, "but they were absent on a scout."[3]

The United States Army was also camped near San Diego in those rough and tumble days: Renegades raiding the area so frightened the residents that 2,000 troops bivouacked there in 1878 and 1879. A shoot-out on the main street of San Diego in 1879 left five raiders dead. When the railroad came through that same year connecting to Corpus Christi, more trouble followed and the Rangers and the army had their hands full.[4] Brooks recounts an odd episode:

"One time when Sebastian Bell and his cowboys left San Diego, heading south to receive cattle, just south of town they discovered what they thought was a wild deer, a shot bringing him down. The pet deer was the mascot of a company of the U.S. soldiers camped near San Diego! There was an arrest, a trial, and so on. That young buck looking for a companion of the same species had wandered too far and had met his death; such is fate."

James Brooks may have wondered where fate was leading him in the fall of 1880. He made at least one trek to San Antonio, and it was there he ran into a young man named Duval West, the grandson of Judge Thomas H. Duval and nephew to Burr G. Duval, one of the biggest railroad men in Texas. The year before, Burr Duval, his eighteen-year-old nephew, and fourteen others formed an expedition that traveled west from San Antonio to the Chinati Mountains around Presidio. They were looking for gold and silver and, although they did not find either that year, interest soared after talks with West Texas rancher John W. Spencer who had mined the area for nearly two decades.[5]

Three railroad companies–the Galveston-Houston-San Antonio, the International-Great Northern, and the Texas and Pacific–made major investments in what soon became the Shafter Mining District. In June of 1882 thousands of acres deep in the mountains were leased to a San Francisco brokerage firm, and the Presidio Mining Company was organized. Silver was discovered soon after, as Spencer had predicted, and the exciting news spread rapidly across the Southwest.[6]

One of those who became interested in the prospects in West Texas was an old Forty-niner and former governor of Colorado, Alexander Cameron Hunt. Hunt's life reads like a pulp western novel, adventuring from his Illinois home to Denver, mining for gold and silver, establishing Aurauria, Colorado, during the 1859 Gold Rush, and Alamosa and Salida nineteen years later. He served in Congress and was also an Indian Agent, and a railroad man. Hunt served as president of the Rio Grande Railway Company, and came to Texas to investigate the mining claims along the Rio Grande. Hunt bought up land in Texas, and before he returned to Colorado assisted in the projection of a national rail line from Laredo to Mexico City.[7]

Reports from the expedition returning to San Antonio, and the arrival in Texas of men like Alexander Hunt, caught the interest and fascination of many a young man, including Bud Brooks. Sketchy evidence and stories handed down by Brooks's family suggest that the young cowboy hired on for the next expedition to Shafter, and may have spent much of 1881 in a fruitless attempt to mine gold and get rich. (His family speaks of a gold nugget mounted on a ring that was handed to two generations: the ring, since lost, may have represented if anything the only gold nugget Brooks ever found.)[8]

Empty handed and discouraged, Brooks drifted down the Rio Grande to the Laredo area, perhaps still employed with Hunt's railroad company that connected the two regions in 1882. Looking for any kind of work, he soon hired on with the coal mining enterprises in and around Minera, located about thirty miles upstream from Laredo, where rich deposits of cannel coal had been discovered earlier by geologist David Darwin Davis.[9]

The little Mexican villita teemed with energy and rowdy behavior, raucous celebrations going on deep into the night to offset the day's tough work of coal mining. A mining superintendent there wrote: "The miners hold a 'baile' (dance) in the schoolhouse every Saturday night, which generally ends in a tequila-inspired brawl toward early dawn. On Sundays they hold cock fights, and every pay day nearly everybody gets drunk at the cantina."[10] It may be no wonder that Brooks never made a single mention of this period of his life other than a casual answer to a question by Ranger William Warren Sterling years later that is the only written reference available.[11] Brooks's own bouts with bourbon whiskey to drown his sorrows may have blotted out those days in his memory. Of some consolation was the fact that the young Kentuckian became fluent in the hybrid Spanish language spoken along the border, a skill that would serve him well in the future.

By the fall of 1882, Brooks seemed to have concentrated his efforts on the rail line that moved the Los Mineras coal from Laredo to San Antonio via Cotulla, for he does mention his several "business" trips that led him to the little town on the line. Cotulla was organized in 1881 by Italian Count Joseph Telferner along the New York, Texas and Mexico Railway, a venture owned by Telferner that connected towns such as Richmond, Wharton, Victoria, and Brownsville, with a trunk to Corpus Christi and another planned for Mexico. Cotulla grew rapidly when the Laredo rail line came through there.[12] Then came the rowdies and the speculators–railroad conductors were said to have shouted, "Cotulla! Get your guns ready!" Then came the Texas

Rangers. Wrote W. W. Sterling in his autobiography: "El Paso, Tombstone, Tascosa and the other widely publicized frontier towns could not equal the deadliness of this cattle center on the Nueces River. In most of the rough places, a noted officer could make his play stand up on the strength of his reputation. This was not the case in Cotulla."[13]

And it was there in Cotulla on a January day in 1883 when J. A. Brooks finally met up with his destiny. Frustrated and going nowhere, dulled by the hardened labor and the alcohol, Brooks met Ranger Lt. Charles B. "Girlie" McKinney in town on the fifteenth of that month. McKinney was acting commander of Company F at that time, Captain Tom Oglesby having just resigned in November to become sheriff in Maverick County. McKinney himself would become sheriff of La Salle County in March, but on January 15 he was recruiting, and Jim Brooks signed up.

Some of the men of Company F who welcomed young Brooks into their fold included corporals W. T. "Brack" Morris and H. O. Edwards, and fellow privates A. J. Adams, Sterling Hardy, A. E. Foster, Charlie Norris, Alford Walker, and W. W. Shely. Adams was an aged forty-one-year-old from England; Wash Shely and Brooks would become lifelong friends.[14]

Private Brooks went to work immediately. "That same day [Corporal Brack] Morris was ordered to pick four men and go to Frio County to investigate a fence cutting. To the Cannon Ranch we went. Many miles of his fence was destroyed, the wire cut at each fence post. That was the beginning of the fence cutting wars in Texas." And the beginning of a storied career for Brooks as a Texas Ranger. On January 20, Corporal Morris and Private Brooks arrested four local cowboys for the crime, although a lack of evidence eventually set them free. "We arrested them at a wedding. Those old Texans were proud of what they had done, that their fathers had fought Indians, bled and died for that land, and no Yankees could come here and fence the livestock from the water holes and lakes."

Stationed in Cotulla for the next two-and-a half years, Brooks and Company F kept busy on the trail of fugitives across South Texas, when

A young Ranger Private James Brooks stands at right with pistol in hand, ca. 1885.

Courtesy Brooks family.

their hands weren't full enough just keeping order in the rough rail town itself. "Ranger or not," wrote Sterling of Cotulla, "anybody was liable to have his hand called. He had to prove that he covered the ground he stood on. [James] Brooks' steely blue eyes, square jaw and panther quick movements were the marks of a good man to let alone. After sizing him up, the array of local gunmen decided to take him at his face value. He quickly became a veteran."[15]

Private Brooks's first assignment on his own came March 27, 1883, ten weeks a Ranger, when a horse and buggy were stolen in Clinton. Captain Joe Shely, who had replaced Charles B. McKinney on March 1 as commander of Company F, sent Brooks to investigate. An elderly woman who owned a store there had been robbed, her carriage used to haul off the stolen merchandise from her own store. Two days later Brooks located the buggy and arrested Bill Brace for the crime. Brace talked freely and the next day Brooks arrested accomplice Bud Wright. Both men were in the Cotulla jail that night, the buggy returned to its owner. Both pled guilty at their trial and served four years in the Rusk penitentiary.[16]

Brooks explained years later in his memoirs that at that time the retired Ranger Capt. Jesse Leigh "Lee" Hall, now a ranch manager, "secured a lieutenant's commission for young [William] Scott and he was placed in command of the eastern detachment of Company F, stationed at Cuero, DeWitt County. Old 'Parson' Edwards as we called him was in charge but resigned and went back to his old home [Grimes] county. Edwards was a splendid Christian man, and he was highly respected and loved by the men who served under him."

While stationed with Scott in Cuero, Brooks recalled that "Bill Thompson, who killed a young cowboy at Rockport the year before, was tried and acquitted for murder. His case had been moved from Rockport to Cuero, where the Rangers guarded him awaiting trial. [Now] fence cutters, thieves, and other desperadoes were on a rampage in the western part of DeWitt and Karnes counties." While Scott took the others to ward off those ruffians, "I was left at Cuero to assist the sheriff and to guard Thompson. Lt. Scott and the rest were absent until the trial was over. Thompson could not be identified as the man who killed the young cowboy at Rockport, and therefore was acquitted."

On April 1 Brooks returned to Cuero from Cotulla to retrieve arrest papers at that sheriff's office, but when he arrived, there were no papers to be found. Hardly had he returned to camp before he was sent back north to Karnes County, accompanying grand juror Steve Rogers to the county seat. While there Brooks was asked by the local sheriff to assist in the recovery of ten head of cattle recently stolen; the Ranger private had the cattle back in their pasture on April 14.[17]

J. A. Brooks evidently was charged with working the northern region of Company F's territory. In June he arrested an alleged murderer, "an old Negro named Griffin who had been hiding out for some years," in Karnes County, and in October he arrested a cattle rustler in DeWitt County. For ten days in November Brooks was security escort for prisoners taken up to the courts in San Antonio and Seguin, and in December he found himself in DeWitt County once more, arresting a horse thief on the eighth and a cattle thief on the thirteenth.[18]

In the spring of 1884 Brooks met John H. Rogers, recently reenlisted after a brief stint with Company B in 1883. Brooks and Rogers would work side by side for many years, eventually colleagues in arms as fellow Texas Ranger captains. John Harris Rogers was born in Guadalupe County, nine miles east of Seguin, in 1863, eight years Brooks's junior. At age eighteen Rogers left the farm and made his way to Colorado City, Texas, where he soon joined the Rangers. Budget cuts for the Frontier Battalion forced him home for three months but he drew his next paycheck with Company F on March 31, 1884.

The two lawmen would be friends for the next forty-five years until Rogers's death in 1930, even though they had almost nothing in common except the shared experiences in the Ranger service and a healthy respect for each other. Rogers always kept his Christian faith and his family as his highest priorities, while Brooks, although a Presbyterian church member, rarely darkened a church door and remained most loyal to law enforcement above all or anyone else. Rogers was a teetotaler and later a "Dry" prohibitionist, and likely admonished his friend for the amount of whiskey he imbibed during his career. Rogers carried a Bible closer to his drawing hand than his revolver, but Brooks relished the opportunities to practice his shooting prowess. Both were respected for their commitment to Texas law and order, Rogers as "the praying Ranger," Brooks as "the fastest gun in Texas law enforcement."[19]

On November 25, 1884, J. A. Brooks was promoted to corporal of Company F, and one week later was promoted again to 2nd Sergeant to replace his friend Brack Morris who had resigned to run for sheriff.[20] Brooks concentrated more of his time at the camp and in La Salle County. Trouble arrived at the company's doorstep in February 1885, not with violence but in a major budget cut by the Nineteenth Legislature in Austin. The appropriation for the Rangers was reduced from $75,000 to $60,000, and Adjutant General W. H. King made the difficult decision to eliminate one entire company rather than parcel out the cuts.[21] Relative peace in the Rio Grande Valley at the time signaled, ironically, the end of Company F.

But the company and Sergeant Brooks's job were spared by, again the irony, an outbreak of violence in Dimmitt County. When Sheriff Joe Tumlinson's posse chased rustlers across the river into Mexico late in January and were subsequently chased back to Texas by the large band of renegades, a series of brazen raids into Texas that followed sent an alarm all the way to Austin. Governor John Ireland arranged for Federal troops and more Rangers to make their way to Dimmitt County. Adjutant General W. H. King headed for Carrizo Springs to set up headquarters, and ordered companies D and F into southwest Dimmit County.

Meanwhile, La Salle County Sheriff C. B. McKinney had already rounded up a posse of ten men and made his way to the William Votaw Ranch just eight miles from the Rio Grande. Accompanying him were Brooks and Sgt. G. W. Farrow from Company F. This region, known as "the Nueces Strip," had a long and violent history of trouble. On February 8 the Rangers and McKinney's posse organized themselves at Votaw's place.[22] Brooks picks up the story of what happened next:

"The rustlers had their headquarters near Presidio, Mexico, eight miles south of the river. Ex Captain McKinney, ex Captain Lee Hall,

Lieut. Scott and [myself] with Capt. Joe Shely made a hurried night ride and joined Capt. Lam Sieker and his [Company D] at their camp. We then went to the Rio Grande and were joined by a number of stockmen at that point, about 250 in all. At daylight [Feb. 9] two hundred Mexicans appeared on the south side of the river. Capt. Shely sent a note across to them to effect a truce on an island in the middle of the Rio Grande.

"Capt. Shely, Lieut. Scott, ex Capt. Lee Hall, [and] Capt. Lam Sieker was the party to meet with them. Capt. Sieker suggested that I go along with them, which was one of the proudest moments of my life." The island was known as Las Ysles Crossing to the locals. The Mexican contingent consisted of a physician named Pope and two others.

"We had a fine time being banqueted by the citizen party, but the [U.S.] Federal agents resented their not being invited to the banquet and ordered an arrest. We got word in time that the soldiers were coming and outrode them. About dark we crossed back into Texas. The trouble soon subsided."

Perhaps the trouble with raiding parties subsided, but not the violence in the Nueces Strip. In the 1870s sheep ranches began to invade the exclusively cattle country of Dimmit County: by 1880 there were over 30,000 sheep in the region, as many as cattle. A long-standing enmity between the two ranching interests exploded in violence, headed up in the mid-1880s by ringleader John Laxton, a cattleman. In March 1885, a string of killings brought the Rangers back into the area to investigate.

Sergeant Brooks and Pvt. J. B. Donegan left their Cotulla camp and arrived in Carrizo Springs just as Sheriff Tumlinson brought in three suspects. The youngest, Felix Taylor, agreed to turn state's evidence against the others. On March 17 Brooks and Donegan accompanied Taylor to the site of one of the killings to retrieve evidence, and then escorted Taylor back to jail. Convictions later that year helped quell some of the violence; a more permanent solution, the deadly drought of 1886–1887, effectively eliminated sheep ranching along the Nueces thereafter.[23]

The good news in all of this was that, after having effected an end to the raids and much of the violence in Dimmitt County, Company F would not be disbanded after all. However, a change of scenery for Shely's company was recommended by General King until he could decide how to address the budget reduction. In June Joe Shely resigned as captain of Company F and was replaced by William Scott; Company F transferred its camp temporarily to Uvalde that same month. Brooks roamed up to Bandera County to make two arrests late that month, and in July he and Private Rogers tracked and arrested the three Wingus brothers north in Edwards County for cattle rustling.[24]

During these first months as a Texas Ranger, Brooks found himself tutored by Captain Scott, a man he later credited for much of the success of his career. The early promotions and the responsibilities given the young man are a testimony to the confidence of his captain and the response in kind. Brooks later noted, "Capt. Scott encouraged me to be a real worthwhile Texas Ranger under all circumstances."

On October 5, Company F and all of the Frontier Battalion companies were reduced by six men each as a result of the cuts by the state legislature. Company A was mustered out of the Frontier Battalion permanently, and Capt. Lam Sieker became the Rangers' quartermaster.[25] In the reshuffling that followed, Brooks kept his job, was promoted to 1st Sergeant, and Company F was sent north to Vernon, Wilbarger County, on the Red River border. Their camp was actually about ten miles east of Vernon near the little town of Harrold, but the first three weeks of December the entire company resided across the river on the Anadarko reservation near Chickasaw Nation territory. There they worked with Federal and Indian agents to round up two Texas cattle thieves hiding out in the hills.

In February 1886, Sergeant Brooks scouted into Hardeman and Childress counties on the trail of fugitives from justice, but the four-day journey failed to locate them. Ten days later Captain Scott left for a trial in Marshall. During his ten-day absence, Sergeant Brooks was left in command of the company, his first experience in charge and a taste of his future as a company commander. After Scott's return to camp, Brooks and three privates tracked four days into Hardeman County, and on April 3 joined the entire company for twenty days in Ft. Worth to help keep order and quell a railroad strike.[26]

On March 1, 1886, 300 workers on the Texas and Pacific and the Katy railroads went on strike in the Ft. Worth area, encouraged by the national union Knights of Labor as yet another effort to confront the domination of Jay Gould and his railway cronies. Women and children sat on the rails to stop the trains, and for a month rail commerce stopped in North Texas. On April 3 railroad officials ordered a mail train to run the blockade: it carried armed guards and other security agents. When it reached Buttermilk Junction at the edge of town, two strikers threw a switch and guns blared. One guard was killed.

Governor Ireland called for U.S. troops and the Texas Rangers to intervene and stop the violence. Company F responded, and peace was soon restored. Gun shops were closed down in Ft. Worth, and federal marshals and Rangers combed the streets making arrests. By April 22 the strike collapsed and the national organizers departed, as did the marshals and the Rangers.[27] Brooks returned to Harrold on April 19 just in time to retrieve a man named Ford Jones who had broken out of the Vernon jail, and recalled years later that the Ft. Worth strike was one of the most dangerous situations he ever encountered as a Ranger.[28] In the next five weeks he would narrowly escape two other of the most harrowing moments of his life.

On May 10, 1886, Sergeant Brooks received orders to ride across the Red River into Indian Territory. "The school lands of Wilbarger County [had been] put on the market for settlement. A crew of men from the Indian country came across the Red River into Wilbarger County claiming to be cattlemen after a herd of cattle. But when they left there were eighteen head of horses and two mules missing that were the property of the school land settlers." Captain Scott, on orders from the governor, sent Brooks on the trail of the thieves, accompanied by Privates Dee Coldwell, a distant cousin of Brooks's, and Henry Putz, a brash nineteen-year-old from Dallas.

"The thieves were two days ahead of us when we crossed the Red River. We took the trail north for about fifty miles, then went to Indian Agent [Robert L.] Owens's headquarters [at Ft. Sill] and requested assistance, which was given: Lieut. Thomas Knight of Capt. Sixkiller's scouts went with us with a pocket full of warrants for the thieves. We learned that the horses and mules had been traded and sold to settlers over in Pauls Valley." A man named Guthrie apparently had purchased the stolen mules; Brooks had orders to either retrieve the mules or have the owner pay a fair price to keep them.

The four lawmen rode east out of Ft. Sill, crossing Beaver Creek and past Rush Springs to the valley situated along the Washita River in the Chickasaw Nation lands. They located the horses, but not the mules, and after explaining the situation to the ranchers, herded the recovered horses westward along the old military road. They spent a night near Erin Springs and then headed up the Washita.

Early Saturday morning, May 19, the stolen stock was brought to Red Alexander's store. W. V. "Uncle Red" Alexander was born in Alabama in 1833 and came with his second wife Martha and their six sons to Indian Territory in 1881, where he built his store on the old military road that ran alongside the Washita. In 1885 Alexander's place was designated as a post office and soon the little town of Alex began to blossom around the general store.[29] On this day in 1886 Red's oldest son Perry was minding the store, and Ridge Whitlock also was clerking for Uncle Red.

Miles to the north of the post office, a round-up was under way and dozens of cowboys had gathered two weeks earlier to join in on the job. Obediah Y. Love of Caldwell, Kansas, was one of the organizers. Tom Burke, Henry Witt, and Price Fulton were among the cow hands, and a twenty-four-year old named Albert St. John had also joined up. St. John enjoyed a rascally reputation across Indian Territory, and had been suspected of rustling over in the panhandle of Texas. On Friday, May 18, Love sent the four cowboys to Uncle Red's store for provisions; they rode into town early Saturday afternoon.[30]

Brooks described what followed: "The stolen stock was brought into the store on Saturday, and Putz and Coldwell took charge of them and tied them to some shade trees." Coldwell stayed with the horses and made camp while Putz rode back to join Brooks and the Indian police officer Knight. "By that time, a big crowd had gathered. Lieut. Knight and I mixed with the crowd trying to locate the leader of the thieves. One of the ranchers thought he had seen one of them, a tall long black haired man, around the store."

Brooks, Knight, and Putz walked over to the store and sat on some chairs on the front porch. It was about 3:00 in the afternoon. Before long three cowboys rode up, dismounted, and strode inside. Brooks nodded in their direction as they walked up, and the one in front, a tall young cowboy with long black hair, Albert St. John, nodded back. He carried a pistol on one hip, a scabbard and knife on the other, and two cartridge belts slung over his shoulder. As they disappeared inside Red's store, Knight turned to Brooks and informed him that the broad-shouldered cowboy was the same man he'd encountered three weeks earlier: carrying weapons inside Indian Territory was against the law except for peace officers, and Knight recalled warning the cowboy and receiving only a curt reply.

Knight said he would need to relieve the cowboy of his revolver, and asked if Brooks would accompany him inside; Brooks agreed. The two men stepped inside, young Henry Putz a few steps behind. Albert St. John had by this time walked to the end of the store and sat up on the counter. Burke and Fulton stood away from St. John who was talking amiably with Ridge Whitlock and a customer named Fleming Stanford. Perry Alexander had just stepped into a large storage closet, and a local resident named Bill Long was the only other person inside the store.[31]

Knight walked purposefully down the narrow aisle and right up to St. John, whose back was turned to him. Brooks moved to the right and Putz stood just back a step. Knight said in a quiet but steady tone, "I'll take that pistol from you now." Startled, St. John swung around on the counter and in the same motion slid his feet to the floor and reached for the gun on his hip. Brooks hollered, "Hold up! Hold up!" Lieutenant Knight grabbed for the gun that now pointed at his side. In the next instant the three lawmen pulled their guns. St. John reached his left hand to grab Brooks's revolver pointed at him and called out, "Let 'er pop!" Four shots fired in what sounded to the witnesses in the store like a simultaneous explosion.

Three of the bullets, two from Brooks's gun and one from Putz's, struck St. John even as his boots hit the floor. The concussion of sound echoed through the small store. St. John took a faltering step backwards and fell on his side, dead a moment later from the bullet that had penetrated his heart before exiting his back.

The other cowboys dashed outside, followed a few moments later by the peace officers. Young Perry Alexander peeked from the closet to see the body lying on the floor. Sergeant Brooks stepped out into the bright sunlight on the porch and shouted for a doctor, knowing that it was already too late.[32]

The story spread rapidly through the little town. Burke and Fulton made for their horses and headed back to the ranch to tell their boss what had happened; Obediah Love rode quickly into town that evening, in time to see St. John's body carried in a hastily prepared coffin to a nearby building.

The four lawmen left town before sundown, the stolen horses in tow. Brooks remembered their taking a circuitous route out of the area, fearing that St. John's friends might come after them: "We camped on a creek where there were a lot of large trees. About midnight sixteen armed men crossed the creek: they were on our trail. We were glad they passed without discovering where we were. The four of us were not anxious for a fight when there was four to one against us." It is not known if this was indeed a posse looking for the lawmen: Brooks admitted later that there were "whiskey runners" in that territory at the time.

"Early the next morning we arrived at the Pauls Valley P. O. and supply store. The postmaster told his clerk to get his horse and guide us another way back to the [Indian] agency." On the way back to Ft. Sill, the four men decided to lighten their load by selling the stolen horses back to the ranchers from whom they had just appropriated them. The two mules were also found, but left behind as well. Arriving at last at the I. B. Ranch near Fort Sill, Agent Owens told the Rangers to "go on back to Texas." Lt. Knight, Henry Putz, and Brooks wrote out affidavits for Agent Owens detailing the incident three days earlier. Then, wrote Brooks years later, "we spent two days at the Suggs Ranch where we learned that those same desperate cowboys had been giving them trouble. Two days later we were safe back in Texas."[33]

But James Brooks's dealings with this affair were far from over.

3

THE SHOOT-OUTS

Judge Parker remarked, "If there were more like them in this land of blood, it would be a better country."

On May 26, 1886, Obediah Y. Love wrote the following letter to Montgomery A. Sandels, the district attorney for the federal court located in Ft. Smith, Arkansas: "Dear Sir, I as a personal friend of Albert St. John, who was murdered at Alex, Chickasaw Nation, Ind. Ty., under direction of Dept. U.S. Marshal Menohan ask that writs be issued for the murderers and they be arrested and carried to Ft. Smith for trial. Albert St. John was murdered at Alex on the 19th of this month by T. R. Knight, J. A. Brooks and two [*sic*] unknown men. The murder was cold blooded as the eye witnesses below will attest." Stanford, Burke, Long, and Fulton's names were scribbled across the bottom of the letter.[1]

Five days later the federal court brought charges of murder against Knight, Putz, and Brooks, who "feloniously, willfully, premeditatedly and of their malice aforethought killed and murdered Albert St. John." A warrant was issued for their arrest, and in late July the three men appeared before the court in Ft. Smith and pled not guilty to the charges. They remained under house arrest into September, and were then discharged under their own recognizance and allowed to return to their jobs until the new court date was set for the following March.[2]

During Brooks's absence from Company F and from Texas, the "Fence Cutter Wars" in Brown County erupted with a new fury. As the railroads moved west of the Brazos and into what had been Comanche country, ranchers and farmers made their way out into the broad expanse of West Texas. With their arrival the free range began to disappear even as the American Indians had a decade earlier, and that brought a frustration among many that resulted in miles of the "cursed" barbed wire being destroyed in a futile attempt to stem the progress of civilizing the frontier. As Walter Prescott Webb described the scene, "When they saw all the lands going under fence, they seized their wire-cutters and used them in the determination to keep the free range. The horse thief was caught with the horse and the cow thief with the cow, but the fence-cutter rode away from the curling steel tendrils with no evidence upon him. He had to be caught on the job through detective work."[3]

Much of the violence was concentrated in Brown County in the mid-1880s, enough so that Governor Ireland sent the Rangers to investigate, and special laws were passed by the state legislature to give law enforcement a stronger hand to play. One of the targets of the fence cutters in Brown County was the defiant rancher L. P. "Lev" Baugh who, after a year of repairing fences, left a note on a post that simply said: "You cowardly cur, this is my fence and you let it alone." By early 1885 a grand jury sat to contemplate charges against a list of local culprits, the list supplied by the Baugh brothers to Brown County Sheriff W. N. Adams. Eight men were indicted but the trial was postponed until the fall of 1886, and trouble continued unabated.[4]

Adjutant General King ordered Texas Ranger Ira Aten to take personal charge of investigating the volatile situation there. Aten went undercover with a rancher named Joe Copeland, infiltrating the fence-cutter mob. Meanwhile, Company F was ordered to move its camp from Harrold down into Brown County in September; they set up shop on the thirtieth.[5] Sergeant Brooks had returned by that time from Arkansas and joined the company as it awaited word from the undercover agents.

Word came the first week in November: a "cutting party" had been scheduled for the night of November 9, and Baugh's ranch was again the target. Captain Scott of Company F took Brooks and privates Jim Carmichael, Billy Treadwell, and John Rogers to intercept the fence cutters. L. P. Baugh sent three of his ranch hands, and Aten and Copeland managed to elude the fence cutters and join the Rangers at the appointed location.

Half a dozen riders arrived at the long fence line at about midnight. In the shadows of nearby brush the Rangers waited. Two of the perpetrators, Amos Roberts and Jim Lovell, had been indicted by the grand jury the year before. Others in the band may have included Ace and John Matthews, Bob Parrock, Frank Johnson, and Wood Runnels, all but the last also on the grand jury's list. Roberts and Lovell dismounted and approached the fence while the others remained on horseback.

As the two men pulled wire cutters, Captain Scott emerged from the shadows and shouted, "Texas Rangers!" The others in his posse stood at the signal, revolvers and Winchesters cocked. The unidentified riders spurred their horses and disappeared into the darkness at the same moment the two men on the ground grabbed for their rifles. Two volleys rang out only seconds apart. Roberts was hit so hard by the rifle fire that he tumbled in a backwards somersault; Lovell clutched at his chest and crumpled to the ground. Both died within hours, and were buried on Lev Baugh's property.

The next morning a confrontation in the city streets between the two factions was narrowly averted by the intervention of Captain Scott. Two weeks later, information led to the arrest by Sergeant Brooks of Wood Runnels, and later Frank Johnson–tracked into Callahan County, both identified as participants in the November 9 incident. An attempt was made on Joe Copeland's life that same month, and the grand jury lumped together five of the fence cutters in an indictment that drifted through the courts until a dismissal of all charges in 1888.[6]

Late in the year Charles B. McKinney, the man who had recruited Bud Brooks in 1883 and now served as sheriff in La Salle County, was gunned down and killed in cold blood near Twohig in the same county where he was sheriff. Twohig, organized in the 1870s and located twelve miles south of Cotulla, later became the town of

Artesia. Bud Crenshaw and McKinney's old nemesis Jim McCoy ambushed the sheriff on the day after Christmas; a deputy named Pete Edwards was wounded during the fracas. Crenshaw was hunted down and killed by Texas Rangers on January 17. McCoy turned himself in and was tried for the murder. Brooks later wrote in his memoirs, "Jim McCoy was hanged by the neck for it so that ended his career. The other man who was also guilty of that murder was shot and killed by the Texas Rangers, another career ended to the credit of the wide awake boys who are at all times true to their own convictions and to this great state."[7]

During December, Company F scouted into McCulloch, Concho, and Lampasas counties on the look-out for fence cutters; no arrests were made. In January 1887, Captain Scott reported that there had been no fence cutting problems in Brown County that entire month. By the first of March, Company F had moved its camp to Sabine County in East Texas: a whole new drama awaited Brooks and the Rangers there.

During Brooks's absence while in court in Arkansas the previous summer, Company F had moved to near Hemphill along the Sabine River to track members of the Conner family accused of murdering two neighbors. The Conners, Uncle Willis and his boys Frederick (Fed), Charlie, Bill, and Alfred (Alfie), holed up deep in the bayou bottomlands east of Hemphill, hardscrabble country they knew like the back of their hands. Captain Scott had another view of it: "I had rather be a pack mule out west than be a million heir [*sic*] in this brush," he wrote. "We have been going out here every day, and each man brings back Ticks. Enough to keep him scratching and Kussing all night."[8]

Charlie and Fed Conner had been arrested and convicted the previous winter for the murder of Kit Smith and Eli Lowe, and both had broken out of jail and disappeared with the family into the morass of the Sabine bayou country. In August after weeks of futile searching, Scott found a trail that led into Louisiana and arrested Alfie Conner there. While the rest of the clan plotted revenge, Alfie was whisked off to jail and Company F returned to Brownwood.[9]

A renewal of violence around Hemphill in March 1887 brought Company F back to the Sabine less than excited about the prospects. "Sure rough country on man and beast," Scott reported. "Can stand it if I can only get back to the prairie alive."[10] He would, barely.

The Conners had forced the last sheriff to resign by sheer intimidation, and the new peace officer adamantly refused to hunt for them down in the bayous. "They terrorized the whole country," a newspaper reporter wrote. "People were afraid to light their lamps after dark. The gang would drive up to a farm, force the farmer to hitch up his team to a wagon, fill it full of corn, and then they would take it to their camp in the woods. And they would move camps frequently."[11]

Two local judges, James Polly and William Wallace Weatherred, had called for the Rangers; they were soon deputized and joined the company along with three other locals: Milton Anthony, Henry Harris, and John Toole. Redden "Red" Alford, another local, was suspected of aiding the Conners, and he soon was enlisted as a scout for the expanded company.[12] On March 25 the posse rode out of Hemphill south along the edge of the Sabine bottom, but after five days of tracking they returned empty handed and not a little frustrated.

Late on the thirtieth, a report came to the camp through Alford's brother that Red was helping the Conners move their camp and that he, Red, would come to guide them soon. When the guide arrived about 3 a.m. the Rangers divided into two parties and moved out. Captain Scott led one group that included Sergeant Brooks, John Rogers, Jim Carmichael, Billy Treadwell, and Jim Moore. Privates Bob Crowder and Ed Caldwell took the locals and branched out in another direction, the two groups hoping to cover more ground in the pitch black darkness until one or both found the Conner camp.[13] Another participant, Private J. Allen Newton, chronicled the action in a newspaper interview some years later, and picks up the story here:

"Capt. Scott ordered us to leave our horses and pull off our leggings and spurs and approach the camp as quietly as we could. Alford said that we would know when we got near the camp because [the Conners] always hobbled their pack horse and tied a small bell on him.

We walked and walked until we got tired out from walking but never heard any bell. Capt. Scott accused Alford of lying but he swore we were on the right trail.

"When we were about three hundred yards from the camp, as we found out later, Alford refused to go any further. 'They're right down there,' he said. 'I don't want to go any further because if you don't kill or arrest them, they'll kill me.'

"'All right, you coward,' Capt. Scott said, 'lie down here.'

"The Conners were at 'Camp Handy' which was situated on a high knoll. It was called by that name because there was a clump of five or six tall pine trees on it, and not another tree for 200 yards around them. The old man with Fed and Charley [and Bill], their pack horse and four dogs were all in them trees. Their dogs were trained never to bark, and all during that fight they never uttered a yelp.

"Quicker than it takes to tell it," Newton continued, "Jim Moore of Kerrville was killed, Capt. Scott got shot through the left lung, and Rogers was shot in the left side and arm." Even at the same instant, according to the official Ranger reports, another Conner, thirty-two-year-old Bill, fell in a hail of bullets from Sergeant Brooks's Winchester. "But," Newton recalled, "they must have fired at the same time, because the bullet Bill shot cut off three fingers of Brooks's left hand and lodged between the thumb and forefinger of his right hand."[14] Conner's bullet apparently caromed along Brooks's rifle barrel, slicing through the first knuckle of each of his three middle fingers on his left hand and slamming into the palm of his right hand as it was curled around the stock.

Rogers and Brooks fell to the ground at about the same moment, and in the darkness managed to bandage one another as the shooting continued around them. Jim Carmichael bent down to see about Jim Moore, but the recent recruit from Company C was dead a moment after he fell. Captain Scott writhed in pain on the ground, and Billy Treadwell's gun jammed after only a couple of shots into the dark. Meanwhile, Uncle Willis, Fed, and Charlie kept firing from behind the cover of the pine trees.

Jim Carmichael stood alone, firing repeatedly at the flashes of fire coming from the Conner rifles. One of his bullets hit Fed, others struck the dogs and the pack horse. Rogers managed to sit up and fire off several shots even as he bled from the two bullet wounds. Brooks tried to help but with both hands disabled he could not even grip his rifle.

The shooting signaled the other group a hundred yards off in the darkness and they soon came running. The three Conners, still alive, disappeared like ghosts; Bill Conner, the pack horse, and all four dogs lay dead. When the others arrived, "Carmichael had reloaded," Newton recalled, "and was firing in the direction in which they had disappeared, cussing the Conners for being cowards."[15] In his official report Captain Scott recognized the bravery of Carmichael as having saved the lives of the wounded Rangers, but noted: "the citizens being more accustomed to hunting deer than desperadoes held their stand, not being more than eighty yards distant from the fight and did not come to our assistance for minutes after the fight was over. Had the squad come," Scott offered a bit optimistically, "we would have captured the entire Conner gang." The captain ordered all of the fugitives' equipment that had been left behind destroyed.[16]

As first light peeked into the bayou country, the situation looked bad for the wounded Rangers. Captain Scott's wound was the most serious, although he managed to give several commands before turning over the duties to Sergeant Brooks. Tourniquets had stanched the bleeding from Brooks and Rogers's wounds, and a burial detail was organized shortly to dig Jim Moore's grave. Judge Weatherred led Privates Crowder and Newton and the deputized citizens the four miles back to the horses, and the three then rode hard to Hemphill and San Augustine twelve miles further to find doctors. Judge Polly scribbled a note on a piece of paper from one of the Ranger's notebooks to be handed to whomever they reached first: "Capt. Scott and two of his men was [*sic*] shot this morning by the Conners," it read, "and wishes that you come at once to this place as they need & wish your service and attention on them. Be sure and come right away as they are badly wounded."[17]

Dr. J. W. Smith was soon located in Hemphill, and Dr. Frank Tucker received Polly's note in San Augustine later that day and headed for the woods. Several citizens in Hemphill, including just by chance Captain Scott's sister, volunteered wagons to help carry the wounded Rangers out of the tangled briar country. Miss Scott went with Smith, the first to arrive on the bloody scene. Smith wrote in his medical report: "I extracted the ball [from Captain Scott's lung] about Noon which relieved the difficulty of breathing to some extent. I was very doubtful as to his reacting," so doubtful that he did not bother dressing the wound. "I amputated three fingers for Brooks on one hand and removed a ball from the other hand." He dressed Rogers's wounds, the bullet to his side having been deflected by the Ranger's pocket notebook in his vest: that likely saved Rogers's life.[18]

Dr. Tucker in his report seemed more optimistic about Scott's condition. "Hope to save his life," he wrote. "His wounds had not been dressed [when I arrived] for he was expected to die. A Winchester ball had carved away Brooks' fingers, and," Tucker agreed with his colleague, "nothing to do but clip off ends of bones and wrap hand."[19]

"Finally we got up some neighbors," Private Newton continued in his interview, "which was a hard thing to find in that country, who helped us make litters of the pine boughs to carry our dead and wounded into Hemphill that night [April 1]. We buried Moore the next day." Captain Scott still in critical condition, "Brooks took charge and ordered me to go to Nacogdoches, the nearest railroad station, to wire the dead and wounded men's relatives, and to get some dogs to track the Conners with. He gave me his horse which I was to change for a fresh one at St. Augustine."

Jim Moore's uncle, Kerr County Sheriff Frank Moore, arrived at Hemphill on April 3 and took the dead man's possessions back to Center Point and his family. "The dogs from the prison at Rusk were brought by a man named Jones," Newton recalled. "John M. Spradley, who was then sheriff of Nacogdoches County and one of the most famous sheriffs of East Texas, joined us when we returned to Hemphill, and stayed with us about ten days."[20]

Sheriff Spradley and Jim Carmichael led a posse in search of the Conners using the dogs from Rusk. They spent weeks in the Atoyac River bottom lands but managed only to arrest five locals charged with aiding the fugitives. On October 25 another posse of Rangers and citizens gunned down Fed Conner not far from the Camp Handy battle site.[21] Newton tells the rest of the story: "The state offered $1000 reward for the Conners dead or alive. A man named Turner went down there [undercover] as a sewing machine salesman. He located [Uncle Willis'] grandson and followed him one morning when the boy went to take his grandfather his breakfast.

"The old man was sitting up against a tree with his gun resting across his knees. Turner got so excited that he killed both the old man and the little boy. The old man's body remained upright leaning against the tree. The citizens were so afraid of him that they thought he was playing possum and wouldn't go near him. They sent for Mr. Polley [*sic*] and he had the body buried."[22]

Over time, the three seriously wounded Rangers recovered. John Rogers eventually left for his Kingsbury home near Seguin where he convalesced for several weeks before returning to duty. He was accompanied to camp by his brother Curren "Kid" Rogers who joined Company F. Captain Scott went back to his post in June, but in 1888 resigned from the Rangers and went to Mexico where he worked successfully as a railroad contractor. Jim Carmichael also resigned in 1888 and left Texas altogether; Billy Treadwell became a cow hand on a ranch near Goliad. And Jim Brooks learned to operate a rifle and a revolver with his bad hand, to such a degree that his reputation as one of the fastest guns in the Ranger service was not diminished in the years that followed this dramatic confrontation along the Sabine.[23]

J. Allen Newton offered one more postscript to the story of the Conner Fight: "The girls [in Hemphill], who had never seen anybody but the country boys in their homespun clothes, thought we were 'it' in our city clothes. [Sergeant] Brooks courted a minister's daughter there." Twenty-one-year-old Miss Martha Peddy's father, Pastor Andrew Jackson Peddy, cared for the small flock at First Baptist

Company F, Frontier Battalion, 1887, shortly after the Conner Fight. Note Brooks's crippled left hand as he is standing third from right.

Courtesy Brooks family.

Church in Hemphill. "He asked her to go to church one day. She came out of the house carrying her shoes under one arm. When they got near the church, she sat down on a stone and put on her shoes. We sure did tease Brooks about his girl."[24]

Sergeant Brooks assumed command of what was left of Company F during Captain Scott's absence for the months of April and May. A train robbery between Benbrook and Weatherford sent Company F there on June 10 but the robbers had already been captured by the time they arrived. The Rangers moved west to the railroad town of Cisco next where elections were being held that some thought would cause violence. With the Rangers present into July, the elections were carried out peacefully.[25]

When John Barber's gang held up a train near Flatonia in early July, Deputy U.S. Marshal William Van Ryper rode to Cisco to enlist the Rangers' help in tracking the bandits who were headed for Indian Territory. He arrived on Sunday, July 10, and enlisted John Rogers–after waiting for him to leave church services–to aid him on the trail.[26] Interestingly, Private Rogers had briefly assumed command of the company two days earlier: Captain Scott had been feeling poorly, and Sergeant Brooks had been called to Ft. Smith to stand trial for murder.

The killing of Albert St. John in Indian Territory fourteen months earlier now came back to haunt James Brooks. Following the indictment by the grand jury the previous fall, the trial had been scheduled for March but postponed twice, and now sat on Federal Judge Isaac C. Parker's docket for July 15 in Ft. Smith. Judge Parker, known across Arkansas and Indian Territory as the "hangin' judge," had served on the bench since its inception in 1875, achieving notoriety for his swift and extreme judgments.[27]

Brooks later wrote, "Putz and Coldwell had both resigned. Deputy U.S. Marshal Ben Cabell notified Capt. Scott to send me to Dallas, Texas, where Putz was living, and that he (Cabell) would take us to Fort Smith, Arkansas. Mr. Bill Butler of Karnes County [a wealthy third generation rancher who lived near Kenedy] wired the marshal at Fort Smith to have my bail bond fixed and that he and other friends in Texas would sign for the money. [But] I stayed with the marshal, therefore no bond was required. Putz and Knight were also there at that time." All three had been indicted. "There was a lot of grumbling around the courtroom that Knight and I were not being held in the Federal Jail, but Judge Parker remarked, 'If there were more like them in this land of blood, it would be a better country.'

"Boudernot [*sic*], a renowned attorney from Indian Territory, was at Ft. Smith at the time. He was a full-blood Cherokee Indian, but a good one. He offered his services to us without pay and we loved him for his magnanimity." In fact the U.S. attorney general had issued an order that the Indian police officer Knight be granted a defense attorney without cost, on the basis of his argument that he had been following orders when he confronted St. John. Elias Cornelius Boudinot came from a prominent Cherokee family; a Fort Smith attorney named Thomas Barnes also helped on their defense team.[28]

Brooks remembered some frontier celebrities who were in court at that same time: "The noted outlaw women, Belle Starr, Cattle Annie, Little Breeches, and others were there that summer of 1887. I saw Belle Starr when she came riding to court on her big black horse. She was really a picturesque character in her black riding habit seated on an old-fashioned side saddle," he wrote, perhaps remembering Mag Hickman from his Collin County days at the same time. "Although summoned again and again [over the years], she was always acquitted by the juries that were composed of sympathizers. That was also the year that hangman Muldoon [*sic*] dropped his sixteenth criminal through the hangman's shoot, and died himself with a stroke just after." George Maledon, a U.S. deputy marshal originally from Detroit, served Judge Parker's court to the grisly tune of sixty, not sixteen, convicted felons plummeting through the hangman's door over a twenty-year period. He retired in 1896 after Judge Parker died from complications of a stroke, went on several promotional tours as "the hangman," and died in 1911.[29]

The trial began on July 15, 1887, and lasted ten days. The prosecution, headed by district attorney M. H. Sandels, sent more than a dozen witnesses to the stand, the most significant being those in or around Alexander's store that day: Fleming Stanford, Price Fulton, H. M. Long, and Thomas Burke. Henry Witt, who had known St. John for two years and had ridden into town with him that fateful day, spoke for the prosecution as did Obediah Love, the man who had sent the cowboys to town. Ridge Whitlock, the young clerk at the store, was absent from the hearings, excused due to his wife's difficult pregnancy at the time.

Young Perry Alexander took the stand and admitted he had been playing dice in the back storeroom when the gunfire erupted. A diagram was introduced that showed the inside of the store and the approximate spot where each of the men was standing when the

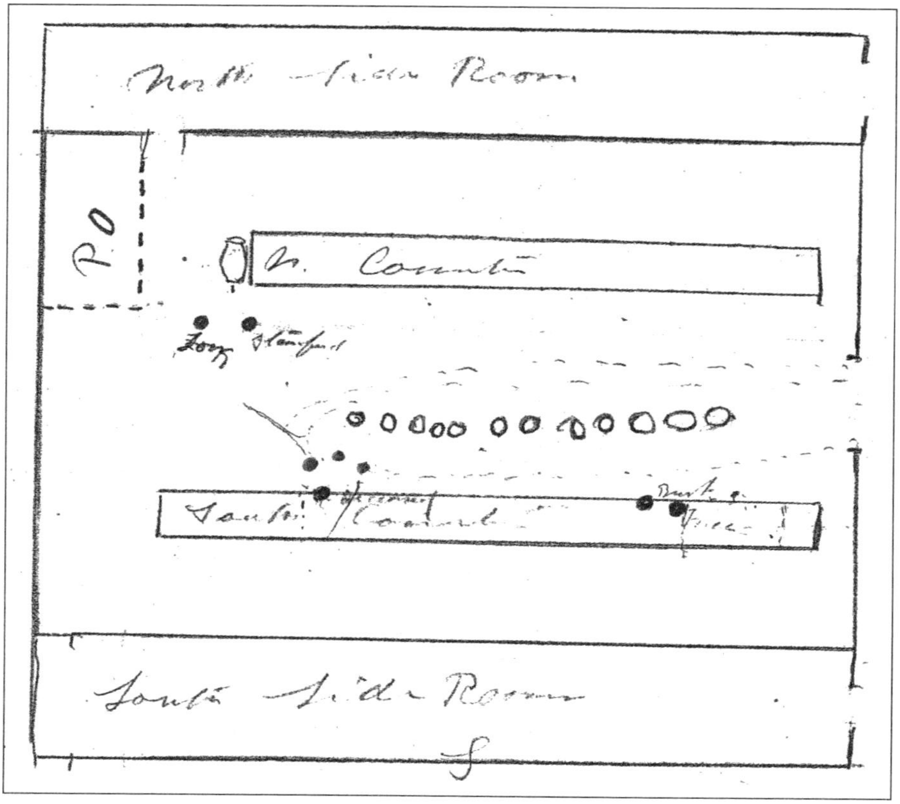

Sketch of interior, Uncle Red's Store, Alex, Oklahoma, from the trial testimony records, Ft. Smith, Arkansas.

Criminal case files, National Archives, Southwest Region, Ft. Worth.

shoot-out commenced. Red Alexander described where two bullet holes were later found in the floor and on one wall.

The prosecution rested on July 22 and the defense called its only three witnesses over the next two days: Knight, Putz, and finally Sergeant Brooks. Henry Putz defended himself when accused by the prosecution of being a quick draw, "traveling on your six-shooter." "No, sir," replied Putz. "I seen he [St. John] had his pistol, I didn't have much time to think, I thought it was time to shoot to get the pistol away from him."

"When St. John jerked Knight up against the counter," Sandels pressed the defendant, "that left St. John free to you: why didn't you throw your arms around him?"

"Well," Putz drawled, "I wasn't in love with him."[30]

Brooks appeared last at the trial, identifying himself as being thirty-one years of age, living in Texas, engaged "in the ranger establishment for five years and as first sergeant when the incident occurred." Defense Attorney Barnes asked, "Your hand seems to be disfigured there."

"Yes, sir," said Brooks. "That was done the 31st of last March, after the killing." Brooks recounted the shooting of St. John as he answered the questions one by one. After noting that St. John had died soon after falling to the floor, Brooks was asked: "Why did you shoot the man?"

"Well, for this reason," Brooks replied. "I did it to keep the man from killing me or Knight. He was a powerful man. I was satisfied he could kill either one or all of us. I was satisfied the man would shoot. I only fired to save myself and these other men. I didn't kill him to disarm him."

"Did it appear to you that you could have done different?" Barnes asked.

"No, sir," Brooks answered without hesitation. "I could not."

Then it was Sandels's turn at the Ranger. He hammered away at the fact that the three defendants failed to note in their original affidavits that Knight had grabbed St. John's drawn gun. "Can you explain why it is the three of you failed to make that statement before [Owens] and yet all three of you make that statement here? Can you tell me why that is?"

"I object," Barnes spoke as he rose to his feet before Brooks could reply. "He cannot answer for anybody, only himself."

"I think it's better to put that to the Court and not argue about it," Sandels shot back.

"I don't need any lectures about it from you," Barnes stood his ground.

"I don't need any from you neither," said Sandels. "I understand my position exactly."

Judge Parker interrupted, "Let the question go," he ordered. The cross-examination moved on.

Toward the end of Brooks's testimony, the D.A. asked him why he didn't help Knight grab St. John's gun instead of drawing his own. "After a man gets his pistol out," the Ranger replied, "there ain't no time to take it from him. St. John was a very large and powerful man and I know well enough to know that when a man has a pistol in his hands."

Sandels interrupted. "And so you concluded to kill him."

"I expect my pistol was the first to fire," replied Brooks.[31]

The trial moved to its final session shortly after with closing statements by Sandels and Boudinot. On the morning of July 26 Judge Parker gave instructions to the jury and sent them to the jury room to deliberate. They were not gone long. Dave Blair, the foreman, read the jury's decision:

"On the charge of murder in the first degree: Not guilty. On the charge of manslaughter, we find all three guilty."[32]

4

THE GARZA WAR

We entered the room, covered the robbers with our six guns and arrested them.

GUILTY!

Based on the affidavits, memoirs, and trial testimony of the three defendants it is clear they believed themselves to be innocent of this crime: each in his own way had presumed he was doing his duty, following the law, and assisting in the lawful arrest of Albert St. John. What a shock it must surely have been when they heard the foreman read the verdict.

Judge Parker may have been just as shocked as the three defendants. On July 28 Parker issued the sentence and had the three men locked up in the Ft. Smith jail, although they spent the next three weeks essentially under house arrest. Late in August the federal judge called the men back into his court and announced his suspension of their sentences effective immediately.[1] Lt. Knight returned to his Ft. Sill assignment, Henry Putz returned home to Dallas, and James Brooks headed back to Company F. Everyone believed the incident was now over and done. But not so.

Political pressure from friends of Sergeant Brooks to blot out the conviction came from all directions in the form of letters and telegrams addressed to A. H. Garland, attorney general of the United States; two dozen petitions arrived from Indian Territory and Texas townships with over 700 signatures. Many believed the jury was made up of cowboys who would naturally side with their own against the three peace officers; some, including Brooks, blamed the brash young Henry Putz's cavalier attitude on the stand for swaying the already biased jury. Others knew that Brooks's reputation would surely be besmirched and a long shadow cast on his budding career as a Ranger unless the conviction was erased.

Judge Parker could suspend the sentence; it would take someone on a much higher bench to overturn it. Capt. William Scott, Brooks's commanding officer, was the first to suggest the appeal to the White House, in a letter dated August 6 asking Capt. Lam Sieker "to assist me in getting up a document in Brooks' behalf to be sent to the president asking a pardon for Brooks." Having contacted the defense attorneys in Ft. Smith, Scott wrote Sieker that "the Judge [Parker] will not sentence the boys until they can hear from the President on their case. Brooks says that their conviction was due to the impudent talk and actions at Ft. Smith of ex-Ranger Putz," he added. "Please do all you can for Brooks. He is a perfect gentleman and has always made a first class soldier."[2]

At the suggestion of attorney Thomas Barnes, who had assisted in the defense, an application for the pardon of Knight, Brooks, and Putz was issued that same day, and a request that those papers be forwarded "as soon as possible." Telegrams flew across the lines in every direction.

The first response on behalf of Sergeant Brooks came from his home state of Kentucky, and immediately. On August 8 letters appealing for a presidential pardon came from James B. McCreary, a member of the U.S. House of Representatives and a former governor of Kentucky, and Joseph Clay Stiles Blackburn, one of Kentucky's U.S. senators. Blackburn wrote in part: "Brooks comes of one of the oldest and best families in Ky. His brother in law, [Will] Morgan, is one of my best and closest friends, which will explain the deep personal interest I feel in the effort of his friends to secure his pardon."

That same day another Kentucky congressman, Col. W. C. P. Breckinridge, descendant of one of the most prominent Bluegrass State

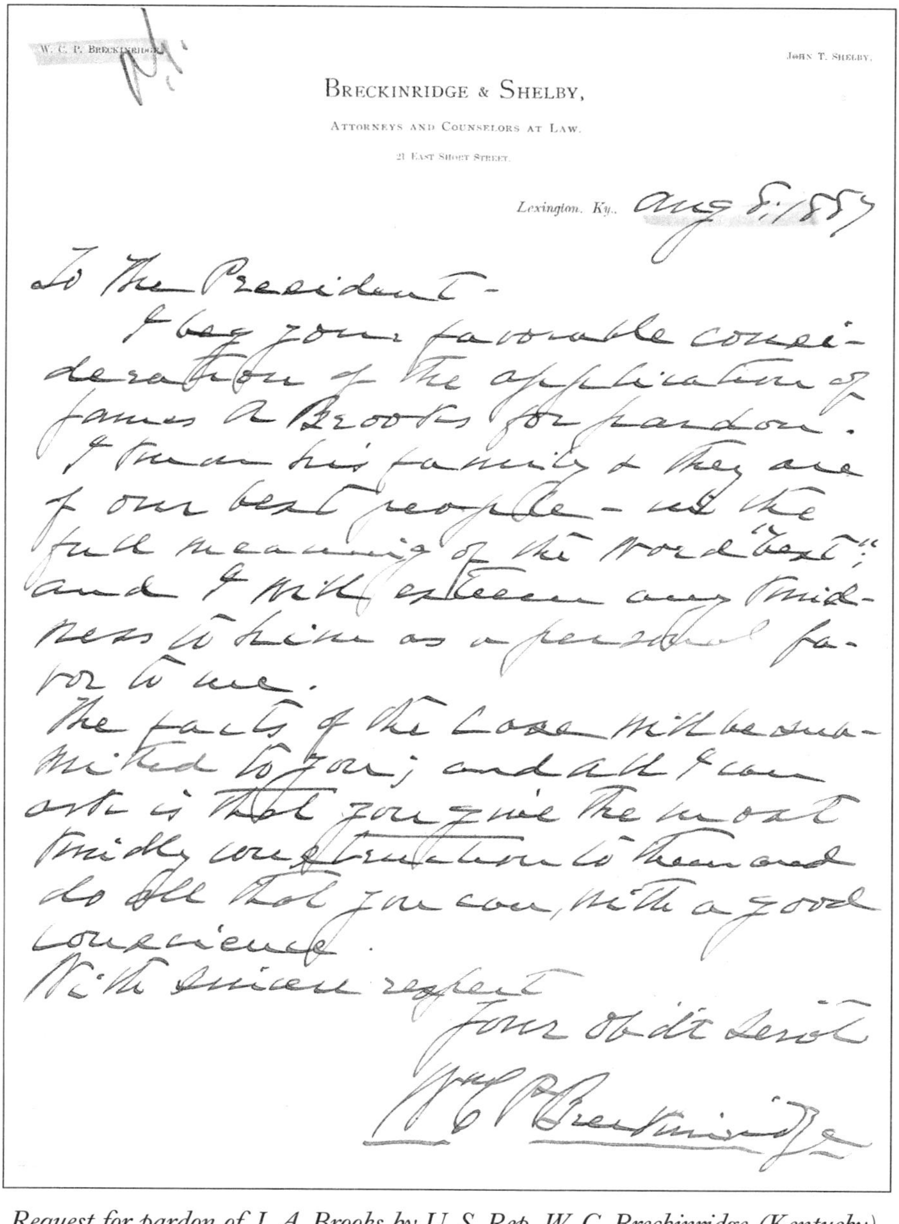

W. C. P. BRECKINRIDGE. JOHN T. SHELBY.

BRECKINRIDGE & SHELBY,

ATTORNEYS AND COUNSELORS AT LAW.

21 EAST SHORT STREET.

Lexington, Ky., Aug 8/1887

To The President -

I beg your favorable consideration of the application of James A Brooks for pardon. I know his family & they are of our best people - in the full meaning of the word "best"; and I will esteem any kindness to him as a personal favor to me.

The facts of the case will be submitted to you; and all I can ask is that you give the most kindly construction to them and do all that you can, with a good conscience.

With sincere respect

Your obdt Servt

Wm C P Breckinridge

Request for pardon of J. A. Brooks by U. S. Rep. W. C. Breckinridge (Kentucky), Aug. 8, 1887.

Criminal case files, National Archives, Southwest Region, Ft. Worth.

families, wrote from his office in Lexington. A day later an appeal arrived from Kentucky Democrat John G. Carlisle as he resided at the Hotel Arlington in Blue Lick Springs. Carlisle, Speaker of the U.S. House of Representatives, brought considerable political weight to the process; he would serve later on President Cleveland's cabinet.

Texas was heard from next, with petitions from Bastrop County citizens and Vernon, the town where Brooks's Ranger camp was headquartered at that time. On August 12, Texas Governor L. S. "Sul" Ross wrote: "I respectfully recommend the pardon of the two Texas Rangers Brooks and Putz." Joseph D. Sayers, U.S. congressman and later governor of Texas, sent a telegram as he traveled by train across Texas. Addressed directly to President Cleveland, the telegram "urged the immediate pardon" of Brooks: "I personally know him to be an honest, sober and law abiding citizen and a faithful and fearless official," likely using the term sober as a reference to a person of high moral character.

Richard Coke, former Texas governor and at that time U.S. senator, sent his appeal from Waco on August 27, and wrote: "Great sympathy is felt in Texas for these young men. They are excellent men and fine officers. They could have refused to have come to Lt. Knight's assistance, but being officers themselves they naturally responded to his request for aid." Wilbur H. King, adjutant general of Texas, wrote: "In the case of Brooks, I can state from my own knowledge and thorough acquaintance with him, that he is a man of unusually trustworthy character and good conduct–*sober*, brave, discreet and obedient as a soldier, and modest, quiet and honest as a man and citizen."

"I am sure he is morally innocent of any wrong in this matter," King's appeal continues. "He has served the State of Texas long and well, and with credit and gallantry–having been but a few months since crippled for life in the fearless discharge of his duty; during his long service in conduct has always been such as to entitle him to the approval of his superiors, and the esteem and confidence of his associates and the good citizens of our State."

On August 15, Robert Owens, U.S. Indian Agent for Indian Territory, secured the affidavit of Ridge Whitlock, an eyewitness to the St. John incident who had been absent from the trial. Whitlock writes that after the shooting, "I heard Knight remark that he [St. John] was a fine looking young fellow and he was sorry that it had occurred. It is my opinion and belief that Knight was in danger before he ever fired a shot." That affidavit, along with a lengthy letter from J. D. C. Atkins, commissioner of Indian Affairs for the Department of the Interior, accompanied the petitions and letters sent to Attorney General Garland and then forwarded to the president's desk.

In an addendum to his report and as a further persuasive argument, Owens's letter echoed the sentiment regarding Brooks: "[He] since that time in the service of his State as an officer, was waylaid with a number of other officers, his own hand shot off and several of his companions killed," the facts being skewed but the point made. "And since this occurrence of the 19th of May, 1886, Knight's two superior officers, Captain Samuel Sixkiller and Lieutenant William Fields, promoted to Captain after Sixkiller's death, have both been murdered. It is not very safe for police officers in this country when they are murdered on the one hand and convicted on the other."

J. M. Perryman, principal chief of the Muskogee Nation, agreed: "Believing that the conviction of Lieut. Knight for an act committed while in the discharge of his duty will have a tendency to render the lawless desperadoes with whom the Police have to deal more difficult to control, I would respectfully urge his pardon."

On September 13, 1887, six months into his first term as president of the United States, Grover Cleveland issued three pardons, including this one that reads:

"Whereas, at the May term, 1887, of the United States District Court for the Western District of Arkansas, J. A. Brooks was convicted of manslaughter, his sentence being suspended;

"And whereas, it appears that the homicide of which he was convicted, was the result of rashness while assisting an officer in the discharge of his duty, rather than of malice or criminal intent;

Grover Cleveland,

President of the United States of America,

To all to whom these Presents shall come, Greeting:

Whereas, at the May term, 1887, of ~~the United~~ States District Court for the Western District of Arkansas, J. A. Brooks was convicted of manslaughter, his sentence being suspended;

And whereas, it appears that the homicide of which he was convicted, was the result of rashness while, assisting an officer in the discharge of his duty, rather than of malice or criminal intent;

And whereas, his pardon is asked for by a number of the most respectable citizens of the region where the killing occurred, and also by influential gentlemen in other parts of the country:

Now, therefore, be it known, that I, Grover Cleveland, President of the United States of America, in consideration of the premises, divers other good and sufficient reasons me thereunto moving, do hereby grant to the said J. A. Brooks, a full and unconditional pardon.

hereunto signed my name and caused the seal of the United States to be affixed.

Done at the City of Washington, this Thirteenth day of September, A. D. 1887, and of the Independence of the United States the one hundred and twelfth.

Grover Cleveland

By the President:

T. F. Bayard

Secretary of State.

President Grover Cleveland's pardon of J. A. Brooks, Sept. 13, 1887.

Courtesy Brooks family.

"And whereas, his pardon is asked for by a number of the most respectable citizens of the region where the killing occurred, and also by influential gentlemen in other parts of the country;

"Now, therefore, be it known, that I, Grover Cleveland, President of the United States of America, in consideration of the premises, divers other good and sufficient reasons thereunto moving, do hereby grant to the said J. A. Brooks, a full and unconditional pardon."[2]

This stunning turn of events made a lasting impression on Brooks, his conviction forgiven, and more importantly a sense of eternal gratitude for those who had come to his aid. He had made his own impression on those who had come to know him in a relatively short time. From the Suggs Brothers and Indian Agent Robert Owens in Indian Territory, to rancher Bill Butler in Karnes County, to his own Captain Scott, and to the adjutant general of Texas, Gov. Ross and the congressmen from two states, the support proved overwhelming and successful. Brooks would never forget his debt to these men; his career would be a testimony of integrity to them.

Sergeant Brooks returned to Texas in early September. Company F had been busy during his absence, and had also moved part of the company and their camp from Cisco 100 miles southwest along the rails to Ballinger in Runnels County. In August the fence cutters in Brown County stirred up trouble once more with an attempt on rancher Joe Copeland's life. John Rogers led seven other Rangers there and arrested four suspects, three of whom had been previously hauled into court by Company F.[3]

Brooks reported first to Captain Scott in Cisco, then traveled on to Ballinger where Rogers nominally served as commander at that camp. Brooks arrived there on September 15 in time to receive the surprising and good news of his pardon by President Cleveland. On the twentieth, Brooks officially reenlisted, having been discharged on July 31 from the Frontier Battalion upon the Arkansas federal court's conviction.[4]

He enjoyed only fifteen days of respite before the job had him on the trail once again. "I joined, or I will say returned, to active service.

The stage coach from Ballinger had been robbed several times by a lone robber. Well, the robber, Jim Newsom, made the mistake of his life when he flashed a $100 bill in front of a friend of mine the night after the robbery. John M. Formwalt, the sheriff of Runnels County, and I were soon on the trail of the marked $100 bill.

"Newsom and his partner had bought a herd of horses. The sheriff was notified and we located the horses about 35 miles south of Ballinger. Newsom and his partner were at Coleman, Texas, waiting for Newsom's partner to go to trial for horse theft. We arrived at Coleman late at night. We went to the hotel and requested the manager to put an extra pallet for us in the room of the robbers," apparently pretending to be friends of Newsom. "When he opened the door, we entered the room, covered the robbers with our six guns and arrested them. Jim Newsom weakened and said that he would plead guilty. The final result was a ninety-nine year sentence in the federal penitentiary."

On November 20, 1887, James A. Brooks turned thirty-two years old; the next day, Company F moved their camp from Ballinger to just outside of San Angelo in Tom Green County. Brooks spent most of that month scouting far to the south in the rugged country of Edwards County, and in December traveled back to Tom Green County and aided John Rogers and Bob Crowder in the arrest of three cattle thieves near San Angelo.[5]

As the new year 1888 arrived Brooks found himself back in Edwards County until the middle of February when he rode the rails east to Crockett County in order to track and arrest a man named R. T. Bailey for assault. Brooks took Bailey to the jail in Runnels County where the warrant had been issued.[6] Since the Rangers were the only law enforcement agency in Texas who had jurisdiction across county lines, this line of work remained steady through the years: a telegram from a sheriff would lead to the trail of the fugitive, an arrest, and then back to the original county for prosecution. All too often, however, a sympathetic jury would find the party innocent, or a mistrial would end in the dismissal of charges, constantly frustrating the efforts of peace officers.

Company F, Frontier Battalion, 1888. Brooks is center front row.

Courtesy Brooks family.

On March 26, 1888, Company F moved their camp back to Ballinger. One month later, Capt. William Scott resigned and headed to Mexico to work for the railroads. Scott had been a mentor and friend as well as commander to Jim Brooks, and the sergeant would remember Scott many years later with kind and generous words: "I owe much of my success to him, not only as a Texas Ranger but in other vocations while passing through this long life."[7]

The Frontier Battalion was dwindling both by natural attrition and the budget reductions of the state legislature who saw little reason for the Rangers to be in existence, certainly not at the level they had been when Indians and desperadoes roamed the frontier. Company A had been the first to go; Company E temporarily disbanded on April 6, 1887, and on November 30, 1888, Company C's demise left only three companies and forty-eight Rangers in service. Four dozen men now took on the responsibility of keeping law and order in the largest state of the Union. "Their services have been necessarily arduous," wrote the adjutant general, "and have proved of great value despite the small numbers. Our frontier is an extensive one, and many of the border communities are largely dependent on the rangers for security to life and property, protection to courts and people, and the execution of the law."[8]

On May 1, 1888, J. A. Brooks was promoted to lieutenant and commander of Company F; John Rogers became his 1st Sergeant. Brooks had steadily moved up the ladder of command and in only five years as a Ranger found himself now in charge of a loyal band of a dozen men and an immense area to scout. In the official records of Company F for the year 1888, in fact, Brooks and his men logged 47,781 miles of travel across mostly South and West Texas, made 230 scouts, and arrested 249 alleged criminals.[9]

The role of the commander of a Ranger company during that period meant plenty of paperwork and reporting to be done. Telegrams arrived from Austin or a county seat asking for assistance and the commander assigned one or more men to the task; on rare occasions the commander himself would leave the camp to take up a job. Lieutenant Brooks logged each scout that took place including the miles traversed, made notes as to which Ranger arrested which fugitive and where and when, and filed a fairly detailed report for the adjutant general at the end of each month. An inventory of camp supplies and equipment usually went on the monthly report, and any comments as to the general conditions of both supplies and horses. Brooks, who was promoted to captain of Company F on May 1, 1889, completed his work faithfully for his company over the next sixteen years.

The years 1888 and 1889 were especially busy ones for Company F, not only because of the drastic reduction in the Frontier Battalion as a whole, necessitating the heavy load of work and even longer-distance scouts, but also because of the constant moving of the camp during that period. Brooks changed camp headquarters from Ballinger to Kerrville to Laredo, back to Kerrville and then to Rio Grande City the first year, and from Rio Grande City thence to Santa Maria, and finally to Cotulla in 1890.[10] Cotulla, where coal train laborer Bud Brooks had joined the Rangers only seven years earlier, became Company F's permanent camp for the next decade. It had been a meteoric rise for the young Kentuckian to the captaincy in the Texas Ranger Frontier Battalion.

It was in Kerr County that Lieutenant Brooks met the woman who would become his wife and the mother of their three children. Posted outside of Kerrville near Center Point in May 1888 to scout for reported fence cutters, Brooks had the occasion to be introduced to Miss Virginia Willborn. Virginia lived on the outskirts of Center Point with her brothers Thomas and Neal, raised by her grandmother after the deaths of their parents. Virginia's mother died giving birth to her in 1869. Grandmother Emeline married Rufus Moore and bore Virginia's mother, then married Thomas Coldwell in 1841 shortly after Rufus died.

Emeline Moore Coldwell endured a well-traveled life. In 1849 the Coldwells of Missouri, now including their children Cornelius and Carrie, followed thousands to California and the gold mines, where Thomas died in 1852. Emeline, twice widowed, moved to Tennessee briefly and then to Texas in 1860, probably with members of the Moore family who settled in Kerr County. When Virginia's father Albert "Lem" Willborn died in 1873, Emeline took the three children into her home and raised them as her own.[11]

Cornelius "Neal" Vernon Coldwell, Virginia's "half uncle," became a highly respected Texas Ranger and captained Company F in 1874 and Company A in 1876 before retiring from the service. Neal Willborn and Captain Coldwell's son Vernon also joined the Rangers.[12] And it was Captain Coldwell who introduced his niece to Jim Brooks in 1888. Enamored by Virginia's cowgirl expertise on horseback and with a gun–did Mag Hickman and Belle Starr come to his mind again?–Brooks took a leave of absence in September 1889, to court her. They were married a year later, on September 16, 1890, at the Center Point ranch, and moved to the Ranger camp in Cotulla.

In between the months of courting, Captain Brooks kept busy moving and coordinating the efforts of his Ranger company. He and

J. A. Brooks upon his promotion to Ranger captain, 1889. His top hat shields his left hand.

Courtesy Brooks family.

his men arrested four of the fence cutters in Kerr County in June 1888, and Brooks himself tracked and captured two horse thieves in July and a cattle thief in September. Company F shifted south to Laredo where, with the aid of Company D, thirty arrests were made in an alleged conspiracy to commit murder.[13]

From October 1888 until the following October, Company F camped outside Rio Grande City, concentrating on horse and cattle rustlers crossing from Texas into Mexico. Brooks rarely left camp during that period, focusing his efforts on maintaining the camp and sending his Rangers on scouts. In May and June he stayed in Roma for several days to guard court proceedings, and in October he divided the forces and sent half the company to camp eighty miles away at Santa Maria, twelve miles southwest of Harlingen, to cover more of the borderlands. Even still, the Ranger ranks proved so thin that only fifteen of the fifty-two requests for Rangers sent through Austin in 1889 proved manageable.[14]

On October 18, 1889, Brooks received a message from the post commander at Ft. Ringgold that one of his Rangers, Pvt. M. R. Daniels, had "roughed up" an army private named Isaac Terrell during a disturbance in town. Dismissing the charge at the time, Brooks received a letter of complaint against Daniels six weeks later from a citizen of Rio Grande City, again alleging rough treatment. When Adjutant General King heard of the complaints, he asked Brooks what was going on. Brooks replied that Daniels had been carrying out his duties and that any rough treatment was likely deserved. Nevertheless, King replied, Brooks was to keep Daniels in camp and send another Ranger into town.[15]

In February 1890, a dispute arose that Brooks managed to keep from becoming an international incident. A physician in Cameron County named G. S. Smith purchased land that skirted along the Rio Grande and included spits of land out into the river itself. When Smith constructed a fence on his property, Mexico raised a fuss that his land included some that was not situated in the United States. When U.S. troops as well as Rangers prepared to march to the border for a

Capt. Brooks and Co. F at their Cotulla camp in 1890. Brooks stands far left.

Courtesy Brooks family.

possible face-off with Mexican soldiers, the fence came down. Brooks wrote U.S. Secretary of State James G. Blaine explaining what had happened and that the situation had been defused.[16]

On March 7, Captain Brooks moved his headquarters from Rio Grande City to Edinburg (today the town of Hidalgo); Sergeant Rogers swapped places and commanded part of the company for the next eight weeks. Between May 10 and 20 the two camps broke and merged in Cotulla where Co. F would remain for the next ten years. John Rogers met and married Hattie Burwell of Cotulla in the spring of 1892, was promoted to captain at the end of that year and assumed command of the revived Company E on January 1, 1893, moving to new headquarters in Alice.[17] The two very different Presbyterians, Rogers and Brooks, parted company as good friends after working side by side for eight years; they would be at each other's side again many times in the years that followed.

Adjutant General W. H. King retired January 23, 1891, after a decade of service to Texas and as Captain Brooks's boss. Of his service an historian wrote: "King had a keen understanding of the legal requirements of the Ranger service, of the delicate balance required between the use of force and the letter of the law, and of the severe demands this balance often placed on the Rangers," a severity including drastic reductions in that force that may have been the final impetus to his retirement. "His vision and understanding of what the Rangers were accomplishing, and the relationship of these accomplishments to the development of the state, was matched by few commanders and probably no elected official."[18]

King himself reported: "I have worked earnestly and singly for what I believed to be the best interests of the State, its good people and its citizen soldiery, both Militia and Rangers." King had been especially interested in the appointment of the "special" Rangers during the years of budget cuts to the regular force. Woodford Haywood Mabry succeeded King as adjutant general, a position he would hold for the next decade.[19]

Another interesting appointment that month was the promotion of William Jesse McDonald to captain of Company B stationed in the Panhandle area of Texas. "Bill Jess" would come to be the most widely recognized Ranger of the next decade, his flamboyant spirit and love for the camera and the reporter making him the best known of the Ranger commanders.[20] When Rogers took over Company E two years later, three of the famous "Four Captains" were now in place; newly promoted Sergeant John Reynolds Hughes would join them soon.

In early September 1891, Brooks sent privates John Natus and Tupper Harris on a scout in the Encinal area to arrest Fernando Gayton, a suspected cattle thief. As they approached Gayton's hideout on the night of the twenty-sixth, the alleged felon attacked the two Rangers, stabbing Natus. Harris shot and wounded Gayton, saving Natus's life. Gayton was taken to the La Salle County jail, where Brooks and John Rogers arrived a day later to finish the investigation.[21]

A much larger investigation awaited Captain Brooks and Company F in the winter of 1891, one that would send reverberations across the borderlands and through law enforcement agencies across the Southwest. A year earlier, on June 18, 1890, Captain Brooks had received a telegram informing him that an armed band of Mexicans had surrounded a small town in Hidalgo County. He rushed with four of his company to assess the situation there, only to find that the alarm was false. The rumor stemmed from an inflammatory article written by Catarino Garza, newly arrived in the Valley and editor of the Eagle Pass *El Libre Pensador*. Along with co-editor Gabriel Botello, Garza recruited in Texas for revolutionaries to overthrow the hated Porfirio Diaz regime in Mexico City.[22]

Catarino Erasmo Garza Rodriguez, born and raised in Matamoros, educated and married to a prominent rancher's daughter, a dynamic speaker and writer, incited the people of the Valley to support their brothers and sisters across the Rio Bravo. An incident with law enforcement agents in the streets of Rio Grande City that year left him wounded and the Hispanic population up in arms against the authorities; the murder of *El Mundo* publisher Dr. Ignacio Martinez in Laredo in 1891 further incited the Mexican population.[23]

Adjutant General Mabry remained unimpressed as he singularly underestimated the situation: "These smugglers are citizens of Mexico who are outlawed by the Mexican government," he reported, "and are always ready to join issues under the banner of any revolutionary leader who promises to create trouble on the border. They are material for ready draft to any movement of the Garza character, of any firebrand smooth of tongue and knowing well the nature and history of the Mexican people."[24]

Three times in 1891 Garza attempted an invasion into Mexico; three times he failed, and the volunteers began to disappear. Still he persisted, enough so that the U.S. Army arrived to quell the trouble. On December 16, Captain Brooks sent Sergeant Rogers and four Rangers to join two U.S. marshals and a company of U.S. troops in a hunt for a band of Garza's followers. This band escaped across the border into Mexico, but other Garcistas ambushed Company C of the Third U S. Cavalry on December 22, killing Army Corporal Charles Edstrom and bringing reinforcements pouring into the Valley. Duval County Clerk Rufus Glover was murdered by a Garza follower, prompting a manhunt that ended in a shoot-out a few days later and the death of the rebel at the hands of Sheriff Wash Shely.[25]

Company C came under attack six days after Corporal Edstrom's death with Brooks's Company F acting in cooperation with them. While on a scout, five Rangers spotted Garza and three others on horseback and quickly gave chase. A running gun battle ensued, as Pvt. E. E. Townsend reported later in a newspaper interview: "Four of McNeel's company of Rangers and I had a running fight with Garza and three of his men on the prairie near La Granjenta Ranch in Starr County. We chased them about nine miles in the brush.

"When the shooting started, I fired 10 or 12 rifle shots at Garza, who was riding a big paint horse, at a distance of about 300 yards. He was running at right angles to me. I could see every bullet hit the sand, but I simply couldn't connect one of them with him or the horse. Probably their (the Garza-ites') fire was painfully regular and had something to do with my nervousness."[26]

These incidents helped engender a new cooperation between the army and the Rangers, with the Texans assuming the role of scouts and trackers, a key role they would play for the next several decades. The so called "Garza War" also produced an enmity between the Frontier Battalion and many of the citizens who lived in the Lower Rio Grande Valley, a volatile and fragile situation that would last for years.

Internally, the Frontier Battalion experienced its own impact from the Garza movement, as historian Robert M. Utley observed: "The Garza war spotlighted the performance of three Ranger officers. J. S. McNeel, a former San Antonio lawman with political connections, captained Company E. His boastful ways and operational lethargy weighed against him, and in August 1892 General Mabry resolved to remove him. By contrast, despite the obstacles, [J. A.] Brooks proved smart, energetic, and persistent, and he displayed his usual qualities of leadership. So did Brooks' sergeant, John H. Rogers, [who] replaced McNeel as captain of Company E."[27]

A warrant was issued for Garza's arrest, and Brooks, Sergeant Rogers, and Sheriff Wash Shely of Rio Grande City took up the trail: An abandoned camp and twenty horses were all they found. On January 5, 1892, U.S. troops and Rangers stumbled onto a camp of the revolutionaries who promptly vanished in the heavy brush; reports indicated that Garza had been among that band. Although he managed another miraculous escape from the authorities, important documents related to his revolutionary plans, some of which implicated government officials in Mexico City, were found left behind by Pablo Munoz, a Garza lieutenant. Catarino Garza would never be seen in Texas again, but his impact continued like a ripple effect well after his death in Colombia in 1895.[28]

Concerned by the activity stirred up along the border, the adjutant general decided to take a personal look at the situation. Captain McNeel of Company E and Brooks met Mabry when he arrived by train in San Diego and escorted him to Corpus Christi. After a brief visit there, Brooks rode with Mabry to Laredo and then up to Cotulla, where the visiting adjutant general was greeted at the camp by a rousing cannon salute. On January 30, 1892, Brooks sent his most dependable private, D. L. Musgrave, back to Nueces County on the trail of what turned out to be yet another false alarm: tension was in the air.[29]

Although not every citizen in the Valley supported Garza, Adjutant General Mabry certainly had that opinion when he wrote, "The resident population of the interior was composed entirely of Mexicans who claimed citizenship in Texas, but were with singular unanimity in sympathy with the Garza movement. They would harbor them secretly, act as spies, and notify the revolutionists of any approach of rangers or United States troops."[30]

By the middle of February Mabry had returned to Austin, Garza was nowhere to be found, and the revolutionary zeal was flagging. Small bands of Los Catarinos still roamed the Valley, however, necessitating constant scouts by the Rangers of companies E and F, most to no avail. Abandoned camps seemed the order of the day, several of which contained the remnants of trenches, huts, and recently dug wells. Before he left, Mabry ordered the temporary expansion of the Ranger companies to allow for the ground that needed to be covered. Brooks, for at least a short period, commanded a force of twenty-four men, fourteen of whom he reported as Special Rangers "on detached service."[31]

As Company F roamed the low counties for the last of the ragged band of zealots, interest in the purported activities arrived in the person of national reporters looking for a story. Frederic Remington and Richard Harding Davis arrived in Texas early in January to follow the U.S. troops along the border, made their way to the Ranger camp of Company F the first week in February 1892, and stayed long enough to get a taste of the Texas frontier character, much of which they would embellish in their published reports.

Frederic Remington eventually became the most famous Western artist and sculptor in American history, but in 1892 he was a thirty-year-old illustrator for the magazine *Harper's Weekly*. Entranced by the western legend and lore ever since he read of Custer's Last Stand in 1876, Remington eagerly pounced on the opportunity to come to Texas with his boss, the magazine's managing editor Richard Harding Davis. The two would also collaborate in Cuba and on San Juan Hill during the Spanish-American War in 1898. Remington's book *Pony Tracks*, published in 1895, reflected his experiences in Texas.[32]

Davis was only twenty-seven years old but already a veteran of the magazine media world, a reporter in Philadelphia and New York when he graduated from college, and an author of juvenile detective short stories published as *Gallagher and Other Stories* in 1891. After his Texas experience, Davis wrote seven popular novels and a score of plays, reported on two wars and nearly got himself shot as a spy during World War I.[33] Later in 1892, just back home from Texas, Davis published *The West From a Car-Window*.

"When [the Eastern man] touches at the border of Mexico, at Laredo, and starts forth again across the prairie of cactus and chaparral towards 'Corpus,'" wrote Davis, "he feels assured that at last he is done with parlor-cars and civilization; that he is about to see the picturesque and lawless side of the Texan existence, and that he has taken his life in his hands." Watching his escort, Sheriff Wash Shely, taking target practice from the rail car window only reinforced the stereotypical picture.

The commotion over the killing of Rufus Glover fascinated the New York reporter: "the killing of one man in an almost uninhabited country. Laredo is one hundred miles from the scene of the murder, but there the popular indignation and excitement were so great that another mass meeting was called endorsing the action back in Duval County, and another petition was made to the Governor." This incident impressed the Easterner that the "Wild West" might be "reconstructed," progressing, after all.

"But the West," wrote Davis, "is not wholly reconstructed. There are still the Texas Rangers, and in them the man from the cities of the East will find the picturesqueness of the Wild West show and its happiest expression. If they and the sight of cowboys roping cattle do not satisfy him, nothing else will. The Rangers are a semi-militia, semi-military organization of long descent, and with the most brilliant record of border warfare.

"These men are the special pride of General Mabry, the Adjutant-general of Texas, who was with them the first time I met them, sharing their breakfast of bacon and coffee under the shade of the only tree within ten miles. He told me some very thrilling stories of their deeds and personal meetings with the desperadoes and 'bad' men of the border; but when he tried to lead Captain Brooks into relating a few of his own adventures, the result was a significant and complete failure."

Both Brooks and his friend John Rogers preferred to keep their exploits to themselves. Rarely did they ever replay any of the myriad dramatic confrontations, and certainly not to a reporter. Some of the Ranger company, however, relished the idea of giving a good story to an Easterner. Being informed before Davis's visit that he wanted to interview a desperado if at all possible, the Rangers dressed up General

Mabry's cook in appropriate gear and tied him to a tree near the camp. Throughout the evening and long into the night, the Mexican cook regaled the two reporters with fabricated tales of his murderous deeds, giving them plenty of copy until the next morning when Mabry hollered out, "Antonio, where's my breakfast?" The hoax was over, the story excluded from a chagrined Davis's book.

"When General Mabry found they would not tell of their adventures," Davis continued in the story that was printed, "he asked them to show how they could shoot; and as this was something they could do, and not something already done, they went about it as gleefully as schoolboys at recess doing 'stunts.'" When Davis's hat flew off in a sudden breeze, Wash Shely stepped up first and fired off several shots at the makeshift target sixty feet away. This seemed to provoke something of a dare among the regular Rangers, producing "an instantaneous volley from every man in the company; they did not take the trouble to rise, but shot from where they happened to be sitting or lying and talking together, and the air rang with the reports and a hundred quick vibrating little gasps, like the singing of a wire string when it is tightened on a banjo."

The reporter's hat now sported twenty-eight bullet holes. Brooks re-told the story years later in a newspaper interview: "He [Davis] carried the hat back to New York to prove that he encountered a band of bandits."

"Then General Mabry," wrote Davis of his frontier encounter, "who seemed to think I did not fully appreciate what they were doing, gave a Winchester rifle to Captain Brooks and myself, and told us to show which of us could first put eight shots into the target.

"It seems that to shoot a Winchester," the reporter wrote, "you have to pull a trigger one way and work a lever backward and forward; this would naturally suggest that there are three movements–one to throw out the empty shell, one to replace it with another cartridge, and the third to explode the cartridge. Captain Brooks, as far as I could make out from the sound, used only one movement for his entire eight shots. As I guessed, the trial was more to show Captain Brooks's quickness rather than his marksmanship . . . When I had fired two shots into space, the captain had put his eight into the board. They sounded, as they went off, like fire-crackers well started in a barrel, and mine, in comparison, like minute-guns at sea."[34]

5

PRIZEFIGHT IN EL PASO

We're here to protect life and property. We are not taking sides in this dispute.

On March 22, 1892, Ranger Pvt. E. E. Doaty of Company E was gunned down by fleeing Garcista rebels, renewing with full force the hunt for the last of these border ruffians. Captain Brooks joined McNeel's force as they combed the Valley. On the twenty-sixth, Private Musgrave happened onto a camp and found himself quickly outnumbered. He managed to escape and return to his company; the bandits had vanished when Company F moved in the next day.[1]

Two brothers, José and Pancho Ramirez, had been accused of the killing of Army Corporal Edstrom the previous December, and Brooks and Rogers came upon their trail late in March in Encinal County. Separating to cover more territory, Rogers and a volunteer named Lee Hall surprised the two brothers in their camp; in the shoot-out that followed, José was killed. Two days later, Brooks tracked and arrested Pancho Ramirez, returning him to the Starr County jail where the warrant had been issued.[2]

In April, four more Los Catarinos were rounded up by Company F and escorted to the jail in Corpus Christi to stand trial. U.S. Marshal P. S. Levy received the prisoners, who would appear in the federal court for violation of U.S. neutrality laws. By May the Garza trouble had seemingly come to an end in the Valley.[3]

But for Captain Brooks the hunt for the latent revolutionaries continued. In June he moved Company F to a camp near Realitos, closer to the center of activity, and where much of the company would remain for the next year. In nearby Benavides, Brooks and a local deputized citizen, J. F. Ruthge, interrogated a young black man named Ashworth who they thought had information that would lead them to suspected rebels Eusebio Martinez and Gribeno Benavides. The trail took them into an area familiar to Brooks, what he called "the gatta," a denizen of thieves in a densely wooded area of the lower Gato Creek in northwest Zavala County; bandits often used this stretch of creek bed for hideouts. No suspects were found on this scout.[4]

Months later Brooks wrote his adjutant general asking permission "to look for Garza-ites and their leader." Mabry in declining replied tersely, "Your zeal may cause you to overlook criminals against the laws of our own State." Capt. Joe Shely, one of several peace officers from that clan, had recently reported that Brooks seemed almost obsessed with hunting the revolutionaries, and Mabry added as a postscript to Brooks: "Such reports as from the interview of Capt. Shely does not do the cause of the Ranger Force any good."[5]

Although difficult to do more than read between the lines of reports and letters, there is a troubling sense that James Brooks was going through his first period of personal problems since he joined the Rangers a decade earlier, problems that may very well have been related to his excessive drinking. On July 5 Brooks asked for and was given permission to visit "the state encampment," a retreat center where he stayed for nine days that month. Although he was active in October and made six arrests in Duval County, on November 16 Brooks took a brief leave of absence "on account of being ill." The physician's billing of $60 to treat Brooks seemed "too excessive" to General Mabry when he received the paperwork: Whatever medicine used was not itemized.[6]

On January 1, 1893, James Brooks said goodbye to his friend and trusted officer John H. Rogers who now assumed command of Company E. D. L. Musgrave was promoted to first sergeant to replace

Rogers in Company F, and W. M. Spindle was promoted to the newly instituted rank of corporal a few weeks later. Others in Brooks's command included George Bigford, Will Evetts, Walter Ellis, John and Joe Natus, George Piland, T. H. Pool, R. C. Lewis, J. C. Thomas, Ed Rowe, John Hess, and the captain's brother-in-law Neal Willborn. Most of the company now stationed at Realitos–there were eighteen on Brooks's roster in January–continued to scout for border bandits, while a handful kept the camp at Cotulla. By June of 1893 all of Company F encamped in Cotulla.[7]

Because of a controversy stemming from the forced resignation of J. S. McNeel as commander of Company E and the subsequent resignation of all of his men in protest, Rogers found himself having to recruit from scratch into the new year. He brought his cousin Tupper Harris and his younger brother Curren "Kid" Rogers over from Company F, and eventually had a full contingent to oversee. On January 20 both company records show the arrest of a horse thief in Starr County, likely an action of Company F but credited to Rogers's new command.[8]

Captain Brooks had his own struggles with company employees as he went through a series of teamsters that year. Abe Temple was replaced by Pablo Flores in April, but Flores was fired a month later and replaced by Tom Williams. Williams left in October, and his replacement Cole Harper lasted out the year. A Charles Willis was soon in Company F's employ, but two more wagon drivers would rotate through in 1894.[9]

This tedious work, in addition to keeping account of and repairing or replacing camp equipment, exemplified the mundane duties of a company commander which kept him busier than the scouts and arrests he might make on occasion. Left at camp while others followed fugitives or scouted may have been one of the several frustrations that kept Brooks in the bottle.

On July 4, 1893, John R. Hughes, sergeant of Company D, promoted to captain. The ascension of Hughes brought together for the first time the commanders who would be known thereafter as "the four captains." They would guide the Frontier Battalion through its final years of existence and into the twentieth century and a revamped organization of law enforcement, the Ranger Force. Their leadership, integrity, and determination fought off the concerns of legislators who believed the Rangers to be antiquated, and stamped this era in the annals of Texas Ranger lore.[10]

Legend and lore notwithstanding, and perhaps to escape the boredom of running a mostly empty Ranger camp after having been dissuaded by his superiors from chasing Garcistas, Captain Brooks boarded a train on May 4 that took him up the Rio Grande to Langtry, a hideaway frontier village and home of the famed Judge Roy Bean. "The Law West of the Pecos," as the sign over Bean's saloon court proclaimed, the erstwhile magistrate enjoyed a reputation for harsh judgment on the bench and intoxicating entertainment when court adjourned, both experiences appealing to the Bourbon County Ranger. Although Sergeant Musgrave would be the Ranger officially assigned to the Langtry area throughout the next year or so, Captain Brooks made many a trek there to visit with his friend the judge.[11]

Langtry also was home to one office of the U.S. Customs Service, and an incident there in 1893 sparked headlines across the Valley. Gangs of smugglers and rustlers crossed the river near Langtry for the most part untroubled by law enforcement. The deputy customs collector stationed at Langtry, Frank A. Cunningham, reported trouble involving threats by a gang leader named Charles Small. Arriving by train in early July, Sergeant Musgrave took the threats seriously and arrested Small, but the suspect soon enjoyed his release and was back causing a stir in the saloon.

On July 22 Ranger Pvt. R. C. Lewis confronted the inebriated Small and attempted to take away his revolver. A scuffle soon turned into a street fight with Small, Lewis, and Sergeant Musgrave firing away at one another. Musgrave wounded Small twice, and a third shot killed him. Musgrave wired Captain Brooks and both of them wired the adjutant general later that same day explaining the incident. Cunningham sent his own report two days later, concluding that "all credit is due to those rangers here but do believe that the force should be augmented by at least two or three others–it would doubtless have a tendency to over awe the outlaws." The only augmentation was Musgrave.[12]

One consequence to the fight had an international flavor to it. Oliver Heyworth, the British consul in Galveston, wired Brooks that a Briton named Hughes lived in Mexico across from Langtry and had had cattle stolen by Small's gang. Brooks sent three men to assist Musgrave in the arrest of one of Small's rustlers. Heyworth complained in September that the bond posted against the suspect was too slight and that he would surely make bail and skip the country, but Brooks responded assuring the consul that the culprit would be prosecuted.[13]

Captain Brooks might have made a personal appearance in Langtry to deal with Charles Small had he not been sent to Temple on July 15 along with other Rangers from around the state to help quell the violent railroad strike there. Temple, organized by the Gulf, Colorado & Santa Fe Railway Company in 1881 and named after one of its chief officers, soon burgeoned with over 3,500 citizens by the end of the decade. When the Missouri-Kansas-Texas railroad came through as well, trouble often erupted among the rough rail workers. Two days of violence under the hot Texas summer sun in 1893 resulted in dozens of injuries and arrests. Captain Brooks was heard to say to the leaders of both parties in his usual calm way: "We're here to protect life and property. We are not taking sides in the dispute." Peace was soon restored.[14]

Brooks left the boredom of camp life often in the latter months of 1893, scouting in La Salle, Encinal, Val Verde, Frio, and Zavala counties, but bureaucratic affairs still tracked him down. Two of his Rangers, George Bigford and Kid Rogers (before he joined Company E), had been accused by Oakville citizens of murder during an arrest the previous year. On November 17, 1892, the two Rangers plus Joe Natus and T. H. Pool had left the Realitos camp and taken a circuitous route towards Corpus Christi scouting for mule thieves. The trail took them a wayward course north to Oakville in Live Oak County.

At nine o'clock on the night of the twenty-second, the Rangers spotted a campfire just off of the road, dismounted, walked in, and

Texas Rangers at Temple, Texas, railroad strike, July 1894.

Courtesy Brooks family.

asked for coffee. One of the Mexicans in the camp, Juan Longoria, offered the coffee but his brother Gabriel refused to identify himself when asked, prompting Natus and Pool to search the camp area while the others kept an eye on the suspected mule thieves. Something spooked Rogers's horse and Kid turned to tie it back up.

As Rogers turned his back, the brothers Longoria jumped George Bigford who jerked himself loose and hollered for help at the same instant. One of the Longorias grabbed for his Winchester, but it was his last act: Bigford and Rogers opened fire at nearly point blank range, killing both Mexicans.

In the ensuing investigation it turned out that these were not the mule thieves being sought by the Rangers, but it remained a mystery why the two Longorias had reacted in the manner that caused their deaths. Brooks wrote up the company report of the incident but failed to telegraph Adjutant General Mabry, who sent a terse message chastising the captain a week after the incident: "The Press has reported this incident and I know nothing of its circumstances. You are to promptly report such occurrences via long telegram and full report by letter; and in the future you will act accordingly."[15]

A complaint was filed by friends of the Longorias over the winter, and Brooks went to Oakville to confer with county officials on March 8, 1893. Brooks dutifully wrote Mabry that no one there believed "the killing was a willful or malicious act, but only an unavoidable mistake." Still, it appeared the case might go to trial, and Captain Brooks wired General Mabry asking for money to retain a defense attorney. Mabry thought the request "exorbitant" and capped the fee at $200. J. M. Eckford was eventually retained for $150, but on March 14 the captain reported that "the boys were not indicted."[16]

In that same letter of March 8, Brooks wrote a lengthy note responding to the accusation against his men: "No good citizen of this place [Realitos] has complained of any misconduct of my men. They associate with the best people here. 'Tis true I have one or two men who drink a little, but I have never known them to do anything very bad.

"A certain element in this section are very much prejudiced against Rangers," Brooks noted, "and will do anything that they can against them. Therefore I have instructed my men to be very careful and keep on their good behavior. If you desire, every good citizen here will write you in praise of the Rangers; several have volunteered to do so."[17]

In his company records closing out the year 1893, Captain Brooks reported that among his camp equipment he had "two worthless tents and two worthless pack saddles," that Corporal Spindle had been discharged, and that he had sent three men to the Smith Ranch near Uvalde to investigate a fence-cutting incident. There the Rangers conferred with "Sheriff Garner," as Brooks identified him. This was John Nance Garner, a young attorney who had just opened his practice in Uvalde and been elected county judge, and who would eventually become one of the most powerful politicians in the United States and a two-term vice-president under Franklin D. Roosevelt.[18]

Although the year 1894 appears to have been especially calm for Company F, the deaths of five Rangers over a relatively brief span troubled the men of the Frontier Battalion and further depleted its already dwindling numbers. E. E. Doaty had been murdered by outlaws in the spring of 1892, J. W. Woods of Rogers's newly formed Company E disappeared–his body never found–while acting as an undercover agent in Menard County, and Frank Jones, captain of Company D, was shot and killed in Mexico while chasing bandits across the border.

The Olguin family had terrorized the areas around Ysleta for years until the adjutant general had had enough: he sent Captain Jones and four privates after them in June 1893. On Pirate Island, a slip of land in the Rio Grande bottoms, the Rangers were drawn into a deadly trap and Jones died in a hail of bullets. The remaining Rangers escaped across into Texas; Jones's body was recovered days later. On the Fourth of July, Sgt. John R. Hughes assumed command of Company D and promoted to captain on the same day he buried his colleague.[19]

Capt. Bill McDonald narrowly escaped death in December 1893, or he too would have been a statistic in the Ranger records. A shootout with Childress County Sheriff John Matthews in Quanah over earlier derogatory comments about the Frontier Battalion left Matthews dying of two bullet wounds and McDonald with a punctured lung and broken ribs.[20]

Joe McKidrict of Hughes's Company D was gunned down by former Ranger Bass Outlaw in the streets of El Paso on April 6, 1894. Outlaw had been discharged from the same company after one too many drunken brawls, and was hard after another bout when Private McKidrict, in El Paso to appear at federal court hearings, noticed him wandering in a back yard. Offering to help, McKidrict was instead met by a bullet in his temple. John Selman, a former brigand but now an El Paso constable, shot and killed Outlaw moments later, being wounded himself in the confrontation.[21]

On September 15 one of Brooks's privates, a young man named Billy Hooker, was found dead, floating in the Nueces River, the fifth Ranger to die on duty in a deadly short span of two years.[22]

Personal tragedy also struck Brooks and his wife in 1894. On June 28 Virginia gave birth to their first child, a daughter they named Mary Vernon Brooks. The captain was not present for his daughter's birth but came quickly to Cotulla from a scout. But on December 12, just five months later, the infant died. Brooks never wrote about the experience, and never spoke of it to his family, but certainly the girl's death left a scar on his heart, and may have had an impact on his marriage and on his attitude toward the children who would be born four years later.[23]

Further depleting the Frontier Battalion, budget cuts by the legislature decreased the company rolls from sixteen to eight men in early 1895. On February 26, Sergeant Musgrave complained that he needed out of Langtry to "be stationed where there is some work to do." Musgrave resigned shortly thereafter and Joe Natus promoted to 1st Sergeant of Company F. On March 30 Captain Brooks discharged six of his privates, and thirty days later two more left. One of those dismissed bore the interesting name of Frank S. Barefoot. Besides the two officers, privates Neal Willborn, George Bigford, Ed Coleman, W. T. Henshaw, Billy Bates, and John Hess, and teamster Charles Willis, now comprised Company F.

Captain Brooks kept on the road in March, traveling mostly by rail to post guard at the district court in Beeville, then to Laredo to help preparations for elections to be held in April, then off to Karnes City and back to Laredo on the last day of that month. General Mabry instructed Brooks to keep the peace during the Laredo voting but, he wrote: "The arrival and presence of the Rangers at Laredo must not be ostentatious, and such as not to attract notice nor comment."[24]

In June Brooks spent nine days attending the district court in Cuero, DeWitt County. From there he made his way to Millett back in La Salle County to investigate a robbery. For several weeks in July and August the active Brooks traveled to Laredo, Dilley, and Pearsall to talk with angry stockmen about a rash of cattle rustling. After an investigation, Brooks arrested Dan Yates and his two grown sons Elbert and Sam on August 20 in Pearsall for stealing some of those cattle. And in

September Brooks took the train to San Antonio to consult with law enforcement agents about a murder there.[25]

He was not the only man in Company F on the move. The drastic reduction necessitated a much broader scouting of the immense territory of the borderlands, and often the Cotulla camp was all but empty. In fact, when on November 14 the adjutant general wired Brooks to send three men to Kerrville, the captain had to deputize a local man named W. E. Campbell as a Special Ranger to go to Frio County and find three of his privates for the assignment.[26]

One of Brooks's recruits that year was Alonzo W. "Lonnie" Livingston, a nineteen-year-old from Cotulla whom the captain characterized as "being of good courage when in the presence of someone who takes charge." Lon Livingston remained steadfast as he also matured, serving for nearly seven years and achieving the rank of 1st Sergeant and often "taking charge" near the end of his Ranger service.[27]

The decreased company roll was not the only culprit emptying the Ranger camps in November 1895. A much larger drama was unfolding far to the west in the El Paso area, a situation that would soon enough engage the entire Frontier Battalion and the adjutant general himself: not rustlers nor rebels nor ruffians, but a prizefight.

"Voluntary engagement in a pugilistic encounter between man and man, or fight between man and bull or between man and other animal, for money or anything of value, or money bet or waged, or to see which any admission fee is charged, shall be guilty of a felony and upon conviction shall be punished by a fine of not less than $1,000, and by punishment in the county jail not less than sixty days nor more than one year."[28]

So stood Gov. James S. Hogg's 1891 state law in Texas: prizefighting was illegal. But sports promoter Dan Stuart, who kept one office in the Coney Island Jockey Saloon on Main Street in Dallas, believed that despite the tightly written law, a prizefight of international significance could still be arranged. And the fight he had in mind was nothing short of that: Robert Prometheus "Ruby Rob" Fitzsimmons squaring off against Gentleman Jim Corbett for the undisputed world championship. In 1894 Corbett, newly crowned world champ after dethroning John L. Sullivan, refused a fight with Fitzsimmons and had his title stripped by the Olympic Club. To put these two men in the ring at last would be a coup for the promoter.[29]

Plans for the fight drifted along into 1895 with sites suggested all over the Southwest. Stuart himself hoped for the bout to take place near Dallas despite the current law, but was realistic enough to look elsewhere for other options. When Arkansas and Indian Territory turned down any entreaties for hosting the slugfest, Stuart set his sights on Texas.

Stuart headed to court and won: a friendly judge decided that the prizefight could take place in Texas after all. But forces across the state, led by ministers' coalitions in several cities and the influential *Texas Christian Advocate*, persuaded Gov. Charles Culberson and his legislators to get in the ring with Stuart. After a special session debate that lasted less than an afternoon on October 3, 1895, Culberson signed into law a prohibition for prizefighting with enough teeth to it to gain Stuart's attention. "To avert an affront to the moral sense and enlightened progress of Texas," declared the governor, "is the undoubted will of the people."[30]

But events were already in motion. Stuart and his backers had put up large sums of money to have a ring built near Dallas. Corbett and Fitzsimmons were already in Texas to establish training camps, Gentleman Jim in San Antonio and Ruby Rob in Houston. As soon as the law went into effect, the governor notified the adjutant general to make whatever preparations might be necessary to ward off the prospective fight.[31]

Mabry wrote Captain Rogers to have him send an undercover agent to trail Fitzsimmons. To Captain Brooks he wrote on October 4: "Send two good men to San Antonio to keep constant and strict watch on Corbett without attracting any attention. Select men who will follow instructions to the letter, men who do not drink and can keep their council. A meeting between Corbett and Fitzsimmons," Mabry warned, "must be prevented at all hazards." Along the bottom of the telegram he added, "This letter is strictly confidential."[32]

Meanwhile Dan Stuart shelved his plans for a Dallas fight and ordered the partially built coliseum disassembled. An offer from a railroad man named B. F. Darbyshire and the ex-mayor of El Paso Doc Albers recommended Juarez, Mexico, as an agreeable site, with the promotions and accommodations–and money–to be headquartered in El Paso. But the Mexican government having gotten wind of the proposal stood fast against the prizefight as well.

Key support from several El Paso businessmen at this juncture encouraged Stuart to not only stay the course but to look all the more at the West Texas area for holding the fight. Thousands of square miles presented themselves on a horizon far from Austin and the governor's mansion, crisscrossed with railroads to manage the hordes of sports enthusiasts who would surely come. Stuart sent several of his people into the area to scout for a site.

Late in 1895 the first blow was struck but not in the ring: Jim Corbett backed out once more and left Texas. Nothing if not persistent, Dan Stuart immediately wired Irishman Peter Maher to fill in against Fitzsimmons. The entertaining Maher had lost a bout with Fitzsimmons three years earlier and was eager for a rematch. Maher wasn't Corbett, but the bout would still be appealing.[33]

As 1896 arrived, it was clear that if the fight was going to take place, El Paso was the focal point. Dan Stuart set up an office there and a flurry of excitement spread across the town, both for and against the match. Ministers and church women's groups barraged the newspaper editorial pages while boxing aficionados and reporters jammed into the few hotel rooms available. By mid-January both Maher and Fitzsimmons were in town setting up training camps and putting on exhibition sparring matches for the growing crowds. Much to the dismay of his trainers, but to the delight of many citizens, Fitzsimmons even participated in a New Years Eve football game.

Captain Brooks received another telegram from Mabry on January 18: "Send two rangers to El Paso by Feb. 4; *discreet, cool,* and *determined* men," he underlined, "able to act as detectives to find out the location of the coming fight and to prevent it from coming off on Texas soil. Remain incognito," he advised, "except to Capt. Hughes until my arrival about the 10th. Report to me on the quiet." Hughes and his company were the Rangers nominally in charge of this part of Texas, but the adjutant general clearly saw the need for reinforcements, and in fact his own presence. On February 1 he wrote briefly to Brooks, "Caution [the men you sent] to be vigilant and on the look for information."[34]

Brooks and the remainder of Company F decided that they couldn't miss the action that was going on in El Paso: by the tenth of the month nearly every ranger of the Frontier Battalion, and including the adjutant general, had come to El Paso. Hundreds of reporters and fight fans came, too, and fight promoters encouraged by Stuart's determination. George Siler, a sports writer for a Chicago newspaper, arrived and was selected to referee the fight now tentatively scheduled–somewhere–for Friday, February 14. The famous western buffalo hunter, gunman, and sheriff Bat Masterson arrived to head up Stuart's security force: most eyewitnesses agree that Masterson was an adequate force of one.[35]

The fight was postponed a week when the Irish slugger came down with an eye problem he attributed to the grit in the West Texas air; the El Paso Minister's Union credited it to their prayers causing a biblical "blindness of Peter." Still others believed that Stuart needed more time to find the right location and build a ring, and a temporary illness did the trick. February 21 now became the target date.

Stuart kept the Rangers busy by moving building supplies on passing trains in every direction and sending detectives and policemen on a merry chase each time. A frustrated General Mabry declared he would have his men "shoot to kill first and do the arresting afterwards," and to Stuart's face he said, "I'm going to board that train of yours with my men at all hazards. You'll regret taking on the power of the government." Stuart calmly offered to arrange for free rail passes for the Rangers.[36]

On Wednesday, February 19, events began to speed up. Peter Maher's eye infection miraculously cleared up and he declared himself ready to fight. Two Rangers shadowed Fitzsimmons around the clock, including accompanying him across the Rio Grande to his Juarez training camp. More than one hundred Mexican troops stood at the edge of the festivities on the look-out. Another Ranger camped outside the Astor Hotel watching Maher's every move, "notwithstanding Mr. Albers' outburst of virtuous indignation," Mabry reported later, referring to the ex-mayor in whose room Maher was staying. A train pulled out of the El Paso station before dawn, again laden with building supplies, and headed apparently for Fort Hancock; two Rangers made the trip undercover.

On Wednesday night a telegraph office in El Paso was ransacked by some of Stuart's "security agents" after the telegrapher, a man named Brooks but no relation to the captain, threatened to reveal the actual location of the coming fight. Rangers put a guard on the office on Thursday: had they not done so, the fight might very well have occurred without being discovered by law enforcement. Instead, when the real message came in, the Rangers were there waiting for it.[37]

On Thursday the Frontier Battalion was persuaded to pose for a series of photographs for the press on the steps of the El Paso courthouse. The photo that survived may be the only one that includes the entire force of that era, with the adjutant general and the four captains who stand along the front row: Brooks stands dead center with McDonald and Rogers on his left and Hughes on his right.

On Thursday afternoon, the fight site was revealed for the first time: 396 miles to the southeast along the Rio Grande near Langtry, an area Captain Brooks by now knew well. It made sense to some: Judge Roy Bean would be the perfect "host" for such an event with huge crowds at his saloon, a brawling contest fit for wagering, and even a possible fight outside the ring. It was far enough from the rest of civilization to attempt the fight yet accessible by rail from two directions. And there was a small spit of land out in the middle of the Rio Grande that technically might not be considered part of Mexico or the United States, thus allaying charges brought by either country.

The train carrying all of the principals, dozens of reporters, and half of the Frontier Battalion, left the station on Thursday night at 9:45

Texas Rangers at El Paso to stop the Fitzsimmons prizefight, Feb. 13, 1896.

Courtesy Brooks family.

p.m. After dawn it made brief stops at Marathon and Sanderson, and on occasion as it slowed the two fighters were seen hopping to the ground and jogging alongside to keep limber. Legend more than documented records tell of Fitzsimmons wrestling someone's pet bear along the way, and of a staring contest between Masterson and McDonald that nearly erupted in a shoot-out.[38]

Rain pelted the train on the afternoon of the twenty-first as it neared its destination. After a journey of over seventeen hours, Langtry came into view and passengers disembarked like a pack of hungry wolves. A narrow wooden bridge had been constructed out to the tiny island and a young boy from Canada took tips to help some make the short walk from the banks. A full prizefighting ring stood in the middle of the island with a large tarp designed to block the view from any non-paying customers.

The sky was overcast that afternoon, prohibiting a camera crew from Thomas Alva Edison's shop from filming the historic event, but several photographs have survived. The Rangers who made the trip, having decided not to disrupt the fight after all now that it would take place on property of undetermined ownership, situated themselves atop some hefty cliffs on the Texas side of the river where they could peer over the tarp into the ring. Mused the *Dallas Morning News* reporter later, "It was amusing to see the flower of the frontier guard sitting on the crags above with their rifles resting lazily on their laps while that great and unpardonable crime, the big glove contest, was taking place a few hundred yards away."[39]

For all of the drama of the days and weeks leading up to this "big glove contest," the fight itself was anticlimactic. Referee Siler met the two fighters in the center of the ring where they shook hands and returned to their corners. The time keeper whistled, yelled "Time!" and struck a small gong, and the two fighters raced to the center of the ring. Fitzsimmons struck the first blows but Maher responded in kind. Siler hollered a warning to Maher when he threw an illegal punch, and the two men clinched several times. Then, ninety seconds into the first round, Fitzsimmons landed a short punch with his right hand onto Maher's chin. The Irishman twisted once and plummeted onto the canvas, never hearing Siler count him out.[40]

"If you are knowing in the chronicles of the ring," wrote the erstwhile New York cowboy Will Porter under his pseudonym O. Henry, "you will recall an event in the early nineties when, for a minute and sundry odd seconds, a champion and a would-be faced each other on the alien side of an international river. So brief a conflict had rarely imposed upon the fair promise of true sport. The reporters made what they could of it, but, divested of padding, the action was sadly fugacious. The champion merely smote his victim, turned his back on him, remarking, 'I know what I done to dat stiff,' and extended an arm like a ship's mast for his glove to be removed."[41]

6

DEADLY STREETS OF COTULLA

On account of old troubles, too much talk, and reported threats the two factions came very near having serious trouble here.

"WHICH ACCOUNTS FOR A TRAINLOAD OF EXTREMELY DISGUSTED gentlemen in an uproar of fancy vests and neckwear being spilled from their Pullmans in the early morning following the fight," concluded O. Henry in his short story *Hygeia at the Solito.*[1] But not everyone who disembarked exhibited gloomy dispositions. The Rangers had not stopped the fight, but what had transpired hardly counted for much of a success for the redoubtable Dan Stuart and his pugilists. Wrote the adjutant general in his official report: "I desire to express my approbation for the intelligent and efficient manner in which Captains Brooks, McDonald, Hughes and Rogers executed every order and performed every duty. The Rangers conducted themselves in such manner as to reflect additional credit upon the name of a ranger–already a synonym for courage and duty well performed.

"They were active in the performance of every duty," wrote Mabry, "quiet and orderly in manner, determined in mien, fearless and vigilant on duty; they naturally incur the displeasure of lawbreakers everywhere."[2] The recognition and tales of "the four captains" had begun.

Captain Brooks made his way back to Cotulla, while Captain Hughes returned to El Paso to clean up the last of the mess left by the contest. Captain Rogers took the train that arrived in San Antonio on the twenty-third and spent the next days in the hospital at the bedside of his in-law and fellow Ranger Will Burwell who had become seriously ill in Langtry. Captain McDonald rushed to Wichita Falls after receiving a telegram about a bank robbery that had just occurred. Without respite from the long El Paso ordeal, McDonald and five men of Company B tracked and finally captured two of the robbers.[3] It is a wonder that with all of the Rangers in Langtry there was no crime spree across the rest of Texas.

Brooks had little rest himself. He tracked and arrested two fence cutters in Zavala County in late February, and made twelve arrests in March of mostly cattle thieves. W. A. Evetts, who had been instrumental in the scouting of Langtry, promoted to first sergeant of the company that month. In April, General Mabry requested that Evetts be sent to Jefferson in East Texas to investigate fishing violations on the lakes nearby, but Brooks sent Private R. J. Tucker instead. Meanwhile, Brooks and Evetts arrested eight men in Webb County for lying to a grand jury about irregular voting practices there; the two Rangers testified before that same grand jury on June 23 and 24 in Laredo.[4]

In August and September Brooks and his men ranged across Webb, La Salle, and Frio counties scouting for cattle thieves. On October 27 Brooks went to Laredo to keep order during the upcoming national and state elections. "Excitement runs high," Brooks wrote into his monthly report, "and trouble is feared." Half of Company F remained in Cotulla for the same reason. There are no reports of violence or arrests through that next week.[5]

On November 11, Captain Brooks received the tragic news of his sister Fannie's untimely death in Kentucky. Fannie Breckinridge Brooks Morgan, only forty-four when she died and James' closest sibling since their childhood, left behind her widowed husband Will Morgan and three children: Brooks, Coleman, and Sallie. The captain did not arrive in Lexington in time for the burial on the twelfth, but stayed long enough to pay respects and visit his family, many of whom still lived in the Bourbon County area, and to celebrate his forty-first birthday back near his old home. Six months later, his baby sister Lillie Belle lost her husband Allan Hudson; he was only thirty-eight.[6]

On December 21, 1896, Samuel Vaughn Edwards was appointed sheriff of La Salle County following a testy campaign that brought some old blood feuds to the surface: "Vote Right or Fight" declared one campaign slogan. Sheriff W. L. Hargus had abruptly resigned after having been elected to his second term only six weeks earlier, and the appointment of Edwards did not sit well with some. Chief among Edwards's vocal opponents was James R. Davenport of the immense and immensely powerful Armstrong Ranch enterprise.[7]

The residents of Cotulla and the surrounding region took sides, threats flew through the South Texas air like Apache arrows, and Company F stepped in. Dick Ware, the man most people believe killed Sam Bass years earlier in the legendary Round Rock shoot-out, served as marshal in El Paso during this period and was a story-swapping friend of Brooks: Brooks of course had his own Sam Bass tales from his cowboying days. Just back from a two-day visit with Marshal Ware who was traveling through San Antonio, Captain Brooks wrote upon returning to camp, "On account of old troubles, too much talk, and reported threats the two factions came very near having serious trouble here [in Cotulla]. Several on each side were armed with Winchesters and shotguns. But I kept them apart, and by going to each party and reasoning with them persuaded them to lay down their guns and drop the matter."[8]

"Myself and four men remained in town [Jan. 26, 1897] until the 29th," Brooks continues, "fearing something might occur to bring the trouble up again. Everything is quiet now." But trouble brewed all year long and throughout Edwards' two-year term. On February 21 Brooks scouted the Armstrong Ranch "to see Jim Davenport who we heard had been waylaid," he reported. "Found signs showing someone had been near the house, but no clues."

"During the month," Brooks continued, "myself and my men did all in our power to preserve the peace and prevent trouble in La Salle County between the two factions, there being a bad feeling existing." Only a month later he wrote that he was still "very watchful fearing there might be trouble between the two factions of La Salle County."

Brooks remained in Cotulla with two of his men for three weeks in September to "keep the peace" between the combatants, and even on the last three days of 1897 the Ranger captain stayed put in town "preventing trouble between Sheriff Edwards and Jim Davenport." General Mabry encouraged Brooks to use his own judgment "to prevent rupture of the public peace" in Cotulla.[9]

This protracted feud and a similar one in San Saba County prompted the adjutant general to expand his comments on such situations. "In the sparsely settled but organized counties it is frequently the case that a lawless element holds the balance of voting power, and officers are elected who are friendly to them and collude at their depredations." "Officers" referring to sheriffs, it is not difficult to see which side Mabry had taken, although there was certainly no love lost between the Rangers and Jim Davenport, who had earlier served five years in prison for murder but not until after wounding two Rangers as they closed in on his hideout.

"Factions are created, and it is only the rangers that preserve the peace, restore order, and offer the necessary protection," wrote Mabry. Never one to miss an opportunity to laud his agents, Mabry concluded that the Rangers "represent the majesty of the State, and belong to no faction, and merely their presence often prevents bloodshed, and peace and quiet are restored."[10]

As usual, the business of a county feud did not prevent other trouble from receiving the Rangers' attention. On March 7, 1897, influential rancher E. B. Chandler reported to Company F's commander that a mile of fence had been cut on the nearby Meredith Ranch near Atascosa in Bexar County; the Ranger investigation turned up no clues. Brooks spent four days that month in Austin catching the adjutant general up on the Cotulla trouble. In April he "kept the peace in Laredo" during that city's hotly contested elections, and appeared in district courts in Pearsall and Cotulla that spring.[11]

There may have been another item on the agenda of Mabry's March meeting with Brooks, for a terse order emanated from Austin on May 26 directed to all four Ranger captains: "You will advise the department whenever you leave your station," it directed in part, "business or pleasure." Apparently telegrams and directives from Austin had been left wanting for someone to be in camp to respond, although four companies and a total of fewer than three dozen Rangers could hardly be expected to scout all of Texas and maintain much presence back at camp. "I hope it will not be necessary to again call your attention to these requirements," Mabry added as a postscript.[12]

On July 7 Pvt. John Moore of Company F suffered a serious gunshot wound accidentally while scouting in Uvalde County. Captain Brooks personally escorted his injured man to San Antonio and admitted him to Santa Rosa Hospital under the care of a thirty-two-year-old surgeon named Dr. Marvin Lee Graves. Apparently Moore's condition was serious enough to justify visits by his company commander on July 19 and again on August 16. When Brooks arrived once more in November he learned that Moore's father had taken him home, where he eventually recovered and later returned to Company F. Dr. Graves would be instrumental in the recovery of Brooks's friend Capt. John Rogers two years later following Rogers's grave wound during the Laredo quarantine violence.[13]

Captain Brooks also received permission to attend a "camp of instruction" in July in San Antonio.[14] This may have been similar to the "retreat center" he had attended before, and perhaps a euphemism for an alcohol-related rehabilitation center. Neither Brooks nor official records elucidate, but it hardly seems plausible that Brooks would need any "instruction" at this point in his already illustrious career.

For four days in late August, Brooks and two of his men joined forces with Kerr County Sheriff John W. Vann to track a gang accused of illegally shearing sheep on the ranches between Kerrville and Comfort. The Moores and Coldwells, relatives and friends of James and Virginia Brooks and sheep ranchers themselves, may have been victimized. Brooks did not report any arrests.

Also in August Brooks had a run-in with a Cotulla saloonkeeper named George Reed, arresting him for firing a pistol out in the city streets. Brooks walked right up to the drunken Reed and

Company F, Frontier Battalion, San Diego, Texas, 1898. Included in this picture to Capt. Brooks's left: Sgt. Winfred Bates, Privates A. Y. Baker, W. A. Evetts, Lon Livingston, Oscar Latta, and D. L. Lynch.

Courtesy Brooks family.

quickly disarmed him before a deadly shot could be fired. Reed would engage in a dramatic stand-off with Captain Rogers the next year when Company E arrived in Cotulla.[15]

On October 1 a young recruit by the name of Allen Mabry joined Company F. His father, the adjutant general, wrote a personal note to Brooks to "please keep a kindly eye on him, and I appreciate it very much."[16]

1897 ended with Brooks and Company F scouting in Kerr and Kimble counties, investigating two cases of fence cutting in Dimmit County, and continuing to watch the ever volatile situation surrounding the La Salle County sheriff's office. Brooks's monthly reports mention the latter problem in February and March of the new year. In June Edwards resigned and Will Burwell was appointed–and later elected–sheriff.[17]

Yet another incident surrounding the apparently hotheaded Jim Davenport occurred on April 16, 1898, and resulted in the death of a La Salle County cowboy. Davenport rode into town with Henry May that day to confront some Mexicans who worked on the Armstrong Ranch with them and had come into Cotulla to relax at Patterson's Saloon. Newspaperman Guy Reed–whose real name was J. Guy Smith–tried to stop the coming fight, but in a sidewalk scuffle shot and killed May and was gravely wounded himself. Reed pleaded self-defense and was acquitted, and eventually reopened his newspaper business. Jim Davenport continued to get into scrapes, mostly drunken brawls, until he was shot and killed in 1900 by Texas Ranger Will Wright while resisting arrest.[18]

But 1898 would bring the kind of trouble that made county disputes pale in significance: a war between the United States and Spain over the rebellion in Cuba. Spanish Ambassador Dupuy De Lôme's controversial February letter to his government suggesting the new American President William McKinley to be "more bark than bite" in his threats to intervene in the Cuban insurrection, and the subsequent explosion aboard the battleship USS *Maine* while anchored in Havana's harbor that was incorrectly alleged to be a Spanish bomb, brought the two nations to the conflict in April.

Concerns that Mexico might become involved in the confrontation, and that the Texas border seemed ripe for related intrigue if not violence, caused a shift in the Rangers' assignments as Mabry sent all but one of the four companies into the Valley. Rogers's Company E came to Cotulla, while Company F headed briefly to Laredo, then Alice, before establishing an additional camp in Brownsville in conjunction with the United States Army's Volunteers unit there.[19]

On April 19 Mabry issued two orders to his four captains. The first directed them to "immediately recruit your company to twelve men and make preparations to move at a moment's notice." The second, issued hours later, sent separate orders to each company. To Brooks: "Go to Laredo. Spaniards may be contemplating the destruction of Laredo in the event of a [U.S.] declaration of war with Spain. Contact C. F. Yeager and J. O. Nicholson," Mabry instructed.

Brooks complied, then went from Laredo to Cotulla and finally on to Brownsville in May, where he served briefly under Capt. Eugenio Hernandez and 1st Lt. Jacob F. "Jake" Wolters in Troop D of the 1st Texas Cavalry Regiment (United States Volunteers). That unit, which included among others Rangers Brooks's colleague and friend Capt. John H. Rogers, did not leave American soil, and saw no action while on coastal patrol. They mustered out in November 1898.[20]

W. H. Mabry resigned his adjutant general position on May 5 to serve in the war effort and was replaced by A. P. Wozencraft. Mabry had been an effective public relations supporter of the Frontier Battalion during his service, while Wozencraft proved to be the more disciplined organizer and bureaucrat. Wozencraft would serve less than nine months in the job.[21]

The "splendid little war," as Secretary of State John Hay called it later, was over almost before it began, the Spanish routed off San Juan and Kettle hills in Cuba, the Spanish navy sunk in Santiago Harbor, and Puerto Rico, the Philippines, and sundry islands in the Pacific awarded to the victorious United States. As an afterthought, Cuba received its independence but continued to be embroiled in uprisings in the years that followed.

In Texas, the war intrigue quickly forgotten, the Rangers reduced in numbers once more, and the companies switched around again, the May 21 assassination of W. J. Bowen in Cotulla arrested the attention of Brooks and Company F well into 1899. And the issue of the very existence of the Frontier Battalion itself loomed large on the horizon.

Nearly a decade earlier, an article headlined the June 10, 1891, front page of the San Antonio *Daily Express*: "Allee Before the Bar. Alfred Allee boarded the south-bound International train at Dilley, June 4th, and a few minutes later emerged with a smoking pistol in his hand,

Brooks, Tom Armstrong, and Capt. John H. Rogers, 1899. The caption identifies Armstrong having served "in Cuba, S. A. War."

Courtesy Brooks family.

while within the limp form of W. C. Bowen dropped between two seats with his life blood spurting from ghastly wounds in the head."[22]

Alfred Allee grew up in DeWitt County and made his way southward engaged in the ranching business. Trouble followed him everywhere he went, with at least three men shot and killed by him in a span of six years: juries acquitted Allee each time. Walter C. and William J. Bowen lived in Cotulla, Walter the editor of the local newspaper and his brother an attorney. Walter Bowen had disputed the self-defense judgments for Allee in an editorial and the quick-draw cowboy seemed intent on trouble finding him once more.[23]

According to eyewitnesses at Allee's trial, when the defendant boarded the train, the Bowen brothers anticipated a fight and shot first. William was permanently injured by Allee's returning gunfire, and his brother killed. Allee was acquitted, but shortly thereafter killed a black porter on another train. In 1896, Allee, having finally sworn off his reputation as a gunfighter, was stabbed to death by a city marshal in Laredo.[24]

The dramatic story followed William Bowen for years. He married into the influential Thomas family, raised two daughters, and eventually returned to his law practice. On the night of May 21, 1898, Bowen was gunned down outside his home as he returned from his office in town, shot four times at close range. Neighbors rushed to his aid, a doctor was called to the home, but the lawyer died within the hour. Neither he nor any neighbor was able to identify the killer.

The citizens of Cotulla reacted with shock and anger, many recalling the events surrounding Bowen's brother's death in 1891, and demanded an immediate investigation and arrest of the villain. Captain Brooks and his company led the investigation before hurrying on to Brownsville–the war with Spain was under way–to join the 1st Texas Regiment, interviewing dozens of neighbors and anyone who had business dealings with Bowen. One of those interviewed was J. A. Poteet, a rancher who lived out from Cotulla and had recently engaged in a heated argument with Bowen over purchase of a piece of property. One witness claimed Poteet had declared the county "not large enough to hold the two of them."

One week after Bowen's death, Poteet was arrested and charged with murder. At the trial in December, a witness for the prosecution named E. A. McCurrey claimed that Poteet had asked him to help murder Bowen. "We could easily kill Bowen," Poteet was said to have told McCurrey. "We could shoot him by his own light while he is reading at night." McCurrey told the jury that he refused Poteet's offer but admitted giving his gun to him to commit the deed.[25]

The trial appears to have resumed in March 1899, in Brownsville, because Brooks reported his presence there, but there are no records in

La Salle nor Cameron county of the eventual outcome. Just as interesting is the fact that for the rest of his life Captain Brooks kept in his private papers the newspaper articles related to both Bowen killings, apparently equally impressed by the drama and tragedy that befell the Bowen brothers, and not a little agitated that the case never came to any resolution.

In the midst of all the trouble that surrounded and embattled the Company F commander, James Brooks appears to have focused his attention, at least for a time, on his family. On December 7, 1898, Virginia Brooks gave birth to their second daughter, who was christened Corrinne Kenny: The captain's older sister Jennie had married Matthew Kenney in 1867 and their daughter was named Corrinne. Captain Brooks was spending most of his time still in Brownsville when his daughter was born, but does report that in April he paid a brief visit to Cotulla.[26]

On August 17, 1899, nine months after Corrinne was born, Virginia delivered a son who was named John Morgan after James's father and his late sister Fannie's husband–and perhaps not coincidentally the old Kentucky Rebel raider as well. Family and friends' stories all agree that, for whatever reasons known only to him, the captain doted on his son for the rest of his life while largely ignoring Corrinne in those later years. Photographs and interviews in Falfurrias a decade into the twentieth century show the captain with young John Morgan ever at his side, while snide comments about his daughter's "fat, ugly arms" scarred her emotionally: she never married and was always was seen in public wearing a long-sleeve dress to hide her arms.[27]

Whatever parenting Brooks exhibited, they seemed rare moments. His absence from the household for extended periods was not abnormal to the vagaries of the Texas Rangers' business, but some of those protracted absences–and even times at home–were alcohol-related binges. Even when Brooks had retired from the Ranger Force and concentrated his time at home, he was wont to take long trips "on business" and ignore the family left behind. His traveling companion was always Jack Daniels, often his son, and never his wife or daughter.

Virginia toiled as the head of the essentially three-person home. When Corrinne was six months old and Virginia nearly six months pregnant, the little girl was kicked in the face by a mule and badly injured. Virginia cared for her daughter for months even while completing her pregnancy prematurely with the birth of John Morgan: His fragile start in life may have had an impact on his father's attitude toward him and his sister thereafter.

As he grew up into early adolescence John Morgan often became the provider, hunting for whatever meat the family might have on the dinner table. Occasional trips to Center Point in Kerr County to visit Emeline Moore Coldwell and Virginia's uncle and brothers proved a respite of some consolation. And it was Virginia and her son, not the captain, who dispatched the rattlesnakes that constantly boarded beneath their house.[28]

Only four days after Corrinne's birth in late 1898, Captain Brooks caught the train to Hidalgo, the tiny county seat nestled on the Rio Grande. But this town was no placid riverside resort; rather, it roiled in the political turmoil of its day. This time, it was *El Club Colorado* that was causing the disturbance.

Twenty-five years earlier the strengthening Democratic Party of Texas had made its way into the Rio Grande Valley to capture the votes of the Spanish-speaking, mostly illiterate, people dwelling along the border. Men like Stephen Powers and James B. Wells, Jr., assumed power in Cameron County by cultivating these constituents with their *Club Azul*: the "Blue Club" colored the ballots to make it easier for the voters. In addition, the politico organization escorted voters to the polling sites, arranged dances and parties and fiestas before the elections, and generally spoon-fed its supporters. Similar clubs had sprung up in Hidalgo, Starr, and Duval counties (in Duval they were first called *club botas*).[29]

As the precursor to "boss rule" assumed control in south Texas, the Republicans, not to be outdone, organized their own voting groups, the Red Club or *Club Colorado* (in Starr County the colors were reversed and the Red Clubs in the Valley counties generally became associated with the Democrats thereafter). The two factions often came to blows along the way, sometimes incidentally and more often for the purpose of intimidation. In 1906, Judge Stanley Welch was assassinated as he slept in a hotel room in Rio Grande City, the murder linked to the *Coloradoes y Azules'* ongoing turbulence.[30]

In the 1890s the sheriff of Hidalgo County was John Closner, a successful and wealthy sugarcane farmer and one of the first to experiment with irrigation systems in the Valley. He was a staunch Democrat and supported by Judge Wells and the Blues. Following the November elections in 1898, controversy surfaced–certainly not for the first time–regarding voting irregularities. A meeting of the inflammatory Red Club was scheduled for December 11. Authorities in the county became alarmed and hurried a telegram to the adjutant general's office in Austin. General Wozencraft instructed Captain Brooks to watch over the volatile situation. Brooks arrived in time to speak with the key leaders of the organization, calm them down, and oversee the peaceful meeting.[31]

Only weeks later, an attempt was made on Sheriff Closner's life. Closner escaped unharmed but blamed the Dougherty brothers and the Red Club for the plot. Pvt. A. Y. Baker of Company F investigated the case and arrested a Mexican gunman who was eventually acquitted. In July Baker was "accidentally" shot by a deputy sheriff near San Diego, but there may have been more to the story than was ever reported. Baker caught the attention of Closner and Judge Wells during his investigation, and after his years as a Ranger, and his involvement in one of the most infamous events of that period, he worked closely with the Blue Club rule in Hidalgo County.[32]

In June 1899, Company F was assigned to the Alice area and Captain Rogers's Company E would switch with them. Company F at this time was scattered across the Valley from its main camp in Cotulla to smaller camps near Brownsville and Hebbronville. In a hasty inventory of camp equipment prior to the move, Brooks noted that of the six company mules, two "can't stand hard service" and he asked permission to sell them. As preparations got under way for the shift, Brooks received a week's leave of absence in July–possibly to be with his wife as she was only weeks from delivering their second child, following which he escorted Private Baker to the San Antonio hospital after the accidental shooting in San Diego.

On July 26 Brooks was sent to Marshall "to do detective work," as he reported. Upon his return to Cotulla to finish preparations for the move, Brooks learned on August 7 that the governor had reconsidered and the companies would stay put after all.[33]

Work resumed apace. In October Brooks was contacted by rancher W. B. Wadsworth who currently served as chairman of the Wharton and Matagorda Live Stock Association. The ranchers in those two counties feared an increase in cattle rustling and requested assistance in curtailing the crime spree. Brooks requested of Austin that a cowboy named McMahan–possibly Ranger Frank's brother–be appointed "special" Ranger and assigned to the association. McMahan was on assignment by October 28.[34]

In December 1899, Brooks asked to recruit more men for his widely spread company. Gen. Thomas Scurry, who had replaced Wozencraft as adjutant general in January, permitted three to be signed up but for a ten-week period only. One of those was Will Scurry, the general's son. On December 18, Pvt. R. L. Miller sustained a serious eye injury in Brownsville, and his captain took him to San Antonio for treatment.[35]

Life for the Frontier Battalion and its commanders seemed more or less routine as the new century arrived. Too thinly spread to be as effective as they wanted, still the Rangers had proven themselves capable of containing the frontier criminal element if not altogether eliminating it. The Indian threat was long since gone, and the wide open west was more civilized now that railroads and towns dotted the landscape.

But the very success of the Frontier Battalion over its nearly four decades in existence now threatened it more than the Comanches or the border ruffians ever had. With the "wild west" fading away, were the Rangers not far behind?

7

TROUBLE IN COLORADO COUNTY

Everyone had a pistol and guns were hidden all over the train.

BEN STAFFORD STEPPED OUT OF THE BARBERSHOP ONTO THE main street of Columbus. It was a cold, blustery December morning. Sumner Townsend was waiting for him in the street. The hot words that had been exchanged for months between the two cattlemen were suddenly replaced by gunfire. Ben drew his pistol faster and his first shot pierced Townsend's arm. Sumner's pistol jerked downward at the impact of the bullet, and his wayward shot imbedded in Stafford's ankle. Ben fired three more times, wounding Townsend in the shoulder, before both men slumped to the ground in pain.[1]

The shoot-out between these two men of Colorado County took place in 1871, and trouble simmered another two decades before boiling over once more, although later stories of an ongoing "feud" were greatly exaggerated. Still, there were plenty of Townsends and Staffords to go around, and everyone kept an eye on the other. Light Townsend was sheriff in 1890, and his nephew Larkin Hope city marshal. Capt. Bob Stafford, Ben's brother, had a son named Warren who drank a bit too often when away from his mother's watchful eye. Bob had an understanding with the law that they would let him know whenever his boy needed attending to.

But on the evening of July 7, 1890, Larkin Hope walked out from a county-wide barbecue going on at The Grove, a park near Columbus, with a drunken Warren Stafford in tow, handcuffed and on his way to the calaboose: Hope deliberately steered the inebriated boy in front of the Stafford house for his mother to see. Several friends of Warren's persuaded the deputy to let the boy go and not insult the family by locking him up, but the word spread quickly and Warren's father, and a few minutes later his uncle John, arrived to confront the city marshal. A shouting match erupted near the door of the Nicolai Saloon where Larkin and his brother Marion Hope relaxed.

Bob Stafford shouted one too many insults at Larkin Hope, however, and the marshal drew his pistol. The first shot dropped John Stafford to the ground mortally wounded. The second struck Captain Bob and he staggered inside the saloon where he was felled by a shot fired by Marion Hope. Larkin stepped inside through a side door to find Bob dead, then walked back to the street and fired another bullet into the dying brother.

Marion Hope dashed out from the saloon and dragged his brother across the street. The two were escorted away by their uncle before any more damage could be done. Larkin Hope went to trial for killing John Stafford and was eventually acquitted of all charges against him; charges against both brothers for the murder of Bob Stafford were dropped. What had been scheduled as a grand celebration for Columbus that July evening–the laying of the cornerstone of the new courthouse–instead became the grist for another round of tales surrounding the mythic "Stafford-Townsend Feud of Colorado County."[2]

A few years after the double killing, Sheriff Light Townsend died; he was replaced by an in-law, Sam Reese. Reese served as sheriff in Columbus for the next four years, and Larkin Hope was back in the county's employ as constable. In 1898 Sheriff Reese was up for reelection and Constable Hope ran against him in what became an overheated campaign.

On the night of August 3, 1898, a mysterious rider dismounted near the saloon, crept through an alleyway, and fired two blasts of his shotgun into Larkin Hope, killing him instantly. Several people saw the rider but could not identify him as he rode calmly out of town and into the night. An investigation led to the arrest of Jim Coleman, a cohort of Sam Reese's: Reese was believed by many to have orchestrated the murder of his opponent but was never charged. Reese lost the election to a replacement opponent named W. T. Burford, an in-law of the Townsends', and Coleman was acquitted after his trial had been moved to San Antonio.[3]

The Reese-Townsend Feud, which actually began with the killing of Larkin Hope, now simmered over the winter months. On March 16, 1899, a furious Sam Reese, still angry at losing the election, went looking for trouble on Main Street, and soon guns were drawn and blazing. Deputy Willie Clements, Marc Townsend, and Marion Hope fired away at Reese and one another, and stray bullets sent citizens screaming. When the last shot echoed away, Reese was dead, shot in the throat. Also dead by his wagon was Charles Boehme, a local farmer and innocent bystander. A little boy named Johnny Williams, standing in his yard when the shooting commenced, took a stray bullet in his hip, crippling him for the rest of his life.[4]

This was enough for the local constabulary, and the Rangers were called to restore order and investigate the shoot-out. Capt. Bill McDonald arrived and talked all parties into backing down, but before he left town someone narrowly missed killing Willie Clements on the night of March 28. On April 1, McDonald left Columbus.[5]

On May 18, Sheriff Burford stationed two deputies, J. G. Townsend and A. L. "Step" Yates, at the Colorado River Bridge with orders to enforce the local law and disarm any citizens on their way into Columbus. When Sam Reese's brother Dick rode up to the bridge in his carriage and refused to give up his weapon, the deputies opened fire, killing him and his black driver Dick Gant. The carriage horses spooked and hauled the carriage and the two bodies back towards Alleyton where they were recovered hours later. Townsend and Yates were charged with murder.[6]

This time it was Capt. John Rogers's turn to restore order. The commander of Company E rode into town a day later and quickly disarmed a cousin of one of the families named Light Townsend as he

Texas Rangers in Columbus, Texas, to control the "feud," 1899. Brooks and Capt. William Jesse McDonald stand in the back row.

Courtesy Brooks family.

arrived to get involved. The young man was so impressed by Rogers's demeanor and actions that week that he, for one at least, swore off the "feud" and joined the Rangers himself, becoming a noteworthy captain years later. Rogers calmed everyone down and left Pvt. Will Wright–who also would command a Ranger company later–and Creed Taylor in charge. Wright stayed in Columbus well into the summer of 1899, and no other incidents occurred on his watch. Step Yates died of natural causes before his trial, and Jim Townsend's trial was set for January 15, 1900, in Bastrop.[7]

On January 5, Captain Brooks was ordered to go to Bastrop to keep the peace up to and during the sure-to-be sensationalized trial proceedings. Brooks and three of his men arrived on the sixth and immediately reinstituted the law to disarm all citizens, which they enforced strictly and occasionally with force. Both sides assumed the other would still be carrying arms, however, and everyone found clever ways to hide pistols and shotguns all over town: some of the men tied strings to the butts of their pistols and hung them down inside their pants legs.[8]

On the day of the trial, events started off calmly when the judge agreed to a continuance and adjourned after only a few minutes. But as members of both factions began to wander toward the saloons, gunfire interrupted the uneasy truce. A Winchester and two pistols firing from inside the Golden Rule Saloon strafed the street. Willie Clements was shot through one lung as he dashed for safety, and Sheriff Burford's son Arthur was killed instantly, shot right between the eyes. Arthur had only just returned from attending law classes at the University of Texas in Austin, and had made the trip to Bastrop as an interested observer.

"Within twenty minutes after the killing," Sterling wrote, "Captain Brooks and his men arrested and put in jail seventeen of the Reese faction. Lieutenant [Winfred] Bates was stationed at the door of the courthouse to prevent the entry of the Townsends. When they started up the steps, the Ranger said, 'That's far enough, boys. This is the end of the line.'"[9]

Jim Townsend's trial was set aside for the time being and the three alleged shooters were arraigned and scheduled to be tried on February 15. Brooks called in reinforcements, and Captain Rogers responded. Between February 6 and 15 the two commanders and a half-dozen Rangers combed the town of Bastrop looking for illegal arms. Reports that gunmen from both factions were making their way to Bastrop sent Brooks down the rail lines that connected with Columbus.

On February 14, Brooks was in West Point, a small stop along the rails, inspecting and disarming travelers as they passed through on the westbound train. He reported later that pistols and rifles were hidden all over the train, behind seats, in the baggage, and lodged in the upper compartment bins.[10]

On the day of the trial the judge issued a change of venue and the three defendants were shipped off to Columbus until another site could be arranged. Columbus seems a peculiar destination given the trouble, but perhaps the Rangers thought that all the gunmen had left that town already. On March 1 six Rangers accompanied Jim Coleman and Walter Reese to the Columbus jail.

Five days later Brooks met Rogers at the Richmond train station where there were reports of armed men boarding the train for Colorado County. The two Ranger captains disarmed more than a dozen men on that train, again finding that "everyone had a pistol," Brooks reported to the adjutant general, and that "guns were hidden all over the train as in West Point."[11]

The trials, Coleman's and Townsend's, eventually were held in San Antonio, where all of the defendants were acquitted. Walter Reese, Sam's oldest son, vowed to stay out of the feud from then on and moved to Rosenberg, but on July 31 he and Jim Coleman were both wounded by gunfire from an arriving train as they stood on the station platform. On board the train were Willie Clements, Marc Townsend, and Frank Burford; Reese and Coleman had been informed the men were on the train and had come looking for this opportunity, but the two were also out in the open when the shooting commenced and got the bad end of the fight. Townsend and Burford were arrested but no trial ever took place.[12]

The Reese-Townsend Feud, eight years in the making, lingered for several more years. In 1906, Marion Hope, Walter and Herbert Reese, and Hiram Clements shot it out following a fistfight near the skating rink in Columbus. The Reeses were both seriously wounded and Clements killed. The participants who survived were arrested but never went to trial. Capt. John R. Hughes and several of his Rangers now took their turn at keeping order; thus, every one of the "four captains" and their companies participated at one time or another in the infamous feud.[13]

The Colorado County violence that had spread across two generations, three counties and four decades, but never saw a single conviction for any of the killings, finally died off, literally. Jim Coleman, Marion Hope, Jim Townsend, Willie Clements, and both Reese brothers died violently but unrelated to one another or the feud. The town of Columbus, battered and beaten by the violence, disincorporated itself and turned over the administrative and law enforcement duties to county officials for the next twenty years.[14]

And the Rangers went back to their work elsewhere, satisfied that the feud had finally ended but frustrated as ever that justice had seen fit once more to fail to complete its work. Records abound of mistrials and acquittals following the diligent work of law enforcement to bring felons to justice, as in the Columbus trouble and myriad cases that involved Brooks and other Rangers. Twice in his own memoirs, Brooks notes "the shame" of watching criminals let off without so much as a fine much less incarceration. Poor judges or prosecutors, or both, constituted much of the problem: evidence often proved insubstantial or unfounded and inadequately presented before the bench. Juries often failed to convict; the few convictions were often overturned by clever defense lawyers or crooked appellate judges. It surely stuck in the craw of many a peace officer whose hours and miles spent on the trail of a felon, not to mention the danger they faced along the way, went for naught in the courtroom.

As the year and century came to its close, Captain Brooks reported his company of ten Rangers: Sgt. Winfred Bates and privates J. T. Armstrong, A. Y. Baker, O. L. Bell, J. N. Evetts, D. L. Lynch, the indefatigable Lonnie Livingston, young Will Scurry, R. L. Miller, and Hayes Wallis. Sergeant Bates, a far better Ranger than poet, published a pedestrian rhyme in January that he entitled "Ranger Boys," just as the Texas legislature was preparing to convene in Austin. Its closing stanza: "The people felt safe with the Rangers about,/ For they always keep a lookout./ Sometimes the old Ranger had mighty bad luck,/ When he used his gun on some hard headed buck./ The Ranger boys' house is where the outlaws roam,/ And that is the place he generally calls home./ This noble little band is everywhere praised;/ They hope the Legislature will give them a raise." [15]

But in 1900 the primary work of the Rangers was for self-preservation more than a pay hike or tracking fugitives. The brewing question of whether the Frontier Battalion was an antiquated agency now past its prime came to the fore, and to the floor of the Texas Legislature that held the budget reins of the Rangers' future in their politicized hands.

As early as January 1899, Adjutant General Thomas Scurry wrote his Ranger captains "to be prepared to defend the Rangers on the issue of retaining the Frontier Battalion." The issue would be before the legislature, Scurry assured them, and to every Ranger he instructed: "Be mindful of the things you do, the actions you take, and your service." Whenever an arrest is reported, Scurry warned, "make your statements of facts as strong as possible." In a follow-up telegram on January 31, Scurry encouraged his captains "to write your sheriffs for help" defending the institution itself.[16]

When the Texas Legislature convened in early 1900, the writing seemed to be scribbled all over the proverbial wall. Minding their business and fighting crime, the Rangers' "good work," as Governor Sayers noted in letters of commendation on March 9 and again June 14, took a back seat to the political fight that aimed to disband the Frontier Battalion. Budget cuts reduced the companies to only six men and a technicality in an old Ranger law became the final weapon of the faction out to close the agency down forever.[17]

Twenty-five years earlier, on April 10, 1874, Gov. Richard Coke signed into law "an Act to provide for the protection of the Frontier of the State of Texas against the invasion of hostile Indians, Mexicans, or other marauding or thieving parties."[18] The Frontier Battalion, the next generation of the Texas Rangers, roamed the wide-ranging Texas frontier for over two decades, delivering for the most part on its objectives. Certainly by the late 1880s the Indian threat had all but disappeared, and the primary task of the Battalion by the end of the century concentrated on the "marauders and thieves."

But as Walter Prescott Webb wrote in his treatise on the Rangers, the frontier force had by that time become "an institutional anachronism."

Capt. J. A. Brooks, Company A, Texas Ranger Force, 1900.

Courtesy Brooks family.

"The Rangers," Webb argued, "had practically worked themselves out of a job by destroying the forces of crime that supported them." Moreover, he contended, the distinctive law enforcement agency had embedded in its own history a general resentment by local peace officers who thought they could control their own situations without outside help, and by the Hispanic population in the lower Rio Grande Valley communities who thought themselves innocent victims of the Rangers's "shoot first, ask questions later" principles of law enforcement.[19]

J. H. King, in his history of the early Ranger service, hinted at the potential problem: "The increase in authority to this semi-military body was an experiment thought by some to be of doubtful if not dangerous character, as it made the Rangers a mounted, armed, and movable constabulary, and yet one not immediately under control of nor responsible to the county officers anywhere; but the necessity was so pressing," King continues, "for some active, potent, and reliable force to face the increasing numbers and defiant boldness of criminals all over the State, that this 'new departure' in exhibiting the power that was represented in the civil authority was put in operation, but not without some misgivings."[20]

Yet another contention of Webb, and others, pointed to the "bad conduct and indiscretion" of the Frontier Battalion, not as a whole but of the few men "who reflected no credit on it." Too often, or at least often enough to resurrect the fear, a gunfighter with little respect for the law and only eager to display his shooting prowess would join a Ranger company. Before his intentions were discovered, an alleged fugitive might be found dead "attempting to escape," or so the Ranger would report. *La ley de fuga* (the law of flight) became a cautionary watchword across Texas and especially in the Valley. A number of the so-called "special" Rangers, political appointees "hired" by ranchers to protect their own interests, fit this category.[21]

By the 1890s the perceived need for a statewide police agency dimmed: the Indians were gone, the wide open frontier mostly a memory, and the very existence of the Frontier Battalion became a politicized issue. Surely, some argued, carrying the antiquated agency into the "modern" twentieth century would serve only to drag the past along with it.

Not everyone clambered onto the bandwagon, however. Where the Rangers had been effective and responsible in curtailing crime, keeping order, and assisting local peace officers–and there were as many of those communities and counties as not–their reputation remained steadfast and their constituency loyal. Here, the efforts of commanding officers such as the "four captains" paid great dividends. For every Ranger or ex Ranger such as a Bass Outlaw, there was a J. A. Brooks or a John H. Rogers to balance the scales of opinion.

And so, during the called session of the 26th Texas Legislature in the spring of 1900, the future of the Frontier Battalion was on the agenda. And it was a technicality in the old 1874 law that provided the trigger to shoot down the Rangers. The key phrase said: "Each officer of the battalion shall have the powers of a peace officer, and it shall be his duty to execute all criminal process directed to him, and make arrests under *capias* properly issued of any and all parties charged with offenses against the laws of this State."[22]

The key to the interpretation by opponents of the Frontier Battalion was the word "officers:" if only officers from the several companies could actually make arrests, then none of the sergeants or privates–who made up ninety-five percent of the entire force–could do so. Such a narrow interpretation would effectively disarm the agency and relegate the powers to only the several captains charged with law enforcement over the entire state.

When the question was brought forth in May, Governor Sayers asked Adjutant General Scurry to find an interpretation: "Get written opinion of Attorney General as to power of a ranger to arrest and execute criminal process," the governor's terse telegram said. "Important," Sayers added. Scurry in turn sent a memo to Attorney General Thomas S. Smith the next day requesting a response.

Ruled Smith in a seven-page statement on May 24: "My conclusion is that the non-commissioned officers and privates of the frontier battalion referred to as rangers, have no authority to execute criminal process or make arrests, and only the commissioned officers of that organization have that power." Quoting from subsequent acts in 1876 and 1879, Smith admitted to "some difficulty in arriving at a conclusion whether by the term 'officers' is meant only commissioned officers, or whether it includes non-commissioned officers, to-wit sergeants and corporals. Ordinarily," he writes, "in military parlance a military force is divided into officers and enlisted men."

Moreover, the attorney general suggested, the acts of 1876 and 1879 did in fact use more distinctive language, employing the terms "officers, non-commissioned officers and privates" as separate entities for execution of the law. "It is a familiar rule of construction of statutes that all statutes in *pari materia* shall be construed together in arriving at the meaning of language used in any of such statutes. These acts," Smith concluded, "intended to confer the power [to make arrests] only upon commissioned officers of the battalion."[23]

In the first round of this political battle, those determined to terminate the Rangers had won. But Thomas Scurry would not go down without a fight. Conferring with Governor Sayers even as the interpretation was being handed down, the adjutant general proposed a reorganization of the Rangers whereby the governor would appoint a company captain and two lieutenants–commissioned officers–as well as three privates. There would be six companies in this plan, four led by captains and two by first lieutenants, and now that would include sixteen "officers" instead of four.

Governor Sayers inquired if he had the authority to do such a thing, and this time the attorney general was again asked to respond. "Considering the large discretion that is given to the Governor by the terms of the Act of April 10, 1874 in organizing, re-organizing, disbanding and reassembling the Frontier Battalion," Smith wrote, "I think the Governor has the legal authority to reorganize the frontier battalion on the basis outlined."[24]

Now it seemed the Rangers still had some life in them after all.

Captain Brooks seems to have been quite interested, and certainly invested, in the proceedings and the debate. On June 15 he wrote General Scurry of a concern that Republicans in Brownsville were agitating against the Frontier Battalion, and that there was "negative talk about the need for the Rangers." On August 4 Brooks received permission for a leave of absence in order to attend the Democratic convention in Waco, where discussion about the Rangers' future mingled with the presidential race that would pit President McKinley against William Jennings Bryan for a second time.[25]

And the work of the Ranger captain continued as well. On March 19, 1900, Brooks sent Sergeant Bates, privates Baker and Livingston, and Special Ranger J. F. Dunn to watch for thieves on the pasture of Alice area rancher Francis Smithers. On the twenty-first, three Mexicans attempted to rope a steer and haul it off the ranch, but were halted by the Rangers. When they resisted arrest, guns blared: Segundo Perez was mortally wounded, Santiago Garcia was shot, and he and the third unidentified thief managed their escape, "the night being very dark," Brooks later reported. A doctor came from Alice and carried Perez to the hospital in Corpus Christi, where he died a short time later.

On the twenty-fifth, a complaint was lodged against the Rangers for the shooting. Brooks went to Corpus Christi and arranged bond for his men, reporting to Scurry that he had heard Garcia was in Mexico, "but think he will die. There should be no more trouble over the killing: Some here thought of putting the boys [Rangers] in jail, but they would have had a lively time doing it."

In an interesting side note in his March 25 letter to Scurry, Brooks recommended a deputy sheriff named A. E. Stockwell for Ranger service with this peculiar remark: "Sometimes he [Stockwell] drinks too much: He accidentally shot William Strickland some time earlier while drunk, [but] with that exception he is all right."[26]

On June 7 Brooks and Adjutant General Scurry accompanied several prisoners to the jail in Nacogdoches, the result of a deal struck to end a bloody feud in San Augustine County. The four men were Wall brothers charged with a series of shootings stemming from the April 18 murder of Sheriff George W. Wall by a local named Curg Border. Brooks then conferred with John Brook, leader of the faction opposing the Walls, on the tenth, leaving Ranger Lynch to keep the peace.

On June 18, the Walls were escorted to the penitentiary in Rusk, and ten days later the newly appointed sheriff Noel G. Roberts was asked to resign to avoid more trouble between the parties. Ranger Lt. Winfred Bates was temporarily appointed sheriff in his stead, but General Scurry ruled on August 1 that Bates was not eligible to be sheriff because he did not have residency in the county, and ordered Brooks to "re-enlist him in Company F or he will be [made] captain of Company A on a temporary basis."[27] Here again, the appointment of "commissioned officers" attempted to address the attorney general's recent interpretation of the 1874 law.

That was not the end of the San Augustine violence, however. In 1902, Curg Border was elected sheriff, igniting tempers once more. A district judge suspended Border in 1904, and he was succeeded by W. Sneed Noble on March 4. Two months later, Sheriff Noble and Border confronted one another and Noble killed the former sheriff, the last act of the feud's violence.[28]

In August 1900, Sergeant Bates and Pvt. Lon Livingston traveled to Palestine, Texas, to stand trial for alleged brutalities in an arrest from the year before; both were acquitted. Their captain was on assignment in Corpus Christi at the time, and on September 6 Scurry telegraphed Brooks to head for Vernon "if you are through in Corpus." Instead, Brooks asked for and received permission to take leave "for a few days" and go home to Cotulla to see his family. Brooks also took an eight-day leave that November to return home, but he and the records are silent as to the reason.[29] Perhaps the uncertainty of his job left Brooks in need of staying closer, for a change, to his wife and two little children.

On Saturday, September 8, a hurricane rambled over Galveston Island during the day, causing substantial wind damage. The storm surge that followed later that evening, however, overwhelmed the island and its city, wreaking destruction and leaving desolation and over 6,000 dead in its wake. The horror of the 1900 storm caused untold tragedy and left the state and the country in shock. In its aftermath, the island city would be rebuilt, the island itself raised and fortified by a seawall, and a new "modern" Galveston would rise up and move forward.

In response to the storm's destruction, General Scurry reported that he recruited Winfred Bates and Lon Livingston from Company F "to patrol the coast on the mainland for the purpose of preventing robbery of the dead and the stealing of effects washed ashore. These officers arrested John and Henry Jacobs for robbery, and recovered $275 in cash and several rings, and also arrested Harry Reagan for burglary in Texas City."[30]

As the politics of 1900 swirled around the state like its own hurricane, the Frontier Battalion limped along through the reelection of Governor Sayers and toward the next legislative session that would determine the Rangers' fate. W. Emmett Robuck was promoted to 2nd lieutenant of Company F on September 16, yet one more "commissioned officer" to enforce the law. In October, Brooks went to Rio Grande City to investigate some pre-election grumbling. Captain Rogers and Company E were assigned to Cotulla in the meantime, but a protest to their presence began the moment they arrived and Rogers ordered all but one of his men back to Alice.[31]

Will Wright, who had just that week left his station as deputy sheriff of Wilson County and joined Rogers's company, stayed behind, temporarily appointed as a lieutenant allowing him to enforce the law. On October 24, a drunk and disorderly Jim Davenport bragged to saloon cronies that he would "run this kid Ranger out of town." Firing his gun into the air outside the saloon doors soon enough brought the Ranger to confront Davenport. As Wright tried to talk the drunk out of his gun, Davenport fired the first shot, his errant bullet poking a hole in Wright's coat. Wright returned fire, killing Davenport where he stood.[32]

A week after his assignment to Rio Grande City, Brooks was ordered north to Yoakum "to preserve order" in anticipation of a railroad strike. He and two of his company rode the rails to San Antonio and accompanied eight machinists to Yoakum who feared for their safety there. The three Rangers remained in town for six days. Brooks then traveled to Carrizo Springs–"go there rapidly with three men," Scurry telegraphed–and spent Election Week there.[33]

J. A. Brooks stayed in Cotulla with his family from November 13 through the twentieth–the captain's forty-fifth birthday, and then headed to Hempstead at the direction of the adjutant general. There he joined Rogers and three of his men in a security detail guarding several prisoners being held in the jail while an angry mob milled about the streets.

As 1900 came to an end, so too the future of the Frontier Battalion flickered dimly in the winds of change.

8

THE RANGER FORCE

5'10" tall, 170 pounds, blue eyes, joined the Rangers on January 15, 1882, in Cotulla

As the Twenty-seventh Texas Legislature convened for its 1901 session, Governor Sayers entered his "Message to Congress" into the records on January 10. Under the title of "The Adjutant General's Department," Sayers wrote this about the Rangers: "This body of men cannot be too highly commended for the manner in which they have discharged the many dangerous and delicate duties incident to their employment. They have been used only where necessary to repress lawlessness, to detect crime, and to arrest and bring to trial the more serious classes of offenders. Their services in this respect have been invaluable, and may be regarded as an absolute necessity to the State."

Clearly, the exigency of the argument to disband or reorganize the Rangers was on the governor's mind as he penned his report to the legislature. "Failure to provide properly for the continuance of this force," Sayers continued, "would involve the assumption of a responsibility which no one at all acquainted with prevailing conditions should care to assume. It is earnestly recommended that the men be invested with such powers of arrest and detention as are conferred upon the officers."[1]

Subsequently, on January 14, Rep. Ferguson "Ferg" Kyle of Hays County introduced House Bill No. 52, "An Act to provide for the organization of a 'ranger force' for the protection of the frontier against marauding and thieving parties." The so-called "ranger force" would consist of four companies, each under the command of a captain and including one 1st sergeant and no more than twenty privates, and one quartermaster for the entire organization. Presumably in the writing of this law, provisions would be clearly stated enabling each ranger to enforce the laws of Texas and make arrests legally.

The bill was sent to the Committee on Military Affairs, and on January 17 committee chair Semmes Parish of Robertson County reported that the committee was sending it "back to the House with the recommendation that it do pass." The next day Representative Kyle presented on the floor for second reading but it was tabled for two weeks. When Speaker Robert E. Prince read the bill on February 4, Rep. John Houts of Jack County offered an amendment effectively killing the bill; that amendment was tabled. A second amendment, offered by Rep. John Ackerman of Grimes County and detailing the furnishing of supplies and weapons for each ranger, was accepted. The amended bill was then ordered engrossed.[2]

Meanwhile, in the Senate chambers a similar bill was being walked through the proceedings by Sen. William Ward Turney of El Paso. Turney, a prominent West Texas lawyer and rancher who had previously served two terms in the House before his election to the Senate in 1896, often represented the ranching industry of Texas whose concerns for security and law enforcement had always included broad support for the Rangers. Turney offered Senate Bill No. 31 on January 14, where it was then sent to the Committee on State Affairs. The bill had its second reading seven weeks later and joined House Bill 52 in joint committee discussion.[3]

Regardless of their future, the Rangers still had more than enough work to do besides listening to the legislators debate their fate. Cattle and horse thieves continued their activities across the state, and a flare-up of the fence-cutter wars sent Rangers from Company F to the John Kenedy ranch in Karnes County late in February. And as interested as Captain Brooks was in the Austin proceedings, a telegram from General Scurry on February 19 hinted at even bigger trouble on the immediate horizon: a prizefight was to take place in the storm-battered city of Galveston.

Following the debacle of the Fitzsimmons-Maher fight five years earlier, a loophole in the enforcement of the ban on prizefighting in Texas was soon discovered. As long as neither boxer was paid for the fight, nor any money waged, nor admission fee charged, such a bout would be considered only an exhibition or, as one promoter called it, a "scientific demonstration." The exchange of money would, of course, be done surreptitiously else no professional boxer would accept an invitation to "demonstrate."[4]

In 1899 the Galveston Athletic Club invited nationally ranked fighter Joe Choynski to be its athletic trainer; exhibitions of his skills would certainly be scheduled. Choynski had been in the ring with the greatest boxers of his time, including Jim Corbett, John L. Sullivan, and Fitzsimmons himself. By 1900 he was on the decline as a successful puncher, losing three "exhibitions" before the Galveston storm disrupted the entire island and its athletics business. The athletic club needed an opponent for Choynski.[5]

Jack Johnson, a black boxer on the rise at that time and a Galveston citizen, had trained in Chicago with fighters such as Peter Maher and Tom Sharkey. He beat another well-known black boxer named Klondike Haynes in 1899 and in early 1901 agreed to an "exhibition bout" against Choynski. The fight was scheduled for the night of February 25 in the still waterlogged Harmony Hall, admission was "free," and the town was abuzz with anticipation.[6]

But not everyone in Galveston was excited about the forthcoming exhibition. Church and temperance leaders appealed to the governor to halt what they considered "a blot upon the fair name of Texas." Since there appeared to be no monies paid or waged publicly, Sayers decided to send the Rangers undercover to find any money source; short of that, they were to arrest the principals as soon as the fight ended and see if the courts would uphold the old law against prizefighting anyway.

On February 20, Captain Brooks and three of his company, A. Y. Baker, J. J. Sanders, and Winfred Bates, arrived in Galveston by train, surely noticing the remnants of the storm's devastation from five months before. There they met with General Scurry and Galveston district attorney John Lovejoy at the Tremont Hotel and immediately began the detective work to uncover the wagering headquarters surely going on somewhere in the city; Lovejoy had agreed to prosecute the fighters following the bout. Brooks spent a night at the Tremont, two nights at the Washington Hotel, and two more at the Grand Hotel, all undercover, but found no money exchange.[7]

On the night of February 25, a huge crowd pressed into Harmony Hall to watch Choynski and Johnson "demonstrate." Brooks and his Rangers were in the crowd as well, managing to establish positions at ringside. Referee Herman Bernau introduced the fighters shortly after the pre-match entertainment of black minstrels and an under card bout featuring two one-legged boxers.

Jack Johnson looked strong and quick for the first two rounds, and swapped punch for punch with the older, more experienced Choynski. But in the third round Johnson dropped his guard and took a right hand cross that finished him in a ten count. The highly anticipated fight was over in less than seven minutes.

But the drama continued. As the referee shouted "Ten" over the fallen Johnson and waved the winner away, Brooks leapt from the crowd onto the mat, crawled through the ropes and headed for Choynski. The other Rangers closed in on the fallen Jack Johnson with a wary eye at a protesting crowd around them. Above the din, Captain Brooks hollered that he was arresting the two fighters at the behest of the governor of Texas, and that they would be duly prosecuted for breaking the law on illegal prizefighting in the state. The crowd roundly booed the intruders as they hauled the two fighters out of the auditorium and to the city jail.[8]

Bond for the two fighters was initially set at a prohibitive $5,000 but soon reduced and the fighters set free. On February 27, General Scurry sent a letter of commendation to Company F for its efforts.

Eleven days later Brooks returned to Galveston to consult with Lovejoy and investigate a rumor that another fight was in the works. On April 29, Brooks and Baker again appeared in Lovejoy's office and spent a week going over testimony before the trial. But three grand juries later, and despite Lovejoy's persistence, no indictments were ever returned, and the fight passed into the minor annals of history.[9]

The larger fight taking place was now on the House floor in Austin, where contestants traded punches over House Bill No. 52 and the fate of the Ranger Force. On February 13, 1901, the bill was read for the third time and the floor opened for debate. Rep. Philip Clements of Mills County, a fervent opponent of the reorganization without proper bonding of all of the Rangers, offered an amendment to add the phrase "and shall give a good and sufficient bond in the sum of $1,000, with not less than two sureties, conditioned for faithful performance of all duties required, said bond to be approved by the Governor and Comptroller."[10]

Such a large bond would make recruitment of non-commissioned officers–the privates–of the Ranger Force prohibitively expensive and certainly prove injurious to the new organization. The principle of bonding made practical sense in that it might also discourage the less than reputable gunmen from joining the Force, but the cost of losing good men, especially young men who could not come up with one thousand dollars nor any sureties, made this argument a bill-killer.

Rep. John W. Stollenwerck, Sr., of Hill County, moved to table the amendment, which was accomplished by a 53–37 vote. The question was raised, and the House voted for H.B. 52 by an 82–14 count. Three of those who cast negative votes, Clements, William McClellan of Coleman County, and William Shannon of Bell County, asked that their reasons for voting nay be entered into the official records. "We voted no," it says in part, "because by its terms each officer and private becomes a peace officer [with powers of arrest] for the State at large, and that without being required to give bond . . . They should at least give such bonds for faithful performance of duty as are required by our constables."[11]

The fight was not over. Semmes Parish moved to reconsider the vote just taken, delaying the final adjudication of H.B. 52 for three more weeks. Finally, on March 7 Parish withdrew his motion, allowing for the joint committees to move the bill to its final step. On March 27, Senator Turney presented the bill in its final form to the Senate where it was passed by a vote of 24–1. Sen. John T. Beaty of District 14 in East Texas, the lone objector and echoing the House concerns, wrote into the record: "While I am not opposed to the ranger service in Texas, believing it necessary for the preservation of life and property, I voted 'no' because I do not think any man should be clothed with all the powers of peace officers and not be required to give bond as other peace officers of this State."[12]

House Bill No. 52, the survivor of the joint committee, was signed by Speaker Prince on March 27, accepted by voice vote in the House and by a vote of 23–3 in the Senate, and signed into law by Governor Sayers on March 29.[13]

The law was divided into fifteen sections delineating the powers of the Rangers, the assignments to captains and the quartermaster, compensation and a list of supplies and equipment for each Ranger, and the general duties. It was noted that the new act would go into effect ninety days from its signing.

Section 2 of the new law provided for a "Ranger Force . . . not to exceed four separate companies of mounted men." The captains and the quartermaster were gubernatorial appointees who would serve two-year terms "unless sooner so removed by the Governor."

Section 3 set the monthly salaries at $100 for captains, $50 for sergeants, and $40 for each private. Section 6 specified that the governor could keep the force "in the field as long as in his judgment there may be necessity for such a force." Sections 4 and 7 detailed the duties of the quartermaster who would serve and be paid at the rank of captain, and Sections 8, 9, and 10 listed the weapons, equipment, rations, and supplies allowed for the force. Each Ranger would supply his own mount, and the cost of the "improved carbine and pistol" given him would be deducted from his first paycheck.

Section 11 contained the key sentence that had been the center of the original controversy: "The officers, non-commissioned officers and privates of this force shall be clothed with all the powers of peace officers, and shall aid the regular civil authorities in the execution of the laws. They shall have authority to make arrests, and to execute process in criminal cases . . . in any county in the State." And although they would not be required to put up a surety bond as many had insisted during the debate, they would be required to "take an oath before some authority legally authorized to administer the same, that each of them will faithfully perform his duties in accordance with law."[14]

On April 1, Captain Brooks received a telegram from the adjutant general that had been sent to all four Ranger captains: "Ranger bill signed few days ago. Won't take effect 90 days. Continue to act under old law."

On July 9, 1901, the Ranger Force was born. J. A. Brooks, formally commissioned by the governor on July 12, assumed command of what would now be called Company A; his new base of operations would be out of Alice. William Jesse McDonald would command Company B out of Amarillo, John H. Rogers's Company C was based in Laredo, and John R. Hughes led Company D out of the Fort Hancock area of far West Texas. Capt. Lambertine Pemberton "Lam" Sieker was appointed quartermaster and based in Austin.[15]

Each captain was required to list his record of service and any incidents of significance while in the Frontier Battalion. Brooks, first describing himself as being 5'10" tall, weighing 170 lbs. and with blue eyes, noted incorrectly that he had joined the Rangers on January 15, 1882, one year earlier than he had. On his list of memorable incidents were the 1886 Ft. Worth strike and the railroad strike in Temple, the 1891 skirmish with followers of Catarino Garza in Zapata County, the fence-cutter wars in Brown County, and the Conner Fight.[16]

Noted Walter Prescott Webb: "Each of [the four captains] was as courageous as the tradition required; all had their mettle of courage tested many times. They were equal to their opportunities, but with the passing of the frontier, the chances for gaining distinction had diminished."[17] But not the chances for performing their duties.

And the Rangers continued to enjoy front page coverage in local newspapers where their service was still appreciated. The Alice *Echo* reported on April 20, 1900, that three Rangers from Company F–Sergeant Bates, Private Livingston, and then-private Baker, along with Special Ranger John F. Dunn–got into a fierce midnight shoot-out with cattle thieves on Francis Smith's ranch twenty miles south of town, killing one rustler and running off the others "with their furious fire." Six weeks later the Rangers were unable to prevent a duel between two cowboys on the Rancho El Lucero, arriving only in time to see that both had been killed in the exchange.[18]

Brooks's old Company F, now stationed in Alice under their new moniker, included Lt. A. Y. Baker, Sgt. Winfred Bates, and privates Alonzo W. "Lon" Livingston, J. J. Sanders, W. Emmett Robuck, Hayes and George Wallis, John Puckett, Floyd Layton, and John Mahon. Privates Tom Franks and John Miller would join Company A later in the year.[19] Brooks moved his family from Cotulla to their new home in Alice that summer, and used his home as the headquarters for the Ranger camp.

A. Y. Baker, Brooks's most trusted officer, did not make the move to Alice with the others. In response to a June 14 directive from the adjutant general's office, Brooks sent Baker to Austin to get orders from General Scurry on a fugitive named George Isaacs, a repeat felon and convict who had been released from prison by an accomplice presenting a fake pardon. Several scouts, including Ranger Lam Sieker who traveled to Nebraska, had been sent looking for the dangerous fugitive. New information on Isaacs' whereabouts led Baker to Roswell, New Mexico, but the Ranger returned empty handed.[20]

During the same stretch of time Brooks was often absent from his camp headquarters and the temporarily commissioned "Lieutenant" Hayes Wallis–the Rangers still operated under the old 1874 law at this point–stood watch in his stead. Brooks had asked permission in May to be in Cotulla with his family, perhaps anticipating the move to Alice, and made a trip with his family to Center Point in late August to visit the Coldwells and Moores. General Scurry had agreed to let Brooks go

Ranger Commanders, 1901. Front row, l to r: Lam Sieker, Major John Armstrong, Bill McDonald; back row: J. A. Brooks, John H. Rogers, W. H. Mabry.

Courtesy Charlie, Lauren, and Carley Reeves, San Antonio.

"whenever you desire provided it does not interfere with the business at hand." And during the first week of June and once more in July, Brooks was back in Galveston waiting to testify to the grand jury sitting for the prizefight trial.[21]

Brooks had only just returned to Cotulla in mid-June when an urgent telegram to captains and sheriffs across Texas suddenly became that "business at hand." The Texas Rangers, in the midst of its largest organizational transformation ever in the summer of 1901, had to contend at the same moment with one of the most dramatic events in its long history: the hunt for Gregorio Cortez.

On June 12, former Ranger W. T. "Brack" Morris, sheriff in Karnes County and one of the first to have befriended the young Private Brooks when he joined up in 1883, rode to the W. A. Thulemeyer Ranch near Kenedy tracking horse thieves. In an encounter with Romaldo and Gregorio Cortez Lira at their ranch, Morris was killed

Capt. Brooks and his three-year-old son John Morgan, 1902.

Courtesy Brooks family.

and Romaldo died later of wounds from the same gun battle. Gregorio headed for Mexico, and hundreds of peace officers and volunteers engaged in the largest manhunt in the history of South Texas.

On June 14 a posse surrounded the home of Martin Robledo, a friend of Cortez, after learning the fugitive might be holed up there. In that shoot-out, Sheriff Dick Glover and land owner Henry Schnabel were killed, most likely by random shots from their own disorganized posse, although Gregorio was in the vicinity at the time of the raid. Cortez crossed the Atascosa, Frio, and Nueces rivers, stealing mounts or on foot along the way, while word spread and Rangers and sheriffs and deputies mounted up in pursuit.[22]

Captain Brooks left Cotulla and went on the trail, leaving "Lt." Wallis again in command at the camp. For a week the manhunt widened even as Gregorio crept closer to the border and freedom. Ten days after the shooting of Morris, Gregorio was captured by Capt. John Rogers as the exhausted fugitive slept in a makeshift tent on a goat ranch near the Rio Grande: Cortez was less than a half day from making his escape into Mexico. The celebrated Cortez–whose *corrido* is still sung today–stood trial in San Antonio, survived at least one lynch mob and several hung juries, and was ultimately pardoned by Texas Governor Oscar B. Colquitt in 1913.[23]

J. A. Brooks fondly remembered Brack Morris, with whom he had served briefly at the beginning of his Ranger career, and he bitterly recalled his old friend's death: "He was murdered by a Mexican bandit, Cortez, the shame of it. Cortez was captured by Captain Rogers but was never hanged for it. Again the shame of it."[24] The nightmare for Brooks that was Gregorio would come back to haunt him again.

On August 19, A. Y. Baker and Lon Livingston were involved in yet another shoot-out, and fellow Ranger William Warren Sterling tells the story: "[They] rode out from their station at Alice to Palito Blanco, which was in the southwestern corner of Nueces County, near the line of Duval County. It is now in Jim Wells County. Their mission was to arrest an outlaw of Mexican extraction [Pablo Flores]." Two suspects had been detained the day before and left under the guard of Pvt. J. J.

Sanders while Baker and Livingston tracked Flores to a neighboring ranch. "This *hombre* not only refused to surrender," Sterling continues, "but he barricaded himself in a house and opened fire on the Rangers with a Winchester. Baker's rifle jammed, and this predicament literally left him in a jam.

"In recounting this incident Lonnie said, 'Old Bake just grinned and started whistling a tune. He calmly got out his pocket knife and used it as a screwdriver to fix his gun.' The redoubtable Livingston, who grew up in Cotulla, did not bother to say that he saved Baker's life by killing their adversary."[25]

On the last day of 1901, Captain Brooks sent Floyd Layton and Hayes Wallis to Hidalgo County to meet with a deputy in Sheriff John Closner's office. They investigated the robbery of a Mrs. King and discovered the identities of two Mexican ranch workers who had disappeared shortly after the theft. The two Rangers tracked the thieves and found them in a camp with the reported stolen property in their possession. When the detectives identified themselves as Rangers, both brigands bolted for the heavy brush nearby. The Rangers fired at the escapees, killing Eduardo de Luna; the other man eluded them.[26]

The Ranger Force was in place and entering its first full year of service. The four captains, along with Quartermaster Lam Sieker, had their work cut out for them recruiting suitable men for their several companies and scouting the still wide-ranging frontier of a "modern," or at least civilizing, Texas: No stronger leaders could have been found. Declared General Scurry: "The fact that the Rangers are kept on the move has a wonderfully deterrent influence over thieves, who are unable to keep track of them and constantly fear being surprised and captured by them . . . The very name Ranger has been a terror to evil doers."

Moreover, Scurry wrote into his biennial report what sounds like a description of Brooks and his cohorts: "The Rangers are frequently thrown into positions which require good judgment, quick action and undoubted courage. They are frequently required to trail criminals who are known to be without fear, desperate, and with a knowledge of the country as good as that of the ranger. To the credit of the force it can be said that they never refuse to face a danger when duty requires it. The moral effect of their presence in any disturbed district is well known."[27]

Detailing the "conditions in the West and Southwest" as being exceedingly large territory with few sheriffs and deputies to keep the peace, Scurry concluded that "the ranger has been of incalculable benefit in restoring peace and good order." In a twenty-two-month period the combined Ranger companies had registered over 155,000 miles traveled in pursuit of their duties, and the adjutant general clearly intended to bolster the value of maintaining the Ranger Force well into the foreseeable future of Texas.[28]

9

THE BAKER/DE LA CERDA INCIDENT

My men are crack shots and I am not afraid of them getting the worst of anything.

THREE YEARS BEFORE THE FOUR CAPTAINS ASSUMED THEIR duties for the Ranger Force, an outbreak of smallpox in Laredo caused a minor panic in the mostly Mexican town that turned into a full fledged riot by March 1899. Dr. Walter F. Blunt, the state's chief health officer, called for a quarantine across the city and ordered fumigation for most of the homes.

The townspeople, misunderstanding the health officer's intentions, reacted as if they were being permanently evicted. The local constabulary called for help, and the Rangers of Company E moved in to assist Blunt and his staff. On March 18 a fight broke out in the streets of Laredo, with snipers firing from rooftops and the Rangers returning fire. Capt. John Rogers was gravely wounded and rushed to a San Antonio surgeon to save his shattered arm. Agapito Herrera, a former deputy sheriff who led the insurgency, was shot and killed. The riot was quelled and the quarantine instigated without further incidents, except for the growing resentment in that community towards the Texas Rangers.[1]

One of the physicians on Dr. Blunt's staff was Isaac Jarrett Jones, a native of Arkansas who had moved to Austin in 1894 by way of a practice in Mississippi. Dr. Jones became Blunt's assistant and chief clerk in 1899 after four years as surgeon in the Texas Confederate Home. He also was active in Texas politics and served as the chair of the Travis County Democrats executive committee. In his biennial report for 1899–1900, Dr. Blunt wrote: "I desire to say that my efficient clerk, Dr. I. J. Jones, has been of great service to me in every department of the service, both in the office and the field, and I desire to express to him my sincere thanks for his service."[2]

During the following year Dr. Blunt became ill and was absent for long periods of time until he was finally forced to resign in October 1901. His replacement, Dr. George R. Tabor, filed this report eight weeks after taking over: "I asked to be shown the books belonging to the department, and found there had been absolutely no system with reference to the bookkeeping, and I also found a small irregularity, to which I called the attention of [Jones], and which he explained by saying it was only an error which he or Dr. Blunt could rectify. He would not pursue the subject further," Tabor wrote, "but left the office . . . and left the city the next day."

Dr. Tabor immediately called in an accountant to go over the books: the "small irregularity" turned out to be an embezzlement of funds totaling nearly $8,700, all of which had occurred since Jones had begun clerking for the health department. In the report, details of the misappropriation included Jones signing checks over to himself or signing someone else's name on a check made out to him, inflated vouchers "in his handwriting without any attempt to disguise it," and more. "Numerous forgeries and other offenses were committed by Dr. Jones to secure money out of this department," concluded Tabor.[3]

On January 5, 1902, a warrant was issued for Isaac J. Jones and, when word came that Jones had fled the city, the adjutant general sent a telegram to Captain Brooks in Alice to take the case. It was rumored that Jones might be heading for Mexico, and the telegram instructed Brooks to track him there. When Brooks asked for any identifying characteristics of the fugitive he would be chasing, the adjutant general replied, "He has a peculiar walk on account of his being extremely pigeon-toed."[4]

With that, Brooks started south. By January 7 he was at the Iturbide Hotel in Monterrey, where he received a telegram that Jones might be in Mexico City. Three days later, informants told Brooks that Jones had cashed a check for twenty-five dollars at a local shop. Brooks kept on the hunt, scouring the capital city for three weeks. On the twenty-first, Governor Sayers encouraged Brooks in a telegram "to be economical" in his paying informants, "but good job so far." The next day Brooks learned that Jones had been spotted "dodging in and out of Mexico City," and Sayers advised that the Ranger captain "try Porter's American Restaurant where Jones has been seen."

But Jones proved elusive. Brooks made his way to Cordoba on January 26, remained there a week chasing rumors, and returned to Mexico City on February 2. In response to Brooks's telegram to Austin, Sayers advised him now to try another tack: "Get the local police to help you, pretend to leave the city and wait for any information. Offer $200 reward."

Nothing worked. On February 10 Brooks returned to Texas, believing that the fugitive had made his way to Guatemala or Honduras. In March, Captain Sieker was sent to Shreveport, Louisiana, where Jones had possibly been spotted, and then on to Arkadelphia, Arkansas. Later that same month, an Austin police captain searched for Jones in Mississippi while Sieker traveled into Mexico, all attempts in vain. The last report indicated Jones had made his escape to Central America, absconding with the $8,000.[5]

Back in Alice, Brooks and Company A had their hands full when the cattle herds–and the cowboys–congregated along the rail lines, at that time the largest cattle shipping point in the country. Ranger William W. Sterling tells a story of one incident in his own inimitable style: "At these times, the streets and wooden sidewalks would be crowded with saddle weary stockmen. The saloons did a thriving business.

"Captain Brooks and his men came to town every night, mainly to watch the fun. They were sympathetic and patient with the revelers, not bothering them unless it became an absolute necessity."[6] Brooks may have enjoyed re-living his younger cowboying days, remembering the antics of Collin County and Denton and Kansas, and likely lifted a few drinks of his own. As a remorseful old man decades later he confessed to "liquoring up" often while on duty in saloons across South Texas, and rowdy places like Alice would have been more of a temptation than Brooks might have been able to handle.[7]

"One night," Sterling writes, "a particularly loudmouthed waddy made his appearance. He whooped and hollered, announcing he was a badman from the salt fork of Bitter Creek, with many other declarations of being double tough. The man eater finally got out of hand, and Captain Brooks told Lonnie Livingston to lock him up. Just as the Ranger started to carry out his order, the cowboy bellowed: 'Whoopeeee! I'm the worst pill in the box.'

"'All right podner,' said Lonnie as he headed him for the calaboose. 'You may be the worst pill in the box, but the doctor says take you.'"[8]

Sgt. Anderson Yancey Baker, "Ancey" as he was known to family and close friends, had his own encounters with the bottle on occasion as well, as did a number of the Rangers according to captains' reports. On May 8 Baker got drunk while in an Alice saloon and fired his pistol into the air. Captain Brooks was forced to write a reprimand into his files: "Baker has an excellent record, I regret to see this blot on it," he wrote.[9] There is some rich irony, or perhaps hypocrisy, in Brooks's report, the company commander having his own propensities to overindulge.

The more or less innocent fun of a rowdy night in an Alice saloon, however, quickly paled when a deadly confrontation in May caused a ripple effect of death and fury that lasted for years.

The massive King Ranch, spread over South Texas, endured cattle and horse rustling year round despite the efforts of security and the recurring presence of Rangers. Its extensive boundaries left the huge operation vulnerable on its outskirts to thievery, and law enforcement was constantly on scouts to deter the criminals. In mid-May 1902, Captain Brooks received a telegram from Austin ordering him to send three men to the King Ranch to investigate an outbreak of cattle rustling in the southern pastures.

Rangers A. Y. Baker, Hayes Wallis, and W. Emmett Robuck rode north out of their Brownsville camp thirty-two miles to the 17,700-acre El Sauz Ranch situated along the Arroyo Colorado near the Cameron

County line, accompanied by a King Ranch cowboy named Jesse Miller. The El Sauz, also listed as El Saenz in some records, had once been owned by Antonio Hinojosa but now belonged within the boundaries of the King operation.[10] On May 15, near the Urracas well, they encountered a *vaquero* who claimed he was scouting the fence lines. However, as there were no fences within a three-mile radius, the Rangers arrested the man and, with no jail for miles, left him tied to a tree until they might return. (He was later carted off to jail.)

They camped nearby for the night and launched their scout at daybreak on the sixteenth. About nine in the morning they spotted several calves tied to trees in some heavy brush. The four men separated in order to cover more ground, the dense brush extending in all directions. Brooks wrote in his official report: "Baker rode down one trail to a windmill where he spotted another calf tied to a tree. In the thick brush he came upon Ramón Serda [de la Cerda] branding a King calf."[11]

Ramón de la Cerda, a young man in his early twenties, and his father owned the Francisco de Asis Ranch which bordered on the King Ranch. In 1900, the elder de la Cerda was shot and killed by a Brownsville police officer, and Ramón and his fifteen-year-old brother Alfredo now operated the family place. Suspicion was aroused earlier in the year that the brothers had been rustling their neighbor's cattle, as they had sold some calves with a "bar-W" brand, only a horizontal line different from the legendary running "W" of the King Ranch brand.[12]

Seeing the peace officer ride up out of the heavy brush, Ramón, armed with two six-shooters, pulled one and shot at Baker, but the Ranger fired his Winchester rifle at the same instant. Ramón's bullet struck Baker's horse in the head as it reacted to the gunfire. Baker's horse fell dead even at the same instant that de la Cerda dropped to the ground, killed instantly by the bullet that struck above his right eye: the gunfight had only lasted seconds.[13]

Edward Burleson Raymond, manager of the King Ranch's Southern Division that included El Sauz, was located by Private Wallis and returned to the scene of the shooting along with Justice of the Peace Estevan Garcia Osuña who arranged for the body to be buried. The three Rangers returned to Brownsville and reported to Captain Brooks, who in turn filed a report with the adjutant general's office.[14]

What appeared to be a straightforward incident soon turned deadlier. The de la Cerdas enjoyed some political clout in South Texas, and Red Club supporters, always looking for any excuse to castigate the Rangers, arranged for Ramón's body to be disinterred six days later to investigate rumors that the Rangers had dragged the lifeless body through the heavy brush after the shoot-out. A magistrate from Brownsville, Hernacion Garcia, and several witnesses, were on the scene and an inquest was held but no official affidavits filed.[15]

But soon thereafter charges of murder were brought against all three Rangers and Miller, and bond was set for Baker at $10,000, which he made with help from the King family and Major John Armstrong, and at the suggestion of his own captain: "Fix the bond at $10,000," General Scurry ordered in response to a telegram from Brooks. "The prejudice against the rangers on the part of the Mexican element is too strong." Friends and neighbors of the dead man, and a large portion of the population in Brownsville, were outraged. Demonstrations in the streets against the Ranger Force, incited by Red Club politicos, accompanied charges of brutality and partisanship by a Mexican newspaper editor.[16]

On June 24, General Scurry wrote Brooks that he "was pleased to hear there was no trouble in Brownsville."[17] Although far from calm, the situation at least simmered down throughout the summer months. Brooks tried to go about his business, sending his men to scout along the border. On August 25 the captain went to San Diego to settle a local dispute involving the judge and the town commissioners. The judge, Sam H. Woods, had been removed from the bench at the climax of a long-standing political fight, but Sheriff Manuel Rogers had then refused to allow the commissioners to meet, locking the doors to the court. When the tax assessor and the district judge began harassing the sheriff, Brooks intervened. "I stopped them at once," Brooks reported, "and they met that afternoon quietly." Both Judge Woods and Sheriff Rogers remained in office.[18]

Meanwhile in Brownsville, where part of Company A remained stationed, trouble brewed. The Rangers, on the defensive and edgy, did not help matters by being overly aggressive on several occasions during the sweltering summer months. Pvt. John Puckett was accused of whipping a man who he said was stealing his clothes from the campsite. George Wallis got into a shouting match with a belligerent customs inspector who had sent a scathing memo to Washington, D. C., about the Rangers, and reportedly slapped the official in the face.[19]

The surviving de la Cerda, fifteen-year-old Alfredo, made his presence and intentions known whenever he rode into town, threatening to get even with the Rangers who had killed his brother. Captain Brooks spent a great deal of time in Brownsville, and was aware of the threats and the danger. In one report he wrote defiantly, "My men are crack shots and I am not afraid of them getting the worst of anything." On September 4 the captain posed with seven of his Rangers for a photograph. Brooks is seated, holding his new issue Waffenfabrk Mauser semi-automatic pistol with its special wooden stock.[20]

About ten o'clock at night on September 9, Sergeant Baker, Pvt. Emmett Robuck, and ranch hand Jesse Miller rode out of Brownsville on their way to the camp on the outskirts of town. Miller had accompanied Company A through much of the summer both for his own protection and as a witness at the inquests. On this night, Baker and Robuck had temporarily traded horses as a result of a saloon wager earlier that evening. To get to their campsite required taking the trail that wound across one of the pastures belonging to Judge James B. Wells, the "boss" of Brownsville Red Club politics.[21]

As the three riders passed a stand of dense brush, shots rang out in the darkness. A shotgun blast killed Miller's horse; another slammed into Baker's thigh. Private Robuck, astride Baker's distinctive white mount and perhaps mistaken for the sergeant, was killed when buckshot struck him in the throat severing his carotid artery. Despite his injury, Baker pulled his pistol and fired into the brush, but the

Capt. Brooks and Company A, Ranger Force, 1902. Brooks, seated, holds his wooden grip Mauser pistol.

Courtesy Brooks family.

assailants–Baker and Miller suggested later that there may have been four or five–made their escape into the night.

Baker and Miller took Robuck's body into camp where Captain Brooks learned of the shooting. The next morning a posse was rounded up, including six of Brooks's Rangers and City Marshal Lawrence Bates (Baker's cousin), and the tracking began. A local named Herculano Berbier gave important information to Captain Brooks that led the posse to a Brownsville warehouse belonging to a Spaniard named Juan Fernandez. Fernandez ran a general store in town and was a friend of the de la Cerdas: earlier in the summer he and Jesse Miller had engaged in a shoving match witnessed by several others.[22]

"Knowing [Berbier,] the boatman who crossed the guilty parties to this side of the Rio Grande," Brooks wrote into his August 31, 1902, report to the adjutant general, "and being in position to get valuable information, I promised him a reward; also promised him a place in my company at $40 per month, in order that he would be protected." Brooks also enlisted Jesse Miller in order to protect him: "Owing to the attempt to assassinate him along with my men," Brooks wrote, "I thought him worthy of the position."

Inside the warehouse on September 10 they found Alfredo de la Cerda and a cache of guns hidden there. Alfredo was arrested without incident and put in the city jail under heavily armed guard. Six others were also arrested as possible associates involved in the killing of Private Robuck. A few days later word came to the Rangers that a lynch mob–probably Blue Club partisans showing support for the peace officers–planned to take Alfredo later that night. Captain Brooks sought out the leaders of the group and told them they would not be allowed to carry out their plan, and "that they would have to kill the captain and every Ranger in Brownsville in order to succeed."[23] The mob disappeared.

But Juan Fernandez, fearing for his life as a friend of de la Cerda, sought protection with the Mexican consulate. Brooks assured the consul and Fernandez that the Rangers would protect him well enough. "I offered to camp my company in Fernandez' yard," Brooks reported.[24]

In response to Brooks's telegraphed report to Austin, General Scurry responded: "Very sorry to hear of Baker's wound and Robuck's death. If you need more rangers wire me. Make full report." In two follow-up messages Scurry raised the reward for capture of Robuck's killer from $200 to $300, and indicated that the adjutant general's office would pay for the Ranger's funeral, "but no more than $60."[25]

Several days after the arrest, Alfredo de la Cerda made bond, thanks to Red Club donations, and was released from the Brownsville jail much to the dismay of the Rangers. By the first of October he was again roaming the streets of the town and allegedly agitating against the men who had killed his brother. Later testimony indicated that Alfredo had offered a $1,000 bounty to anyone who killed Baker if he didn't accomplish the task himself.[26]

On the afternoon of October 3 Alfredo stepped to the doorway from inside the Fernandez and Brothers dry goods store at the corner of Elizabeth and Thirteenth streets. Coincidentally, or so it seemed, Sergeant Baker and Sgt. Winfred Bates were walking down the sidewalk in front of the store at the same moment. According to Bates's testimony, Baker saw Alfredo out of the corner of his eye and, thinking the fifteen-year-old had been lying in wait for him, jerked his 30-40 caliber Krag Winchester rifle in a flash and killed de la Cerda. Both Bates and Baker swore at the ensuing trial that Alfredo made "a threatening movement" a moment before the shooting. Wrote Baker years later: "[Cerda] hastily rose and threw his right hand behind him as if to draw his gun, and mindful of his threats, and fearing that my life was at stake, I instantly shot him in order to save myself."[27]

As angry crowds pressed in, Captain Brooks arrived minutes later and took Baker into protective custody. "I arrested Baker, disarmed him, and took him to Fort Brown [two blocks away] for safe keeping," Brooks reported. "Bail and bond were made before [County] Judge [Thomas] Carson, I gave him his arms and put him on duty." Later in the year Brooks sent Baker to scout in Comstock, midway between Del Rio and Langtry and plenty of miles away from the roiling crowds.

Three days after Alfredo was shot, Herculano Berbier was gunned down by unknown assailants. Berbier had given important information to the Rangers that had resulted in the arrest of Alfredo de la Cerda and was to have been a witness for Baker's defense as well.[28]

While Brownsville boiled in the October sun, the adjutant general arrived at the behest of Governor Sayers to investigate the entire matter. General Scurry filed his report on November 11. He noted that accusations against Baker for killing Ramón de la Cerda in May were "the endeavor of these witnesses to show that Cerda had been roughly handled before death but the evidence is so conflicting on the part of the witnesses for the State and so flimsy that it appeared to be manufactured by the enemies of the rangers. However," Scurry added, "it was enough to create a strong prejudice against Baker, Wallis, Robuck and Miller on the part of a large portion of the citizens of Mexican parentage."

"After Ramón Cerda was killed," writes Scurry, "prominent members of the 'Red Club,' a political party, took up the cry against the rangers. In-flamatory [*sic*] speeches were made against them and articles were written in a small Spanish paper condemning them by names as official assassins and murderers. Ramón Cerda was extolled as a martyr." Scurry refers to an editorial in *El Cometa* written by J. M. Longoria and entitled "Official Assassination" that was actually written one day after Alfredo's death on October 3. In it, Longoria details the shooting on Thirteenth Street and scoffs at Baker's claim that Alfredo drew a gun on him.

"Most of the charges made against the rangers grew out of the exciting conditions connected with the killing of Ramón Cerda," Scurry opines in his report to the governor. "The frequent charges to the effect that the rangers were murderers etc. and occasional threats made against their lives made them apprehensive and under the excitement they resented the remarks and acts of the leaders against them and in some instances treated them harshly but in my opinion the extenuating circumstances should excuse them."

In his concluding remarks to Sayers, Scurry writes, "I am of the opinion that no further action should be taken in reference to the matter, further than to direct the removal of Captain Brooks's company to some other location on account of existing conditions and that another company be directed to occupy his territory." Accompanying his report was a list of fifteen citizens who had claimed harassment by the Rangers, and a letter of commendation for Brooks and Company A written by Robert Kleberg, chief executive of the King Ranch enterprises.[29]

General Scurry ordered Company A to switch places with Capt. John R. Hughes's company then stationed at Fort Hancock. But three days later Scurry rescinded that order and told Brooks to meet him in Laredo. The two men met on October 12 with Captain Rogers, and nine days later the adjutant general switched Company A with Captain Rogers's company; a portion of Hughes's company moved its camp to Alice under the same "General Order No. 268." However, Brooks remained in Brownsville through the end of February 1903, in order to participate in A. Y. Baker's murder trial.[30]

At the grand jury hearing presided over by Stanley Welch, district judge of the expansive South Texas Trans-Nueces region and a notable figure in Red Club politics, the jury returned an indictment against Baker while at the same time praising the Ranger Force for its service in the Valley and commending Captain Brooks for his leadership. And upon learning of the switch of Ranger companies, Judge Welch even offered a protest: "All the ills of the Cerda killings have settled themselves, and I believe that with the aid of the Rangers under Captain Brooks, crime can be eliminated from Cameron County."[31]

While waiting for the trial to commence and for the move to Laredo, Captain Brooks kept busy with the other duties of his company. In September, cholera swept into San Antonio and a quarantine was ordered by the state health office. Brooks sent privates Livingston, Tumlinson, and Franks to assist; the three Rangers were there into November.

On November 16, Brooks traveled to Live Oak County to investigate cattle rustling on the ranch of George W. West. The fifty-year-old West, who had come to Texas from his Tennessee home in 1880, still owned 10,000 acres and thousands of cattle after selling off much of his property the year before; he represented a strong voice for the cattlemen in that area. Less than a decade later he would help found the Live Oak County town that bears his name.[32]

In the official records of the adjutant general for 1901 and 1902 as compiled by Captain Brooks, Company A registered 134 arrests in a twenty-two month period, the same as Rogers's Company C and far fewer than the 211 arrests made by Captain McDonald's Company B. But Company A did record the most arrests of horse and cattle thieves, with forty-five. In May 1901, Brooks's men recovered fifty-six head of stolen cattle, more than any other one-month period and more than any other company's two-year total. Three criminals were killed by Company A, the only deaths registered among the four companies for that period.[33]

A. Y. Baker went to trial twice in 1903, for the killings of Ramón de la Cerda and his brother Alfredo; both times he was defended by James B. Wells and both times acquitted on the plea of self-defense. Early in March Captain Brooks turned over the duties of his area to Captain Rogers and made his way to Alice to pack up Company A for its move to Laredo; they settled into their new camp by the end of the month.[34] Brooks left his wife and two young children in their Alice home, commuting to see them but rarely over the next three years.

A. Y. Baker quit the Ranger Force in 1904 and went to work as a mounted customs inspector. In 1908 he was elected treasurer of Hidalgo County, and four years later he "switched" positions with Sheriff John Closner. When Closner was ousted in 1918 for misappropriation of county funds, Baker inherited the "boss" rule of Hidalgo County, an advantageous political position which he maintained until his death in 1930. Along the way Baker shrewdly turned inexpensive land purchases into a multimillion dollar enterprise, became president of the Edinburg bank, and was considered a philanthropist by some and the "millionaire sheriff of Hidalgo County" by his enemies.[35]

The de la Cerda story is rich with high drama, sensationalized trials, murders and ambushes, and most importantly as a venue for the growing frustration by many citizens along the border aimed at the Ranger Force. Despite the brave and magnanimous efforts of men like J. A. Brooks and, in turn, captains John Hughes and John Rogers, the Rangers continued into the twentieth century under a veil of suspicion and resentment.

10

BATSON PRAIRIE OIL

There is no way of holding a prisoner here except to chain him to a tree with chain and lock

THE ASSIGNMENT GIVEN CAPTAIN BROOKS ON MARCH 18, 1903, must surely have opened a festering old wound in his soul. Even as he was making preparations to complete the move of Company A out to Laredo, Brooks was ordered to Yoakum to assist Atascosa County Sheriff Matthew Avant and two Rangers from Captain Hughes's company in escorting Gregorio Cortez Lira to his trial in Pleasanton. Gregorio, the man who had killed Brooks's friend Brack Morris two years earlier, had been in a San Antonio jail most of that time awaiting this next turn in the judiciary system. His stay in a Yoakum jail resulted from one of many changes of venue. Brooks reports only that he met the Rangers and Avant at the depot in Floresville where they headed to Yoakum, and that Cortez was safely brought to Pleasanton.[1]

The story of Gregorio Cortez's many trials and acquittals stretched on into the next decade. In a personal letter, Capt. John Rogers, the Ranger who captured Gregorio, recalled seeing the just released defendant walking along a San Antonio street some years later, noting the revulsion he felt. One of Cortez's several trials was presided over by Judge Stanley Welch, a key figure in South Texas politics who had also presided at the Baker trial in early 1903.[2]

Captain Brooks was ordered to Zapata County on May 20 by General Scurry to investigate the murder of a Dr. A. D. McCabe.

McCabe had a mysterious past when he moved to Zapata in 1899, but he quickly befriended A. P. Spohn, the county boss, and was appointed county physician. The two outspoken men soon parted company over political differences: McCabe quit his position and bad blood between the two boiled over into open confrontation. The doctor organized a reform party to defy Spohn's political machine, and took to wearing a six-shooter on his hip when in public. On the night of May 19, McCabe was gunned down in his own home by an unknown assailant. The Rangers' investigation turned up no leads and no arrests were ever made.[3]

Brooks's trek to Zapata was one of Scurry's last orders as adjutant-general: Ten days later he retired, accentuating his pride in the Ranger Force and its commanders in his letter to the new governor Samuel W. T. Lanham. Lanham appointed John Augustus Hulen to succeed Scurry in Austin.

The thirty-two-year-old Hulen, born in Missouri and raised in Gainesville, Texas, had already enjoyed an adventurous life. A military academy graduate, he became a successful agent for the Missouri, Kansas and Pacific Railroad Company, organized a volunteer state guard unit, and served as lieutenant colonel of the First Texas Cavalry (U.S. Volunteers), in which Brooks had served, during the Spanish-American War. He was awarded the U.S. Army's Silver Star medal for his action in the Philippine insurrection in 1900–1901, and upon his return to Texas was rewarded with the adjutant general appointment.[4]

On June 2 Captain Brooks received a telegram from General Hulen ordering him to send two men to Carrizo Springs to investigate a crime. Brooks decided to go himself and spent ten days there before returning to the Laredo camp. It is possible that Brooks met Carl Groos during his stay in the small Dimmit County town. Groos and his partner E. J. Buckingham were surveying land north of the town and would soon purchase the 100,000-acre Cross S Ranch in Zavala County (misspelled "Zavalla" until 1928), one of the largest ranches in the Southwest, subdivide it, and sell lots to create the town of Crystal City. One of those buyers would be J. A. Brooks.[5]

On August 20, Brooks learned that his eldest brother-in-law, Annie's husband James Henry Kerr, had died in Kentucky at the age of seventy-three. Kerr was buried the next day in the Lexington Cemetery where many of the Brooks kin would find their final resting place in the years that followed. Brooks went to Bourbon County to visit with his surviving siblings who had gathered for Kerr's funeral, but it does not appear from the family records that he took his wife and children with him on the trip. While in Kentucky he spoke at length with Annie regarding her late husband's estate: apparently some funds were to be directed to "Bud" Brooks. As a result of the visit and probate of the will, the captain was able to purchase additional properties the following year when he invested in the Crystal City land, 640 acres of what was deeded as the Brooks-Kerr tract less than a mile south of the San Antonio Road and adjacent to one of many artesian wells in that region.[6]

At the close of 1903 Captain Brooks listed his company as a part of his December report. His loyal sergeant Winfred Bates continued to serve Company A, along with privates Clyde McDowell, W. D. Blackmon, Tom Franks, Marcellus Lowe, Lott Tumlinson, and J. R. Brown; Brown resigned in March of 1904. McDowell was a Comstock farmer; Lowe was only twenty-one and from Del Rio; and Tumlinson hailed from Carrizo Springs. Twenty-two-year-old Robert Rumsey was recruited out of Laredo in January, and S. B. Bates out of Maverick County.[7]

An incident the first week in January garnered a detailed report by the Company A commander to General Hulen. Brooks had sent Private Tumlinson and three other of his men to the Los Hermanos Ranch not far from Laredo to look for a man named Santiago Mata. Mata claimed he had been shot at by a *vaquero* named Serna. When Tumlinson confronted Serna about the incident, the Mexican ranch hand raised his rifle at the Ranger, whereupon Tumlinson pulled his pistol and fired, killing Serna just as he got off an errant shot. Brooks reported that Serna and Tumlinson were so close in the shoot-out that the Ranger private "had powder burns from Serna's rifle fire."[8]

In the latter days of December 1903, and from January 5 to 15 the next month, Brooks reports that he was "sick" and assigned Sergeant Bates to command most of that time. Whether it was a winter illness or yet another bout with alcohol is impossible to tell from the records, but for four days in July Brooks also reports that he was absent from camp.[9]

Cattle rustling along the Mexico border was on the increase in 1904, and Company A made scouts across Webb, Dimmit, Maverick, and LaSalle counties, with a dramatic number of arrests made around Encinal throughout the year. In his biennial report the adjutant general made special mention of the excellent work of Brooks and his company to curtail the rustling along the Rio Grande; Brooks and Company A received special accolades from the cattlemen across South Texas for their efforts that year. The company registered the recovery of 362 stolen horses and cattle between September 1902 and August 1904, twice the total of the other three companies combined, and arrested forty-three rustlers.[10]

While scouting over in Starr County, Captain Brooks met rancher and Republican boss Ed C. Lasater, and the two quickly became good friends. Edward Cunningham Lasater was forty-four years old when he met the Ranger captain, a native Texan raised near Goliad and a successful cattleman in Live Oak County before he turned his attention to the wide open spaces of South Texas. In 1895 Lasater purchased 7,000 head of cattle from the Kenedy Pasture Company with the intention of becoming one of the largest cattle breeders of Jersey dairy cows from Kerr County and later his son Tom's original Beefmaster brand in the Southwest. He succeeded. At the time he and Brooks met the cattleman owned over 300,000 acres across what was then the massive Starr County.[11]

Copying the ideas of entrepreneurs like Groos and Buckingham, Lasater formed the Falfurrias Immigration Company, named after his South Texas ranch, and encouraged investors to purchase tracts of land. The result would be the incorporated town of Falfurrias in 1904. One of its first land owners was Capt. J. A. Brooks, who in June put $240 down on eighty acres of Lasater's "Falfurrias Farm and Garden Tracts," the remaining balance of $960 to be paid out over four years at seven percent interest. The modest ranch of what later became 267 acres in size was located near the railroad tracks eight miles south of where the little town was being organized. Eventually Brooks purchased five more land tracts in the vicinity totaling over 1,400 acres.[12]

To further promote his enterprise, Lasater persuaded the San Antonio and Aransas Pass Railway to swing south from Alice through his new town. The little community boomed over the next several years, with the Falfurrias Creamery Company, eventually run by Lasater's son Garland, becoming world famous.

J. A. Brooks's purchase of land in Crystal City and Falfurrias over a twelve-month period hints at his moving towards retirement from the Ranger Force. In 1903 he turned forty-eight years old; he had been a Ranger for twenty of those years and had three fewer fingers and plenty of scars to prove it. His bouts with alcohol had certainly not diminished over those two decades; if anything, his several absences from command may account for his thoughts now of giving up the active life for a small ranch in the land that he knew so well. Retirement before an embarrassing incident connected to his drinking seemed an idea of unusual clarity.

Whether his family had any impact on his coming decision is hard to tell. The year he would turn fifty his two surviving children would be seven and eight years old; Virginia, his wife of sixteen years, was still more a stranger than a companion. She had raised the children essentially alone in Cotulla and Alice: would a home in Falfurrias be any different? Giving the captain the benefit of the doubt, however, at least the contemplation of retirement during this period in his life meant the possibility of his spending more time at home.

But not in 1904, not yet. Captain Brooks's twenty-first year in the service would prove to be one of his most active and adventurous, in a strange world new to the Rangers and new even to Texas.

With the gushers and subsequent oil boom at Spindletop just two years removed, Judge William Douglas and his Beaumont business partners Stephen W. Pipkin and William Wiess organized the Parrafine Oil Company, and drilled their first Hardin County well in October 1903. Their first two wells produced enough to encourage them, and Well No. 3 broke through the cap rock at a depth of over 1,000 feet and pumped at more than 10,000 barrels per day until it was capped. The three wells were located northwest of Beaumont and Sour Lake on a flat plain known to locals as Batson Prairie. When the J. M. Guffey Company came in right behind, the nearby village of Otto picked up its sidewalks and moved on to the prairie. Renamed Batson shortly thereafter, its population became a rowdy, lawless 10,000 overnight.[13]

Ranger William Warren Sterling tells a remarkable story that follows up the Batson boom. "One December day in 1903 my father and I were passengers on a Southern Pacific train en route from Beaumont to Houston. Occupying the two seats facing us were former Governor James Stephen Hogg and his business associate, James Swayne, of Fort Worth.

"As our train passed Sour Lake Station, which is now called Nome, the gentlemen's conversation centered on the lawless conditions that had arisen in Hardin County since the discovery of oil. Sour Lake had simmered down somewhat but Saratoga and Batson's Prairie were running hog wild. Batson held a thin edge over the others for sheer deviltry in the rough. Human life was cheap. Shootings and cutting scrapes were common occurrences while thieves stole any property that was not guarded day and night.

"My father, who had been in all three fields, stated that the local officers were both unwilling and unable to cope with the situation. Pointing his finger toward the new oil fields, Hogg said in emphatic tones, 'There is only one way to stop that lawlessness. If I were still governor, I would have Rangers in Batson before sundown tomorrow. When I get to Houston, I am going to wire [Gov.] Sam Lanham and urge him to send them there.'" According to Sterling, Lanham wired Captain Brooks the next day. Brooks went hurriedly to Batson Prairie, surveyed the situation and reported to the governor that in fact there was a desperate need for real law enforcement in those oil fields.[14]

On January 20, 1904, Captain Brooks arrived once more at the Liberty train depot, nearest stop to Batson, this time in company with Sergeant Bates and privates Tumlinson and McDowell. Sterling recalls from his conversations with Brooks and Bates years later: "Captain Brooks and his men made the rest of the trip by hack. Upon arrival at their destination, the Rangers put up at the local hotel, which was a typical example of the rooming houses found in the early oil fields. It was a long, barn-like structure made out of cheap, unseasoned pine lumber with resin still oozing out of the unpainted boards."

"After spending one miserable day in the so-called hotel," Sterling continues, "the Rangers procured a tent, borrowed some cooking utensils and pitched camp in a grove on the edge of town." There the four peace officers would remain for the next eight days. "The coming of Brooks, Bates and company was hailed with relief and delight by the substantial citizens of Batson but viewed with alarm by denizens of the underworld. The crooked officers particularly resented the Rangers. These badge wearing grafters could see an early end of their corrupt practices, as well as the termination of the reign of terror they had imposed on inoffensive working men."[15]

That same day, former governor Hogg wrote oil millionaire John S. Cullinan: "To prevent the threatened outbreaks of lawlessness around Batson, I beg to say that [Governor Lanham] has ordered Capt. Brooks of the Ranger Force to go there to cooperate with the local officers, if necessary to this end. He is a careful, capable officer from whom much good can be expected, in the performance of his duties."[16]

The new situation created by the dramatic southeast Texas oil boom would have been sufficiently dangerous and daunting to clean up with the cooperation of local law enforcement; the fact that many of the deadliest crooks there were the local police made the situation only worse for the Rangers. Sheriffs Billy Bryant and Ras Landry, the latter from Beaumont, were notable exceptions to the lawless brigands who sported a badge and an attitude. "There is bad feeling between the officers and the men who work in the oil fields," Captain Brooks reported during his initial visit to Batson Prairie, "and it will be only a few days before they have it in for me as I have notified all of them that I hoped to keep this place quiet as long as I remain here."[17]

One of the first encounters between the Rangers and a deputy occurred the second day the peace officers were on the scene. The tall, wide-girthed lawman had shot and killed a drunken oil field worker some time earlier and bragged to those at the scene that he "liked to shoot 'em to see 'em kick." When he heard the Rangers had come into his self-proclaimed territory, he blustered that he was unafraid of them and would teach them a lesson or two.

When Brooks learned of the braggart and that he was engaged in extortion and bribery out of his office, he commented to his sergeant that the inevitable confrontation might end in a shooting. But Winfred Bates convinced his commander to let him have first crack at the over-sized buffoon. Later that same day the deputy was reported to be beating up a dance hall girl in town and Bates hurried to the scene. When the deputy turned his attention to the Ranger, reaching for his pistol, Bates drew faster and knocked the ruffian unconscious with the butt of his gun. The Beaumont newspaper delightedly reported: "120 Pound Ranger Whips 220 Pound Deputy."[18]

The town of Batson did not have a jail for arrested felons, so the Rangers dragged the dazed deputy to a large tree at the end of the only street and chained him there for the time being. According to the tales from this incident, when he came to, the prisoner threatened to kill Sergeant Bates. Bates returned and offered him his gun back to see if he might be up to the task; the deputy refused. The next day another crooked constable and the justice of the peace both tried to physically intimidate Private Tumlinson, and both received similar treatment from the Ranger.[19]

Reported Brooks, "There is no way of holding a prisoner here except to chain him to a tree with chain and lock. It is very unpleasant for one Ranger to be compelled to police a tough place like this . . . The sheriff has not asked for Rangers and I don't think he will." General Hulen replied that he "would order as many Rangers to Batson as you like. I certainly do not want you to jeopardize your life." Over time, however, Captain Brooks and Sergeant Bates, who spent much of 1904 in the oil town, managed without reinforcements.[20]

Ethel Stivers, an oil field worker's wife, echoed the story in her memoirs: "The Rangers would come in to Batson and they'd clean it up and it would be decent for awhile. Then the gamblers would come back and start up again. The Rangers would return, the judge would fine everybody $10 and they'd pay it and go back to what they'd been doing. The old judge made his money off the [prostitutes], too. Didn't have a jail most of the time. Just chain them up to a tree, men and women, six, seven, eight at a time."[21]

Brooks essentially commuted between Laredo and Batson Prairie, an arduous trek, for most of 1904. He left the oil field on January 28 only to return again on February 7. He stayed eight days, returned February 20 for two weeks, six more days later in March, then a week in April and so on, leaving Sergeant Bates there during that time.[22]

On his first night there in February, Brooks reported a shooting that left one man dead. "The next night one of the same crowd put on two six-shooters and went out to the west side and run some of the women out, fired off his pistol, and caused some little stir. We got him and chained him up."[23]

Bud Coyle came to Beaumont in 1901 seeking his fortune, and moved on to Saratoga and then to Batson Prairie early in 1904. "You couldn't hardly go up there to Batson without a gang robbing you," Coyle wrote years later. "And so the Rangers came in and said, 'We're going in and running them s.o.b.s out of town.' All the gamblers took off with their women and the pimps and others and took off into the woods. But a fellow named Lang stayed, him and his bartender, and they would walk up and down in front of their saloon.

"And a boy walked up and shot one of them right in the stomach. And before the Rangers could get there a mob was gonna hang the boy for the killing. Someone told [oil entrepreneur] Jim Sharp that they were going to hang the boy, who worked for him. Sharp had two 30-30 rifles and a six-shooter, and I had a shotgun," Coyle remembered. "We went to a fence where the mob was coming to hang the boy. They never got over that fence." The arrival of Brooks and Bates calmed the situation and the mob dispersed.

"And there was another fellow in a saloon with two girls and he wouldn't leave," Coyle continues. "He had a shotgun and every time somebody'd stick their nose inside he'd take a pot shot at them. Captain Brooks just walked right in that door and closed the place down. Someone asked the fellow why he didn't shoot Brooks, and he says, 'Why, I knew he was a Ranger just the way he walked in that door, and I wasn't about to shoot him.'

"This other fellow came down from Liberty and he told me he wanted to see 'the jungle,'" writes Coyle in his memoirs. "That's what they called the mean hang-out over in the thicket. It was the worst place in the whole world. I said we'd wait until Sergeant Bates got there and maybe we'd go down if he was going. And the man didn't know who Bates was and I told him he was a Texas Ranger. And he asked me if I was yeller to go down to the jungle without the law.

"I said, 'Dadgum right I am! Why, a man's a fool to go down to the jungle without the law, without a Ranger. Why, I wouldn't go down there with a deputy or a constable, just a Ranger. You're liable never to come back.'"[24]

In his monthly report Captain Brooks indicates that he made seven arrests that first week in February, and a dozen more during his next visit; those numbers continue right on through to November. Perhaps none of the arrests was more interesting than the one Sterling relates: "When the Batson businessmen saw the large number of prisoners the Rangers were forced to chain up, they got together and built a small jail. It was made out of two by fours, wide side down." This was where the women were usually detained, while the men stayed chained to trees or posts.

But the first occupant, says Sterling, was a Scotsman, a boxer of note and, when drunk, a brawler of some notoriety. "The Rangers had to lock him up during one of these battling sprees, although they liked him personally. The next inmate of the new jail happened to be one of those unspeakable creatures who live on the earnings of unfortunate women," a pimp. "He had unmercifully beaten one of his harem because she was not making enough money to keep him in the style he desired.

"The Rangers knew very little about this type of vulture," writes Sterling, "and they believed that the punishment should fit the crime. They decided to handle this case in their own way, instead of taking him before a judge where he would get off with a light fine. The Scotch [*sic*] pugilist was just sobering up and had a magnificent hangover when the procurer was thrown in with him. Sergeant Bates made a fair proposition to the Scot. If 'MacDuff' would work over prisoner number two in a manner befitting his means of livelihood, the Rangers would release him from custody.

"The Scots are a very thoroughgoing race," Sterling concluded.[25]

Distasteful crooks were to be found roaming all over Texas, not just in the oil towns. The Alice *Echo* ran its June 21, 1904, front-page story on the cooperative effort of Captains Brooks and Hughes, along with four other Rangers, in rounding up three particularly offensive characters –"a mescal smuggler, a mescal vendor, and a horse smuggler" –who had been shopping their illegal wares for some time in the Alice area. They confiscated and destroyed nearly 2,800 bottles of mescal and tequila in the raid.[26] Just the fact that two Ranger captains were involved underscores the serious nature of the arrests, as well as the subsequent relief in the community.

During one of his frequent visits to Hardin County, Captain Brooks made the acquaintance of a young enterprising feed store owner named Ross Sterling. Sterling came to the oil field towns from his home in Chambers County and before his thirtieth birthday opened feed and merchandise stores in Sour Lake, Saratoga, and Batson. His successful ventures and business acumen earned him wide respect in those communities, and his support for law and order, and the Ranger Force, ingratiated him to Brooks. Sterling turned his attention to politics in the years that followed and became governor of Texas in 1931. He and Brooks enjoyed a long friendship that began in Batson.[27]

On another stay in the rowdy oil town, Brooks intervened in a bar room brawl described in detail some years later by a local named Ed Cotton who was only twenty years old at the time. "One time a big fight started because someone hit a porter is all. There was a pool table and the dance hall and the saloon all together, and the fight started in the back when someone knocked the porter down while he was carrying a tray of about eight bottles of beer. The men and the women were fighting, and the floor manager couldn't handle it. They were throwing billiard balls and breaking pool cues over each other's head, and they were scattering all over the place.

"Two women were fighting under the pool table and they pulled it down on top of them. They were pulling wood off the walls–the place hadn't even been finished yet–and hitting each other with the boards. The bartender pulled out a shotgun and shot at a fellow and blew an eighteen-inch hole in the wall. The Rangers got there, and it stopped."[28]

On October 2 a thunderstorm roiled over Batson Prairie and lightning struck a series of poorly protected oil tanks. The resulting fire destroyed most of the oil field derricks and equipment, killed a number of field workers, and burned up an estimated three million barrels of oil. The fire spread rapidly across the oil-soaked prairie and right down the main street of the town. The flames from the conflagration could be seen for miles in every direction.

By the first of November the town was rebuilding and new wooden derricks again dotted the prairie. The brigands who had fled after the fire returned, as did the violence, and once more, the Rangers. Brooks and Bates arrived November 5 and stayed seven days, making several arrests, running a handful of crooks out of Hardin County for good, and handing over the law enforcement duties one last time to the honest constabulary. As the Rangers departed Batson on November 11 for the last time, Ed Stivers summarized their impact: "I'll tell you, when they would come in, they would clean up the place, and it would look pretty decent for a while."[29]

11

KEEPING THE PEACE IN THE VALLEY

My private business being such that I could not do justice both to myself and the state, I tendered my resignation.

IT MUST HAVE BEEN AN INTERESTING ASSIGNMENT FOR CAPTAIN Brooks in the middle of the summer of 1904, ordered to Minera to halt a violent railroad strike. Twenty-two years earlier as a too-often drunken laborer, the Kentucky wanderer had spent the miserable part of a year working in those same coal mines, loading rail cars and helping with the transport to Cotulla and San Antonio. Perhaps the bourbon-induced fog of those early days prevented the Ranger captain from remembering any of those moments now; perhaps a sense of pride welled up within him for the successful career he had managed since. Either way it made for interesting serendipity that Brooks would purchase "retirement property" the same month that he would return to the scene of the sordid days that propelled him into the Texas Rangers.

In between his many treks to Batson Prairie that summer, then, Brooks was in Minera June 28 and 29, and the violence quickly came to an end. Minera boasted a population of just over one thousand mostly Mexican immigrants, almost of all of whom worked in the mines. A deadly outbreak of yellow fever four years earlier had trimmed the labor force dramatically for a time, but soon more desperate men came across the Rio Grande looking for a paying job, no matter how dangerous or debilitating. Organized briefly by labor leaders, the subsequent strike produced violence and little improvement of their conditions. "The men returned to their work," Brooks reported. "The agitators were discharged and ordered to leave the mines."[1]

Minera's future was to be short-lived. In 1912 the mine shafts flooded, and three years later the town was abandoned and the small village of Santo Tomas sprung to life nearby. The railroads, the coal companies, and the laborers went elsewhere, and the ghost town that was Minera vanished but for leftover heaps of clay and slag.[2]

It is only speculation that Captain Brooks may have factored in his visit to Minera in his considerations of retirement. Over two decades had now passed since his joining the Frontier Battalion in Cotulla in 1883; this next year he would turn fifty years of age. He hardly knew his immediate family living in Alice, and there are some indications from his recorded leaves of absence in 1904, and fifteen more days in 1905, that his closest partner, Kentucky bourbon, continued to haunt him. He owned land now and would be purchasing more, and the thought of ranching a small spread may have seemed more and more appealing, especially after the exhausting scouts and the trips to and from Batson in East Texas.

One of his absences had nothing to do with "liquoring up," and only marginally related to his duties as a Ranger commander. In Alice, Brooks had joined the Woodmen of the World, a fraternal organization and insurance company. Begun in 1890 by Nebraskan Joseph Cullen Root, the Woodmen spread quickly through communities in Texas, even electing Texan Morris Sheppard as its national treasurer. (Sheppard would serve Texas in the U.S. House of Representatives and as a powerful political voice for four decades.[3])

In August 1904, the St. Louis Exposition and World's Fair opened with great expectations and international fanfare, and attracted thousands of Texans to its gates over the next five months, including Captain Brooks. It is unclear exactly what prompted Brooks to head for St. Louis in early September, but one guess might be the calendar of events: the Woodmen fraternity held parades and a national conference there from Sept. 5–14; Texas Day was celebrated at the fair on Monday, September 12; and a large cattle auction took place that same week.[4]

Whatever prompted the trip–it does not appear initially to have been for any official reason–Brooks arrived at Ft. Sill in Indian Territory on his way to Missouri, whereupon his journey became more official than he may have planned. A very important resident of the Ft. Sill Indian reservation was preparing to visit the St. Louis Exposition as a special guest. The Apache Chief Geronimo had lived at Ft. Sill under "house arrest" for more than a decade and had been asked to attend the fair as something of a frontier celebrity.

Geronimo himself was less than enthusiastic: "When I was first asked to attend the St. Louis World's Fair I didn't wish to go," he wrote in his 1906 autobiography. "Later, when I was told I would receive good attention and protection, and that the President of the United States [Theodore Roosevelt] said that I would be all right, I consented." One of his escorts to St. Louis was Ranger Captain Brooks, who extended such kindness on the trip that the Apache leader whittled a child's bow and arrow as a gift to be taken back to Brooks's five-year-old son. A commemorative belt buckle from the fair accompanied the Indian bow that young Morgan kept for the rest of his life.[5]

Brooks returned to Texas in mid-September, stopping off for a few days in Alice to be with his family. For the next eight weeks he scouted in Mitchell, Webb, and La Salle counties. But as he celebrated his forty-ninth birthday at his Laredo camp, Brooks still had a busy two years ahead of him before he would give in to whatever dreams of retirement he may have fancied. One of the first incidents in the new year 1905 was a trip back to the oil fields, but not to Batson this time.

In northeastern Harris County, thirty-five miles west and south of Batson, Houstonian Charles F. Barrett discovered oil on a patch of land in May 1904, at about the same time oil was also being found two miles farther west at a place named Humble. By the end of the year the Moonshine Oil Company and the Higgins Oil Company were drilling in that same area, and on January 9, 1905, the first gusher on "Moonshine Hill" blew in.[6]

The boom was predictable and by March there were thirty-seven producing wells and an estimated 10,000 eager workers seeking their respective fortunes on the Hill. And trouble, as always, accompanied them. On January 25 Captain Brooks went to Moonshine Hill to restore order as he had done myriad times the year before on Batson Prairie. That task accomplished by the end of the month, Brooks returned to Laredo. It appears to have been his last visit to the oil fields.[7]

The next four months seem to have been routine for Brooks and Company A. Except for a brief trip to Falfurrias in April to visit with Ed Lasater and finish the paperwork for the deed to his land there, the captain and his Rangers spent their days scouting Webb, La Salle, Zapata, Duval, and Nueces counties for cattle rustlers. On one notable trip back to camp in February, Brooks arrested three men for disturbing the peace–maybe his own peace–on the train. Brooks notes in his records the particular accomplishments of his sergeant Winfred Bates and privates Henry Ransom and Vernon Randle.[8]

Sergeant Bates related an anecdote a few years later about an incident involving the captain, a notorious cowboy, and a judge apparently new to the territory. It is difficult to tell how apocryphal the tale may be but it underscores the prevailing attitudes on the Texas frontier and the general respect for this Ranger captain. "Captain Brooks came up sudden-like on the cowboy leader of a gang of cattle thieves," Bates said in a newspaper interview. "Of course there wasn't any way out of catching him when, as you might say, he already had him. So Brooks larruped him up and took him over to the judge for trial.

"In those days, the cowboys sort of arbitrated the manners of this country, which Brooks knew a sight better than did the judge on the bench. Yet he sat through the quick arrangements which at that time passed for justice, and calmly allowed the best cow puncher in Texas to undergo the shame of being sentenced to hang. Then, rising out of his chair and hitching up his breeches with a quick motion subconscious to Western riders about to mount, the captain reached in the pocket of his coat, drew out a paper and passed it over to the judge, remarking hurriedly:

"'Here, judge, take this puncher's pardon. I got to go get the rest of his gang.'

"And in three minutes Brooks was a small cloud of dust on the prairie."[9]

As if Southwest Texas was not enough "prairie" to spread the tiny Ranger company in search of the criminal element, General Hulen added a huge section of west-central Texas to Company A's jurisdiction as of June 1, including Kimble, Menard, Tom Green, Kent, Irion, Midland, and Mitchell counties. In the first one and a half years of his tenure as adjutant general, Hulen moved the four Ranger companies around Texas for a hopefully refreshing change of scenery as well as to prevent personal conflicts with citizens and authorities from boiling over.[10]

In his biennial report for 1905–1906, General Hulen reiterated the growing demands placed on the Rangers and the need not only of retaining the unique law enforcement agency but also for expanding it into a larger force. "Hardly a day passes without receiving in this department a request for the detail of one or more men on some very important duty that cannot be complied with, owing to the very small force we now have . . . There are a great many more requests for rangers than has ever been before, and there is every indication of this condition continuing for some time to come."

Pulling no punches, Hulen reported, "The law under which this force is maintained is antiquated, and should be materially revised, and the force should be very considerably increased. There is enough work, that by all means should be done, to employ from 75 to 100 officers and men continually. The law should provide for this force to be organized into companies of at least 40 men each . . . 1 captain, 2 lieutenants, 6 sergeants and 6 corporals for each organization, and the men should be enlisted for a period of five years, and required to remain in the service for the entire term of their enlistment.

"In such a service it takes at least two years for a man to become efficient in his duties, and the State should be able to receive the benefits of his training after having schooled him for that period. The officers and men should be better paid, more especially the men, and the State should mount and equip them. The officers should be permanently in their places during good behavior and promoted by seniority," Hulen concluded, "and a system of enforcing discipline should be prescribed."[11]

The Rangers of Company A during this period were a fluid group of young men being recruited, some for only six month stints, and discharged on a routine basis. When Lott Tumlinson was discharged on the last day of 1904, Brooks went seven months without a sergeant until he promoted twenty-three-year-old Edgar Timberlake of Floresville; Timberlake's brother Delbert also joined up that year. Twenty-one-year-old Laredo stockman Vernon Randle enlisted as did Homer Henderson, and D. G. Robinson, a carpenter from Kent County.

Henry Lee Ransom enlisted in March 1905, leaving his deputy sheriff position in Mitchell County. Ransom later served as a Ranger captain, and was killed in 1918. J. D. Harkey had been enlisted into Company C by Captain Rogers, and transferred into Company A in June designated as a Special Ranger. For all the comings and goings, Company A rarely counted more than six men at any one time serving under Brooks.[12]

J. A. Brooks, still based in Laredo, concentrated his efforts now to the north and west of his headquarters. Captain McDonald moved Company B to Brownsville, while Captain John Rogers worked out of Fort Hancock and John Hughes's Company D took on east and central Texas. On June 22, 1905, Brooks traveled to the northern end of his new territory and visited for eight days with the ranchers and businessmen in and around Colorado City. Brooks and his men would find themselves addressing crime in Abilene, Odessa, San Angelo, and Midland over the next two years.[13]

In Tom Green County, the Busk breed of Hereford cattle was introduced in 1904, and with the new and hardy bovines came rustlers eager to get their hands on them. Numerous visits to the San Angelo area for Captain Brooks meant consultation with the local authorities, notably Sheriff J. S. McConnell and Judge Milton Mays. The most prominent cattleman at that time was Claude A. Broome of the Loma Vista Ranch near Coleman, the site of much of the rustling that went on in the early 1900s. Broome served years later on the board of directors of the Texas Cattleman's Association.[14]

Disasters also struck Tom Green County during this period and the Rangers responded. On March 19, 1904, a fire ravaged through the city blocks of San Angelo, and two years later a freak late summer flood inundated most of the city and the surrounding region.[15]

But far South Texas needed law enforcement still, and on June 9, 1905, Brooks found himself in Brownsville handling a potentially deadly situation. William Thomas Eldridge, a businessman from Eagle Lake who had helped organize the Cane Belt Railroad for the burgeoning sugar refining industry in southeast Texas, was marketing his wares in the Valley when trouble boiled over between him and two other merchants. Someone had shot at Eldridge in a botched assassination attempt and Brooks went to investigate.

In Brownsville, the captain first met with Eldridge, who had at one time served as a city marshal, and after interviewing several people confronted a man named Will Merriwether who had been implicated in the plot. There seemed to be open conflict between these two men, and Brooks reported that he "got them together to resolve their differences." Believing he had calmed the matter satisfactorily, Brooks returned to Laredo. Shortly thereafter, however, Merriwether and another man were gunned down, and Eldridge was arrested and charged with murder. He was eventually acquitted, circumstantial evidence once again haunting the peace officers, moved his business to Sugar Land, Texas, and became manager of the Imperial Sugar Company plant there.[16]

In July and August Captain Brooks traveled along the Texas Pacific Railway lines that stretched out across West Texas, making stops in Odessa and Midland and Big Spring. Big Spring was a growing town of over 2,000 citizens in 1905 and the presence of the Rangers was always a welcome sight. Brooks was there on July 1 conferring with J. W. Ward of the railway company, bargaining towards a contract that would discount the tickets for his Ranger company as they moved around the state. The captain, like most of the other Rangers, carried up to eight railway passes with him wherever he traveled, as each railway company required a separate identification card. In addition, Brooks carried a Western Union card to credit the telegrams he wired while on a scout.[17]

Nine days later the captain was in Colorado City, where he took time from his visits with the local business leaders and ranchers to respond to the adjutant general's wire regarding renewal of his oath of office to the Ranger Force. The Texas legislature had required an oath to be taken every two years by the officers, and Brooks dutifully signed the papers in 1901, 1903, and now in the summer of 1905. In returning the paperwork to Austin, Brooks included a letter thanking General Hulen for his reappointment as commanding officer of Company A. He also reported to his boss that privates Ransom and Randle had just been sent on to San Angelo to speak with Lee Wilson, inspector for the cattle raisers association, about the presence of a gang of rustlers in that area.[18]

Into the fall of 1905 Captain Brooks and his men continued to scout the wide country of Southwest Texas, the commander duly reporting myriad visits to Ector, Martin, Tom Green, Irion, and Kent counties with protracted stops in San Angelo and Midland. A train robbery in early November brought Brooks to Midland again where the stolen property was recovered and returned to the Texas Pacific agents. No arrests were made but Brooks assigned Private Robinson to ride the rails for a time "to protect the conductors" as well as discourage further robbery attempts.[19]

On November 20, J. A. Brooks turned fifty years of age and celebrated his twenty-second year as a Texas Ranger. Consideration of retirement now loomed large on his personal horizon, and he may have at least decided in his own mind that 1906 might very well be his

Capt. Brooks and seven-year-old John Morgan Brooks with Rangers of Company A, August, 1906, Colorado City, Texas. Seated: Special Ranger J. D. Harkey; standing: Ivan Murchison, N. P. Thomas, J. D. Dunaway.

Courtesy Brooks family.

last year in law enforcement. Brooks notes several weeks being on leaves of absence, probably to make trips to Alice and Falfurrias arranging for moving his family to their new home in upper Starr County. A small ranch house was built on the eighty acres at the outskirts of Falfurrias; many in that part of the country were constructed up off the ground to keep "critters" out of the house. The Brooks family vividly recalled chasing possums under the porch by day and hearing the eerie whirring alarum of the rattlesnakes beneath the floorboards at night.[20]

But through most of 1906 Laredo was still his home away from home, and from that Ranger camp the captain continued to send scouts in all directions. Company A traced and retraced the railway lines to Midland and Odessa, scouted the upper Rio Grande for cattle and horse thieves, and assisted county sheriffs in tracking down and returning fugitives. Brooks reported several visits to Colorado City and San Angelo, and scouts west to Ector County and as far north as Kent County. From July into November, in fact, Captain Brooks lived in camp at Colorado City more than in Laredo and made more visits to Falfurrias than to Alice.[21]

As 1906 unfolded, Company A was comprised of six Rangers: Brooks, his sergeant Edgar Timberlake, privates Ivan Murchison, E. B. C. McCullum, N. P. Thomas, and W. M. Wolf, and J. D. Harkey "serving without pay from the State." Murchison was from Odessa, Thomas had been a deputy sheriff in Weatherford, and Wolf was a twenty-five-year-old stockman from Scurry County when he enlisted in January. In February all of the privates received, from the State, brand-new "self-loading rifles," as Brooks described them.

Thirty-two-year-old J. D. Dunaway enlisted from Austin in April and was promoted to sergeant in May following Timberlake's discharge. The company shrank dramatically for two months that summer when only Dunaway, Murchison, Thomas, and Special Ranger Harkey were in camp.[22]

J. A. Brooks was dealing with cattle rustling in Mitchell County in August or he might very well have joined Captain McDonald in Brownsville to deal with the dramatic events unfolding there, events that would ripple angrily across Texas to the halls of the United States Congress and the White House.

Late in July, the African-American troops of the U.S. Army's Twenty-fifth Infantry were ordered to leave their base in Nebraska and move to Fort Brown. Their chaplain and only black officer, Theophilus G. Stewart, reported with clairvoyant foreboding: "Texas, I fear, means a quasi battleground for the 25th."24 The confrontation about to take place in Brownsville would be more than "quasi," and the stony silence that met them as they paraded through the streets only underscored the suspicion and intolerance that would soon erupt into violence.

After several individual scrapes between "Buffalo Soldiers" and Brownsville citizens brought the tension to a peak, gunfire erupted along an alleyway next to the Fort Brown barracks around midnight on August 13. Over the next half hour a Brownsville citizen was shot and killed, others wounded and several homes over a two-block area shot at and damaged. As the rioters vanished into the night, accusations and racial epithets filled the air, and an investigation soon commenced.

With only circumstantial evidence and more than enough bias, the citizenry and authorities of the town raised enough fuss to alert Governor Lanham and General Hulen. While Austin cautiously deliberated its jurisdictional responsibility, the flamboyant and assertive Ranger Capt. Bill McDonald took matters into his own hands, leaving his post at the Democratic state convention in Dallas and making his way to Brownsville. Aided by two of his company and Judge Stanley Welch, McDonald arrived in Brownsville on August 21 and managed almost single-handedly to make the volatile situation even worse: Determined to take the suspected soldiers into custody, McDonald caused such a fury on both sides that further violence seemed imminent.

The situation eased when McDonald agreed to hand over his "warrants" to Judge Welch, who in turn allowed the army to reassign the Twenty-fifth without delay. On August 25 the Buffalo Soldiers left Brownsville at dawn without fanfare and settled at Fort Reno, Oklahoma Territory. The men of Companies B, C, and D were subsequently dishonorably discharged by President Theodore Roosevelt, and the distasteful affair roiled on in Washington, D. C., until 1910.[23]

In the summer of 1906 Brooks spent a great deal of his time in Mitchell County, and in October he reported a scout north to Kent County where he kept the peace during trials in the Clairemont District Court. On June 18 the Odessa newspaper reported an incident in its streets that involved most of Company A. Sgt. J. D. Dunaway was confronted by Deputy Sheriff Gee McMeans and the squabble over an unidentified issue soon became a wrestling match, whereupon Dunaway "hammered McMeans over the head with his six shooter." Pvt. N. P. Thomas intervened and grappled with his sergeant while the deputy rode away.

Privates Wolf and McCullum returned the next day to investigate the incident but were encouraged to leave town rather than instigate any more trouble. Dunaway reportedly told Thomas he would discharge him from the Rangers for interfering in the confrontation; instead, Captain Brooks arrived on the twenty-fifth, calmed the situation down, and suggested the sergeant take a leave of absence, which he did. Thomas remained a Ranger, but Company A moved its camp out of Ector County in July at the request of the Odessa town leaders; Wolf and McCullum completed their six-month tour of duty that same month and were discharged.[24]

In October, Brooks enlisted three new recruits: Alfred Randolph Baker, twenty-two, of Uvalde; Thomas White, twenty-five and a lanky 6'3", from Colorado City; and Parker Weston, a twenty-six-year-old ranch hand from Ft. Bend County. This brought Company A to its full contingent of one sergeant and five privates, plus J. D. Harkey.[25]

As the fall elections loomed on the horizon, and the Red and Blue Clubs organized voter rallies that promised conflict in dozens of Texas counties, the Rangers prepared to fan out across the state to keep the peace during the first week of November. Those fears became reality on the night before Election Day when Judge Stanley Welch, a friend of Captain Brooks and a man he had come to respect, was assassinated as he slept in a Rio Grande City hotel room. It would take a year of investigating before his killer was brought to justice, and would have its own profound impact on Captain Brooks's career.[26]

Captain Brooks had asked for, and received, leave at the end of October to be in Falfurrias. During his absence Sergeant Dunaway sent out the men on scouts, and reports to the adjutant general's office were submitted by Dunaway–one in which he noted that he "didn't know the whereabouts of Capt. Brooks"–as well as telegrams from Thomas, Weston, and White.[27] In his own records filed in Austin, Brooks reported the following activities over the next two weeks to the adjutant general's office:

"November 3, 1906. Having arrived at Falfurrias by permission of Gen. Hulen for few days leave of absence, was called upon by citizens to keep the peace until election was over, there being a good deal of bad feeling by reason of several special Mexican deputies having been appointed. Pvt. Murchison and myself kept the peace.

"The 7th by order of Governor Lanham myself and Pvt. Murchison left Falfurrias to join Capt. McDonald at Rio Grande City, Judge Welch having been assassinated at Rio Grande City the night before the election. We joined Capt. McDonald the 9th.

"The 12th by permission of Gen. Hulen I left Rio Grande City for Falfurrias where I arrived the 14th.

"The 15th my private business being such that I could not do justice both to myself and the state I tendered my resignation."[28]

12

TEXAS LEGISLATOR AND COUNTY JUDGE

When you come to your senses, I'll send you your gun.

"Nov. 14, 1906
"General Hulen, Austin:

"I desire to tender my resignation as captain of Company A of the Texas Rangers, said resignation to take effect on Nov. 15, 1906, which action on my part is due to pressing private business which demands my personal attention and which renders my further service in such position detrimental to my best interests. Trusting this will meet with your kind attention and acceptance, I beg to remain, Yours very truly, J. A. Brooks"[1]

The abrupt nature of this letter belies the long months of meditation on Brooks's decision, and the mysterious and vague pronouncement that his "best interests" would be jeopardized is curious if nothing more. He could have been making reference to a family issue, his own personal health, or a politically motivated objective: his move to Falfurrias had an impact on all of these.

The most likely scenario was the last of these, with the others as complements to his decision. Brooks's age was largely irrelevant and his wanting to be with his family more unlikely and at best hypocritical. His drinking problems were no less severe than ever and he still managed to keep them under some control in relation to his professional business.

The most pressing agenda in his life at this time was a political one: working as an associate for Ed Lasater in the high profile Republican's attempt to establish his own political fiefdom in South Texas. Believing in what Lasater stood for as a newcomer to a territory ruled by the old bosses like Manuel Guerra, Brooks looked forward to a new kind of battle for a new cause, a political one. In retirement the Ranger captain could concentrate on aiding Lasater in carving out, literally as well as politically, his own niche in this part of Texas. When the day of decision arrived, Brooks seemed certain of it.

On November 20, 1906, James Abijah Brooks celebrated his fifty-first birthday, the first such celebration "out of uniform" in twenty-three years. In his hand was a letter from the adjutant general containing these kind words: "The Governor, as well as myself, deeply regrets that it becomes necessary for you to leave the service. You have been a Ranger since 1883, during which time you have served from private to captain; having served as Captain since May, 1889.

"You have made an enviable record, and the loss of your experience to the State cannot be estimated. You have always most faithfully and excellently performed your duties, and you can and doubtless will, look back upon your long service as an officer of the State with pride and satisfaction."[2]

Brooks would be the first of the "Four Captains" to retire, but he was quickly followed by Bill McDonald the next year as well as General Hulen himself. McDonald became a state revenue agent and in 1913 a United States marshal; Hulen worked as a passenger agent first for the San Francisco Railway Company in Houston and then for the Trinity and Brazos Valley Railway Company where he later served as its president.[3]

James Brooks, thinking perhaps that he would simply retire to the small ranch outside of Falfurrias, instead became a celebrity and unofficial peace officer in northern Starr County. The "office" was more honorary–and politically charged–than real, and as Brooks said to Ranger Captain W. W. Sterling years later: "Whenever you make a constable or policeman out of a Ranger, you destroy his usefulness."[4]

And although the following anecdote from Captain Sterling's autobiography may have been slightly misplaced on the timeline, it certainly exemplifies the character of J. A. Brooks at most any time during his law enforcement career. "At a hotly contested school election before the organization of Brooks County was completed," Sterling writes, "the citizens of Falfurrias named Captain Brooks 'officer of the day.'

"A former Ranger who lived in Alice came down to watch the excitement. He did too much drinking, and was always dangerous in that condition. The ex-Ranger, who was afterward killed by another ex-Ranger, was rated one of the fastest men in the country with a pistol. Captain Brooks went to him and said, 'Jim, you used to be in the Service, and I have always liked you, but you are heading for trouble. You can't vote in this county, and I wish you would get on the train that is leaving in a few minutes and go home.'

"The man was just drunk enough to be reckless. He had told many men to get out of town, but he didn't like to be on the receiving end himself. He asked, 'Cap, what are you going to do if I don't leave?'

"'I'll have to take your gun away,' was the reply.

"The visitor exclaimed, 'No man in the world can take my gun.'

"Captain Brooks' eyes blazed, and with one lightning movement, he disarmed the recalcitrant ex-Ranger. 'Now get on that train. When you come to your senses, I'll send you your gun.' Liquor had made the younger man forget with whom he was dealing," Sterling concluded.[5]

Ordinarily the retired Ranger captain would have been of some counsel to the sheriff, but for two reasons that turned out to be unlikely. First, the sheriff Brooks may have expected to be working with was his old friend Warren W. "Wash" Shely, a former Ranger whose brothers, also Rangers and peace officers, were known across Texas. But after twenty-two years in Starr County, Wash Shely officially retired the same month as Brooks, having left his post earlier for treatment of a nervous disorder that made his work impossible to continue. His successor was Deodoro Guerra, elected November 6, 1906, someone Brooks did not know personally but was already embroiled with politically.

The second reason why the captain may not have been actively involved with Guerra was the sheer distance for him to travel from Falfurrias to the sheriff's office in Rio Grande City, the Starr County seat. "If a citizen wanted to reach Rio Grande City [from Falfurrias] by rail, he would have to take a most circuitous route. First, via the San Antonio and Aransas Pass Railway northward to Alice. Thence eastward via the Tex-Mex to Robstown. Thence southward via the St. Louis, Brownsville and Mexico Railroad to Brownsville. There he would cross over to Mexico and take the Mexican National Lines to Camargo. Then he could recross into the United States and Starr County at Rio Grande City.

"The alternate and most used routes were by rail to Sam Fordyce." Sam Fordyce was the rail town at the end of the St. Louis, Brownsville and Mexico rail ten miles west of Mission, incorporated in 1904 and named for a railway financier. "From there to the county seat, twenty-three miles by hack, or a ninety mile journey overland." Wagons made the trip with six mules, four to pull at one time and two kept as the others wearied; the trip often took a full week. Added Brooks in a memoir written years later: "There was nothing between Falfurrias and Rio Grande City but sand dunes, cactus and heavy brush." A trip to the sheriff's office would have been an ordeal.[6]

And it was that arduous route, in part, that took J. A. Brooks to another road of his life, a new career in law enforcement far more complex and challenging than being an honorary deputy sheriff. On the way, however, Brooks first would deal with the harsh, and in this case deadly, politics of boss rule in South Texas.

The political war pitting Starr County boss Manuel Guerra and newcomer Ed Lasater swept ex-Ranger J. A. Brooks to the front lines of the battle even before he formally announced his retirement from the Force. At the time of Lasater's arrival in South Texas in 1904, Guerra had ruled his political fiefdom for a decade. Born in Mier, Mexico, of old Spanish ancestry, Guerra made his home and headquarters in Roma in the 1880s, ran a mercantile business as well as the family ranching enterprise, and operated the local Democratic Party on behalf of power broker James B. Wells.[7]

An uneasy truce existed during the late 1890s between warring political factions when Guerra, Sheriff Wash Shely, and County Judge John R. Monroe agreed to coexist in the Starr County region. That truce broke apart by 1904 with the combination of Shely's illness and Ed Lasater's arrival on the scene. Lasater, a redoubtable Republican certainly in a foreign land, carved out his own territory in the distant northern area of the expansive county while Guerra fumed in the Valley. Lasater turned a bankrupt ranching business into a powerful enterprise with remarkable acumen, gobbling up over 300,000 acres from destitute Hispanic ranchers and reigning over the immense territory from his vantage point in Falfurrias.[8]

By the 1904 elections in November, the contest was engaged and the political temperature was approaching the boiling point. When Lasater arrived in Rio Grande City on Election Day eve, he reproached Guerra that the numerous armed "deputies" patrolling the streets would only cause trouble, whereupon the Starr County boss countered that the only trouble would be that started by Lasater's people. The Falfurrias rancher made this proposition in front of a gathering crowd of witnesses: "Tomorrow on election day, suppose we de-deputize every deputy sheriff in Starr County, and as the polls open at seven in the morning you will sit in your chair on one side of the entrance of the voting place and I will sit in my chair on the other side.

"We will each hold a cocked .45-automatic pistol pointed at the other. Should any of my men get out of line in any way whatsoever, you will shoot me; if any of your men get out of line in any way whatsoever, I will shoot you." Guerra couldn't help but accept the challenge: the two men sat across from one another for twelve hours the next day, and no shots were heard in Rio Grande City.[9]

As the 1906 elections heated things up all over again, and the truce now a distant memory, James Brooks, merely by purchasing a tract of land from Ed Lasater, stepped right into the middle of the brewing confrontation. Manuel Guerra put up his cousin Deodoro Guerra in the campaign to replace the ailing Sheriff Shely, and Lasater countered with Deputy Sheriff Gregorio Duffy, a Democrat but on the outs with the Guerra faction. Two other members of the Guerra clan were up for key county offices as well, making the sheriff's election especially crucial.[10] When Brooks mentioned "pressing personal business" in his letter of resignation, this may very well have been what was on his mind.

Ed Lasater's son Tom remembered the November election eve melodramatics: "When the entourage left Falfurrias for the two-day trip to the [Rio Grande] river, it had more the appearance of a war party going to the battlefront than a group of citizens preparing to travel to the county seat to vote in one of the world's largest democracies.

"The convoy included a number of carriages and a large group of men on horseback." According to Captain Brooks's report ten days later, he remained behind in Falfurrias as likely the only law enforcement agent for miles. "All of the men were heavily armed," Lasater continues, "and L. D. Miller was in charge of a buckboard loaded with Winchester rifles which was camouflaged as a load of grain.

"Rob Miller, wearing a Stetson hat, resembled Ed Lasater. Someone in the group suggested that Rob be seated in a prominent position in the lead carriage so that if the group were ambushed and an attempt were made on Lasater's life en route to Rio Grande City, they would shoot Rob and the loss would not be as great. Everybody in the group except Rob Miller found this suggestion very humorous."[11]

Whatever humor still engaged the Falfurrias party came to an abrupt end as they approached the county seat. District Judge Stanley Welch, an ardent Democrat and associate of the Wells-Guerra organization, had arrived in the Starr County seat to oversee the election and do what he could to ensure the partisan results. Forty-one special deputies joined the nine already in town to form a daunting patrol designed more to herd the "right" voters to the polls than keep the peace. When the estimated fifty Lasater men rode into town, the chances of a major confrontation seemed imminent.

That night the streets and saloons were filled with the raucous sounds of voters being liberally encouraged by one side or the other. One of many scuffles resulted in one of Lasater's men being badly beaten up and left for dead. As the beer and whiskey spilled over the revelers, no one heard the shot that echoed inside Judge Welch's hotel room. At dawn on Election Day Tuesday, a deputy concerned that the judge had not appeared to watch over the opening of the polls found Welch dead in his bed, shot at close range.[12]

The shock of the district judge's murder rippled through the crowds all day; few noticed that Deodoro Guerra won the sheriff's race by sixty-three votes over Duffy.[13] Brooks and McDonald arrived the next day to lead the investigation, a case that would careen through the courts for two years. A Republican and Rio Grande City bartender, Alberto Cabrera, was eventually charged and convicted of the crime, only to escape from prison into Mexico in 1912. Gregorio Duffy, appointed as Roma's customs inspector by Republican sympathizers, was killed in 1907 by Sheriff Guerra and two of his deputies after an alleged confrontation on the Rio Grande City streets.[14]

By the summer of 1908, the "retired" Ranger Captain Brooks continued to participate in the power struggle for northern Starr County, taking some limited time to work his small ranch and be with his family. Out of the many hours of conversation with Ed Lasater and other political cohorts, Brooks realized that one option in this political war was to separate the Falfurrias area from the county power base in the south: carving out a new county now became the first objective.[15]

To accomplish this objective meant active work inside the Texas Legislature in Austin, and that meant getting someone elected to represent District Ninety-five. No politician himself, Captain Brooks nevertheless maintained a high level of respect across the district boundaries for his two decades of law enforcement service. In the fall of 1908 Brooks announced his intention to run for a seat in the state legislature, campaigning primarily across the northern part of the county and into Hidalgo County which claimed part of the legislative district. Ed Lasater got the votes out; Brooks won the race and headed for Austin, aware of the daunting task awaiting him: "The Rio Grande politicians fought my mission with all the vim that was in them."

The Brooks family poses in front of their homestead eight miles south of Falfurrias.

Courtesy Brooks family.

The Thirty-first session of the Texas Legislature convened on January 12, 1909, under second-term Governor Thomas M. Campbell of Palestine and Speaker of the House Austin Milton Kennedy from Waco, the latter of whom was forced to resign on the last day of the regular session as a result of a political spat and alleged scandal. Brooks took his own place as a freshman representative, intent on pushing a bill through to create a new county in South Texas. He was appointed to the Public Building and Grounds Committee, the Commerce and Manufacturing Committee, and, with clearly some political clout behind him and his singular agenda, chair of the Committee on Counties.[16]

H.B. 238, the bill that Representative Brooks presented on the floor of the House on January 25, proposed a county that would encompass and include parts of Starr, Hidalgo, Nueces, and Duval counties, with its northern line at the town of Premont and its county seat in Falfurrias. Read and referred to his own committee, Brooks was forced to write the minority report on February 9 when the committee voted against the proposal, an effort led by Rep. William Perkins of Alice who stood to lose a considerable constituency in the proposed county realignment.[17]

Brooks needed some "professional" help, and it arrived in the person of Ed Lasater, who quickly engaged in a public debate with outspoken Democrat and Starr County landowner W. W. "Bill" Jones. A newspaper article described the debate as "waxing exceedingly warm. Mr. Jones and his friends charged that those who would create the county of Falfurrias were seeking to establish an outright Republican county. Mr. Lasater sought to show that it would be to the best interests of a great territory to organize the county, and said that he would have to spend less money by letting the whole matter drop."[18]

On February 17 the Committee on Counties' report was read as the last item of a late night session, where it squeaked by in its second reading but was summarily withdrawn by Speaker Kennedy after a strident debate led by legislators who stood to lose parts of their respective counties. On March 2, with the session fast approaching its close, H.B. 238 passed a third reading by a comfortable 71–33 vote, but died on the speaker's table on March 13 as the regular session adjourned.[19]

The 31st Legislature stumbled through two special sessions that spring, and two more in the late summer of 1910, but Brooks's proposal never made the legislative agenda. Nor did he give up, making trip after trip between his ranch and the state capital, familiar territory not unlike his many Ranger years on the railways. His family still largely bereft of his presence and influence, they recalled years later that the captain would "make his way to Austin each time with a starched white shirt and a bottle of Kentucky bourbon."[20]

That statement became all the more ironic when Brooks was asked to appear before Sen. C. M. Cureton's special investigating committee during the called session of the Thirty-second Legislature. Prohibition was the hot-button issue of the day in Texas, and the war between the "wets" and the "drys" had reached its zenith in 1911 when accusations flew through the Austin air that legislators were being bribed by anti-prohibition lobbyists.

Representative Brooks testified before Cureton's committee on August 10 but had no information on the alleged bribery schemes. When asked if he had talked over the issue with a lobbyist named J. F. Wolters, who had reportedly been given several thousand dollars to spread around the state legislature, Brooks replied: "I served under Wolters when we were in the Volunteers in Brownsville during the Spanish-American War, and he and I were intimate, and I don't know but what some time during the session he and I met and there might have been something said, but there was nothing in regard to any money and nothing in regard to my vote at all. This matter was very likely talked about. I was an 'anti.'"[21]

Interestingly, just two days prior to the testimony that Brooks gave to the legislative committee, he was officially deputized in Starr County by just elected Sheriff John Closner. Again, it seems, the political atmosphere created in the South Texas region was charged with punches and counter punches by both sides. Brooks accepted the office but spent most of his time preparing for the next round of battle in Austin.

During his two years as a state representative, Brooks had learned valuable lessons about dealing in state politics, a battlefront sometimes as dangerous as tracking armed felons across the wide expanses of Texas. For one, he knew he could not return to Austin for a second term with the same proposal: slicing up counties other than his own would get his bill nowhere, again. Cultivating the necessary votes would take more effort than the first time; compromise in committee work and on the floor would be the rule.

In his memoirs, Brooks wrote, "Many of [my opponents] lied about the situation, but my friends knew the truth and used their influence to win. John Garner our Congressman knew about the situation and also knew that there was justice in my proposition. Now I was a Jim Hogg man, but Senator Joe Bailey did not desert me and did not fail to tell the opposition that old Capt. Brooks was right."

Better prepared this time around and with staunch support from key political voices, Brooks was re-elected in November 1910, and headed for Austin to join the Thirty-second Legislature as it convened on January 10, 1911. A new governor, Oscar B. Colquitt, and a new Speaker, Sam Rayburn, also made their way to the session. Brooks carried with him a petition signed by sixty-five citizens from northern Starr County "vitally interested in the creation of a new county in order to secure relief from the almost intolerable conditions under which we suffer," it read in part. "We, as citizens, tax payers and voters, hereby and now desire to give public expression of our confidence in the integrity and ability of our said representative the honorable J. A. Brooks; and request of him, in the event of the possible failure of his present plan, to use his own discretion and his best efforts, in securing the formation of another new county as will afford relief from present conditions."[22]

On January 19, H. B. 94 was presented, read, and referred to the Committee on Counties, on which Representative Brooks did not serve this time around. The bill barely made it through the committee debate, but on February 7 it was amended to specify several boundary lines. The bill's progress now quickened its pace. Rep. D. B. Chapin of nearby Hidalgo County proposed the new county be named after Civil War hero Sul Ross, and renowned orator and Democrat William Jennings Bryan's name was also considered. H. B. 94 was passed by the House 103–2 and sent to a joint committee with the Texas Senate.

On March 2 the bill passed through the Senate and a five-member conference committee was appointed to clean it up for final passage. On March 7 the unanimously recommended bill came out of committee with a new moniker: Brooks County, in honor of the

Ranger and legislator who had battled for it from the beginning. Both houses voted in favor of its passage, 107–1 in the House and unanimously in the Senate. Speaker Rayburn signed off on the bill on March 9 at 4:45 p.m. and sent it to the governor's office. Governor Colquitt signed the bill into law on March 11, the final day of the regular session.[23]

Representative Brooks returned to Falfurrias to accept the accolades of a grateful citizenry. Four hundred people attended a rally in his honor, where ten effusive speeches were made honoring the legislator's success. Following the spontaneous rally, the captain was carried on the shoulders of the cheering crowd to Garcia Hall for more celebration, and a silver tea service was presented to him and Virginia.[24]

Brooks County was to be organized by September 1, 1911, and elections for county officials were to be held the next day. The legislature appointed Ed C. Lasater, F. S. Rachal, E. R. Rachal, Sr., Ralph McCampbell, A. C. Jones, H. D. Thomas, and Amado de la Garza as the organizing committee. A surveyor, F. C. Rahlmann, was hired, polling places were designated and staffed by election judges, and Falfurrias was officially chosen as the county seat. Of the committee, De La Garza was elected sheriff and the senior Rachal tax assessor, but the real power and authority now belonged to Ed Lasater.[25]

Unsettled political disputes still made for a potentially violent Election Day in the new county. Mrs. E. R. Jenson, a long time Starr County pioneer, wrote the governor requesting Rangers to keep the peace, "that their presence may avoid any trouble between the two partys [*sic*]. The Democratic Party being the white man's party is composed of white men, while the Republican Party headed by Ed. C. Lasater and a bunch of Mexicans for a selfish motive contrary to the interest, and peace, to the new formed County of Brooks." Governor Colquitt ordered three Rangers from Company B to Falfurrias, and Brooks found himself in the unusual position of being protected by the Force.[26]

Capt. J. A. Brooks, who had resigned his House seat after the regular session adjourned so he could concentrate his own efforts in Falfurrias, was elected county judge, a position he would hold for the next twenty-eight years. He was replaced in the House by D. W. Glasscock of McAllen, who served in the special session held that summer and later led, and lost, a political fight against Duval County's boss Archer Parr.[27]

Like his ancestor of six generations before, James Abijah Brooks would now embark on a second career in law enforcement, from the constabulary to the bench.

Rep. Brooks on horseback, 1911.

Courtesy Brooks family.

13

FALFURRIAS, BROOKS COUNTY

For some reason kind Providence has been good to me for which I am truly thankful.

Judge James A. Brooks, who preferred to be called "Captain" for the rest of his life despite three decades on the bench, worked diligently to make the county named after him a viable entity. He presided by virtue of his office over the county commissioner's court and as ex-officio superintendent of the public school system that he helped create. He oversaw the initial laying out of the county roads and the bridges, and in 1912 steered the county citizens through a deadly smallpox epidemic. On a monthly salary of $150 plus $600 annually as school superintendent, Brooks led the groundwork that established the new county.

A courthouse was built in 1914 on the Falfurrias town square and the captain was honored at the festivities for his efforts to bring that project to fruition. The original plans for a courthouse had been shelved when most of voting Precinct Four was carved away into the new Jim Hogg County, and a construction bond issue of $68,000 did not pass until February 1914. Construction began in the spring and was completed on October 29, when two cornerstones were laid under the watchful eye of the county judge; meanwhile, court sat in session in the Donaho building near the square. On November 5 schools in Falfurrias were closed, the citizenry gathered behind the high school band as

County Judge Brooks with Ranger captains William Gillette and W. W. Sterling, ca. 1920.

Courtesy Brooks family.

they paraded around the new edifice, and a brief ceremony took place prior to a community picnic served on the school grounds.[1]

Brooks County was not the only new county of that period, for the huge influx of new residents into that area and the subsequent power struggle among the South Texas bosses–Judge Wells, Don Manuel Guerra, Archie Parr, Ed Lasater, Brooks's Ranger colleague A. Y. Baker, and John Closner–led to a melee of political lobbying activity in Austin to carve out new kingdoms. Willacy County was sliced away from parts of the old Cameron (1848) and Hidalgo (1852) counties the same year as Brooks County organized, and Jim Wells County followed the next year as it bit off a portion of Nueces County surrounding Alice. Archie Parr and his cohorts failed to create what would have been named Dunn County in a 1913 legislative battle, but Jim Hogg and Kleberg counties came into existence that year, the former wrenching 990 square miles away from Brooks County.

Obviously in opposition to the move by powerful Brooks County rancher W. W. "Bill" Jones to split the new county and diminish the power of the Lasater political machine, Judge Brooks wrote to the state legislature that the proposed county "would be absolutely dominated by men who are wholly concerned in holding it as mere ranch properties and in perpetuating intolerable conditions which have existed and now exist in Zapata and Starr Counties." Despite the efforts of Brooks and Lasater, Jim Hogg County peeled away, with Hebbronville as its county seat.

The final division came eight years after the initial flurry of activity when Kenedy County was incorporated in 1921 as Willacy, Cameron, and Hidalgo–together with Starr County known collectively as "the Valley"–were reorganized by the state legislature.[2]

The Prohibition issue rambled through Texas and the country for the next two decades; Brooks County voted itself "dry" in December 1912, long before the 18th Amendment to the U.S. Constitution was ratified in 1919. Brooks preferred to stay publicly neutral on the subject, although there was little doubt among family and close friends that his "marriage" to bourbon whiskey was insoluble; his daughter castigated him for his drinking all of her adult life.

Judge Brooks outlasted six county attorneys, five sheriffs, and three county clerks during his twenty-eight years in the courthouse. In his first bid for reelection, the captain ran a vigorous campaign in the Democratic primary race during the summer of 1913, defeating Dr. Henry M. Bennett by a count of 148–119, and running uncontested in the general election. In fact, for the next two decades Brooks ran essentially unopposed. However, in 1932 L. A. Dickey announced his candidacy and ran a campaign serious enough to prod the incumbent to publish a letter in the *Brooks County Texan.* In it, Brooks sounds pitiable and even desperate: "For the part I played in putting this county on the map, so far, my reward has been only honors and the respect of my fellow men. I am possessed of very little worldly goods, therefore, I need the office in order to be reasonably comfortable in these my last years.

"I appeal to you not for sympathy but for what is justly due me. After my long life of service and devotion to you I cannot believe that you will desert me now," he wrote. Following a paragraph lauding his fellow county commissioners, Brooks concludes that "the Spanish speaking people have no reason for complaint. I have looked after their interests, and fight for their just rights. For over forty years 'Old Captain Brooks' has never failed them, and I have no fear that they will desert me now."

In the July 23 primary Brooks defeated Dickey by a margin of 591–322; he won the general election in November running unopposed.

Six years later, announcing for his fourteenth and what would be his final term, the aging and ill judge faced three opponents in the primary, one of whom, Roy Bennett, Ed Lasater's former bookkeeper, ran a hard and well-funded campaign for seven full months prior to primary day. Brooks polled 482 votes that day, enough to lead J. H. Darby (376), Frank C. Rachal (323) and Bennett (220), but not enough to win outright. In the August 27 runoff the captain defeated Darby 856–736, and won the November general contest polling 1,413 votes to one cast for Darby. He took office on January 1, but his term would be cut short by the infirmities that now plagued him.[3]

The ex-Ranger had put his guns away soon after his first election as Brooks County judge, but Bill McBride of the King Ranch remembered that in the 1920s he "saw Captain Brooks shoot five shots at a knot on an oak tree. He fanned the hammer of an old forty-five so fast that it sounded like an automatic and hit the target four times. It made him mad when the fifth shot was a little wide of the mark." Captain Sterling, who met Brooks in 1911 when he went to work at the Rachal Ranch as a twenty-year-old cowhand, recalled years later what an impact that friendship had on him, and remembered presenting the unarmed judge with a Peacemaker pistol in his later years.[4]

Brooks maintained a distant relationship with Ed Lasater's growing political machine, supported in his several election campaigns by the county boss's faction but never known to be a significant "lieutenant" after the county organized in 1911. In his biography written by grandson Dale, Lasater was said to have directed the judge to fire school teacher Florence Schuetz in 1918 shortly after her father announced his opposition to the Lasater-backed ticket in that fall's elections. Brooks did what he was told, but his name rarely appears again in any significant relation to Lasater's operation.

Ed Lasater amassed a fortune in the cattle and dairy business, his wealth estimated at more $1.5 million in the early 1920s, and the Falfurrias Creamery Company's butter put the South Texas town on the world map. He served as president of the Cattle Raisers Association of Texas in 1911, owned the largest Jersey cattle herd in the world at one time, owned the Falfurrias State Bank out of which he operated his fortune, and ran an unsuccessful gubernatorial campaign on the Bull Moose ticket in 1912. He continued to make astute investments and beat back any political opponents, and was in Oklahoma preparing to step into the burgeoning oil industry when he died suddenly in March 1930.[5]

The day-to-day responsibilities of the Brooks County judge operated in a mundane fashion at best, as both the newspaper and judicial records show, with only occasional bursts of activities worth noting. In 1926, for example, three bootleggers were gunned down by federal officers at their camp southwest of Encino, and 347 bottles of tequila confiscated; the two surviving crooks stayed in the Falfurrias jail until their transfer to San Antonio. A day later a fierce and unusual snow and hail storm battered Brooks County and made the front page headlines. Also in 1926, the gypsum mine opened operations nine miles south of Falfurrias and about one mile from Brooks's ranch.

That same year Brooks helped the city leaders finish the paperwork to build the town's second two-story edifice, an office building located on its lone main street, and a new high school building and a "picture house" went up at the end of the year. In May and October the judge was in Austin lobbying for a trunk of a proposed federal highway to make its way from San Antonio through Falfurrias on its way into the Valley; a designated "first-class" highway eventually ran through the county and later became State Highway 281. And on October 5 of that same relatively busy year Brooks joined 1,500 other local citizens in a celebratory throng as the Southern Pacific Railroad's president W. R. Scott drove a symbolic silver spike into the ground, marking the arrival of the first major national railway into Brooks County and marking too a new era of growth for Falfurrias.[6]

Judge Brooks kept his finger on the pulse of Falfurrias and the county that surrounded it, leading the citizens through the growth spurts of its first two decades, and the Depression days that followed. Brooks County was spared the ugly racial violence that swept through the Valley between 1915 and 1918, in part because of the support of Lasater and county officials for the Hispanic populace and their reciprocal loyalty. The tarnished reputation of the Texas Rangers during that era did not carry over to Falfurrias or the captain himself. In his memoirs Brooks mentions a positive relationship with J. T. Canales, the Brownsville attorney who prosecuted the "Special Rangers" accused of myriad abuses against the Mexican citizenry.

The population nearly doubled in Brooks County's first three decades, and agriculture–primarily cotton and citrus–and livestock proved the mainstays of its local economy. Jersey cattle and the creamery in Falfurrias provided a support base during the hard times along with the "gyp mine," and oil discovered in 1935 swept the area toward recovery by the early 1940s.

Captain Brooks spent the vast majority of his days on the bench dealing with petty crimes, marriage licenses, automobile violations, and such, among his other civic activities presiding as judge, school superintendent, or county commissioner. His name appears in the *Falfurrias Facts* only on rare occasions over the three decades of his service–one day, for example, to note that "Captain Brooks spent Sunday at his ranch," and another that he was promoting the citrus growers of the county against all comers.[7]

In July of 1912 Captain Brooks learned that his mother had died in Kentucky. Mary Jane Kerr Brooks was ninety-three when she was laid to rest in the Lexington Cemetery alongside her husband whom she had outlived by forty-nine years. During the course of the next thirty years Brooks lost all of his sisters except Lillie, and his one brother John in 1924. On January 3, 1928, his wife of thirty-eight years, Virginia Willborn Brooks, passed away from complications of an intestinal obstruction. She was buried following a quiet family funeral in the Alice Cemetery where the captain had purchased lots years earlier.[8]

John Morgan Brooks, the captain's sixteen-year-old son, accompanied his father to the San Francisco World's Fair in the summer of 1915. "The Panama Pacific International Exposition" had been ten years in the making, celebrating the completion of the Panama Canal as well as the four hundredth anniversary of Balboa's discovery of the great ocean. The two Texans were captivated by the wondrous sights as they strolled along what later became known as the Marina area on the bay, from the Great Scintillator light show to the rollicking Aeroscope, the State of Texas pavilion, the fourteen-ton type-writer, and even a chewing gum factory. Perhaps most exciting was viewing the Liberty Bell, on loan from its Philadelphia perch. On the plaza called The Zone, filled with kiosks and minstrels beneath the shadow of the two giant Toyland Soldiers, a sidewalk artist drew a caricature of Judge

"A Lone Ranger," caricature of J. A. Brooks drawn at the San Francisco World's Fair, 1915.

Courtesy of Heritage Museum, Falfurrias, Texas.

Brooks which he entitled "A Lone Ranger." The teenager proudly kept the drawing of his father, its title predating the more famous moniker of two decades later, and donated it years after to the museum in Falfurrias.

John Morgan Brooks attended Texas A & M University, and served in World War I as a motorcycle military policeman in France until after the war ended. He helped his father operate the ranch–"The Place" as it was known–outside of Falfurrias when he returned home, and served as a school traffic officer and then deputy sheriff until 1939. Morgan married Gladys Spark, a local debutante and music teacher, in 1933, and they adopted an infant daughter in 1941 whom they christened Beverly.

Corrinne remained in Falfurrias for the rest of her life. She never married, never forgave her father for his alcoholism nor for the way he treated her all her life, and moved into her brother's home in town in the 1930s. She died in 1980, two years after her sister-in-law and three years before her brother, all three of whom were buried in the Falfurrias Cemetery.[9]

Brooks kept up with the state politics of his day, voted Democrat most of his life, but did not actively participate in his later years. In 1927 the captain received an invitation to attend the inaugural of Texas Governor Dan Moody, and he traveled to Austin to participate in the January 18 festivities. Four years later Brooks and his son attended the inauguration of Governor Ross Sterling, the captain's friend from the old Batson oil field days.

On June 15, 1934, the local newspaper *Falfurrias Facts* published what it called a special "Pioneer Edition, dedicated to those who settled Falfurrias." Included within its pages are lengthy articles on entrepreneurs Ed Lasater and Frank Rachal, and the almost legendary old Mexican faith healer Don Pedro Jaramillo, all of whom had contributed to the history and organization of the area. A photo of Judge Brooks appears in the center of the third page, with this caption: "Captain Brooks has seen this section change from a longhorn cattle, brush covered area to a fruitful agricultural community. He has guided the destiny of the county from the very first moment of its inception to the present date."

"His troubles are thousand fold," it continues and peculiarly echoes Brooks's plea for reelection two years earlier, "for he shoulders the tribulations of every inhabitant of his county. Few men have so completely dedicated themselves to a people, and he is rewarded by the devotion and love of those for whom he lives." Brooks is recognized later in the edition in a long list of salutations, as one "who carries the load of every person in the county on his shoulders and in his mind."[10]

In 1935 James Brooks turned eighty and was feted around the county, making several speeches and receiving honors and awards for his long service to Texas. He spent his November 20 birthday in Corpus Christi at the home of old friend Sheriff Will Shely, and received congratulatory telegrams from, among others, Texas legislator Edwin D. Dunlap from Kingsville, Oklahoma oil man Lawrence Miller, Brooks's sister Lillie, and the W. W. Sterling family, whose greeting was addressed "To a great man, our most worthy citizen."

The next evening, November 21, the judge attempted a letter to an old friend, Judge George P. Brown of McKinney, in response to birthday greetings. George Pearis Brown's family was one of the first to settle in what became Collin County and the town of McKinney, and George married Brooks's cousin Margaret Darnall and settled in McKinney for the next fifty years. Brown served as Collin County judge for four years and four more as assistant U.S. district attorney for the Eastern District of Texas, and was respected as a biblical scholar and attorney until his death in 1940 at age seventy-five.

Reflective and perhaps melancholy, his writing only a scribble, Brooks's letter to George and Maggie Brown begins: "Long years have passed since we met yet you have not been forgotten; now in 1889 you almost got me married to a Miss Love, you remember of what caused the trouble, she went back to the state of Tennessee." His grammar increasingly peculiar, Brooks began to reminisce: "Now long before that time from Kentucky to Texas I hiked your parents to see, now the record to keep straight we will go back to 1855." Three pages later, the rambling missal fades to nothing. It was never mailed.

Brooks penned this wistful poesy on his eightieth birthday: "Still healthy and contented at both work and play, why should I not be happy and gay? Three score years and ten have been allotted to men, the good book doth say, Now the law was amended, the time extended, for some good reason I dare not say. The divine law having been obeyed, right living observed, why not preserve this body of clay until it is in a state of decay, worthless I pray.

"I have often passed with the throng, sometimes right sometimes wrong, now destiny has seen fit my life to prolong, and I still love to hear a good song. But if kind providence should decree that it is time for me to pass on and leave my place for the strong, good bye to the passing throng and my heritage will be happy, care free, and long.

County Judge Brooks poses in his Falfurrias courthouse office.

Courtesy Brooks family.

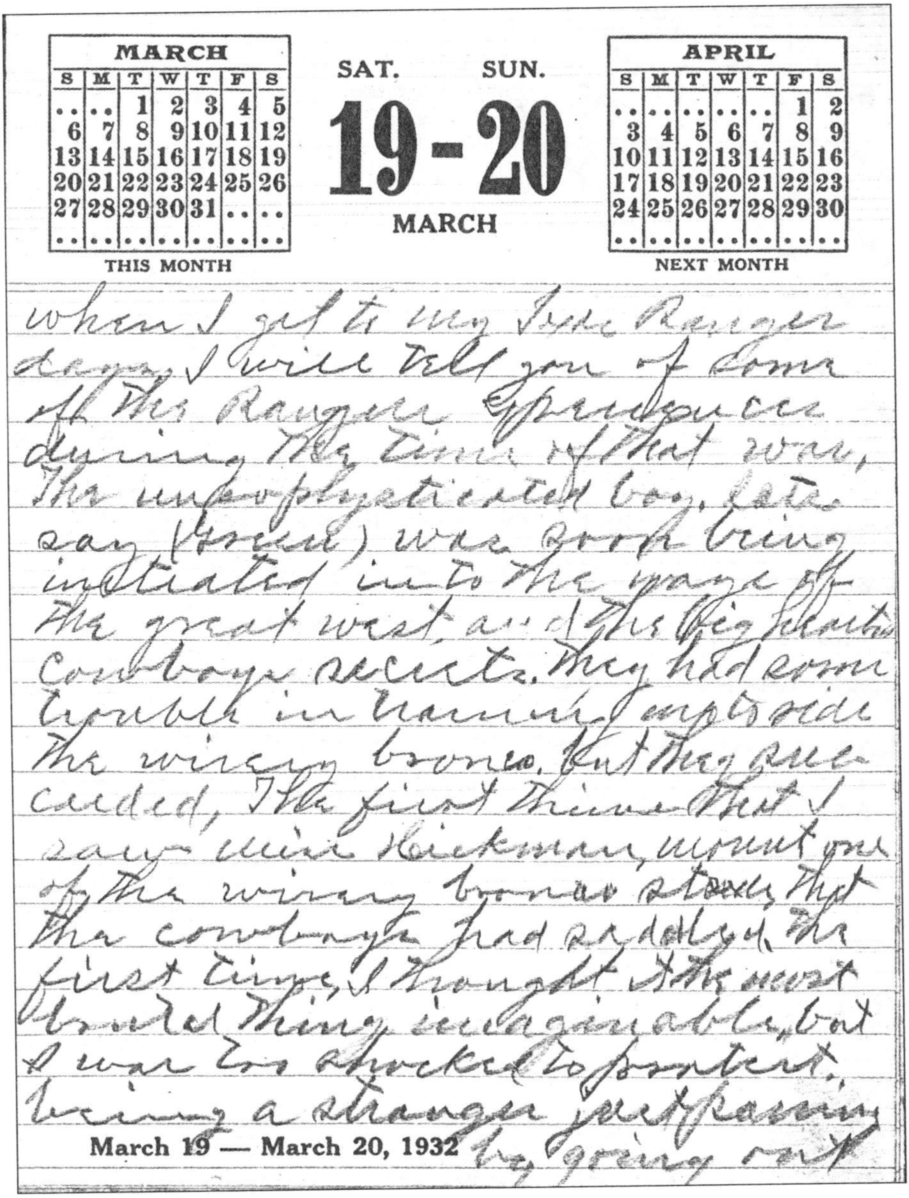

MARCH

S	M	T	W	T	F	S
..	..	1	2	3	4	5
6	7	8	9	10	11	12
13	14	15	16	17	18	19
20	21	22	23	24	25	26
27	28	29	30	31	..	..
..	..	..	..	..	..	..

THIS MONTH

SAT. SUN.

19-20

MARCH

APRIL

S	M	T	W	T	F	S
..	..	..	..	..	1	2
3	4	5	6	7	8	9
10	11	12	13	14	15	16
17	18	19	20	21	22	23
24	25	26	27	28	29	30
..	..	..	..	..	..	..

NEXT MONTH

when I get to my Texas Ranger days I will tell you of some of the Rangers experiences during the time of that war, The unsophisticated boy, let's say (Green) was good being initiated into the ways of the great west and the big hearted cowboys secrets. they had some trouble in learning up to ride the wiry broncs. but they succeeded, The first time that I saw Will Hickman, mount one of the wiry bronco steers that the cowboys had saddled the first time, I thought it the most bould thing imaginable, but I was too shocked to protest. being a stranger just passing by, going out

March 19 — March 20, 1932

Page from a calendar on which Judge Brooks wrote his memoirs in 1935.

Courtesy Brooks family.

Formal photograph of Judge J. A. Brooks, ca. 1939, prior to his retirement. Note portion of cancerous left ear removed.

Courtesy Brooks family.

A rare smile seen on the face of retired Brooks with his granddaughter Beverly, 1942.

Courtesy Brooks family.

"The County the State have treated me great, for which I am grateful; friends I have many, yes a plenty, they have been true except a very few, and to them I hold no enmity, for I try to be forgiving and friendly. Unselfish friendship is a jewel that is hard to obtain, but if once gained it is no trouble to retain; for all time we have loved the beautiful, the good, and the true, now why refrain for we have everything to gain–it is up to you."[11]

The captain attempted to write his memoirs that year, struggling to get much beyond his childhood and cowboy stories and leaving most of his drafts unfinished. At one point he began making notes on a small desk calendar, the stories pouring out around the date on each page and scribbled almost illegibly. A number of the handwritten papers he left behind show a clear difference between his sober and not so sober writing moments. He seemed more clear-headed on occasions when interviewed for books or newspaper articles: During this period of his life he spoke at length with Walter Prescott Webb, William Warren Sterling, Dora Raymond, and Zachary Taylor Fulmore, all of whom wrote those stories into their books. During two days in 1937 the judge interviewed with Lloyd Dyer, a graduate student at Texas A & I in Kingsville whose 1938 masters thesis on Brooks County includes several quotes from the old Ranger captain.

Nearing his eighty-third birthday, the aging judge appreciated his membership in the Old Trail Drivers Association, even though he admitted he had never attended any of its meetings, and made contact with some of the men who still could recall the adventures from six decades before. One of those was W. H. Atkins; another, E. R. "Newt" Rachal, had passed away some years earlier. Another old cowboy was Lake Porter, an old friend and former county sheriff who became a cowboy musician and something of a local celebrity until his death in 1945.

In 1938 a county marker was erected near Falfurrias and dedicated in a ceremony to the judge who had been so instrumental in bringing the county into existence twenty-seven years earlier. An extended article in the Corpus Christi paper that December related many incidents in Brooks's life and career.[12]

In the fall of 1938 Judge Brooks was reelected to the local bench once more, but at eighty-four his health now began to fail him. He had half of his cancerous left ear removed, and battled the debilitating effects of alcohol and a rough frontier life, a battle he was now losing. On February 1, 1939, thirty days after assuming office for his fourteenth term, Brooks knew he could no longer carry out his duties effectively, and he resigned his post as county judge. His son Morgan was appointed to replace him; Judge John Morgan Brooks served in that capacity until 1970.

The captain was the longest serving, and oldest, county judge in Texas when he retired after twenty-eight years; he and his son were the only magistrates in the first fifty-eight years of the county's history. The local paper announced nine days later: "Capt. Brooks Steps from Office after Twenty-eight Years," noting that "James Abadiah (*sic*) Brooks is bringing to a close more than fifty years of public service. Rancher and trail driver and then captain of the Texas Rangers, Captain Brooks today is a storehouse of interesting experiences accumulated throughout the many years he was associated with the development of this south Texas section." The paper noted that in a recent "good will" visit from a Harris County entourage, the senior Texas judge had met with "the youngest county judge in Texas," twenty-five-year-old Roy Hofheinz.[13]

The Brooks County commissioners passed a "Resolution of Gratitude" in honor of Brooks's career, which read in part: "Be It Resolved, That owing to the past illness of Judge J. A. Brooks and his advanced age he has deemed it best that he resign in order that the County Judge's office may function in a more business like manner; we wish to commend [him] for his past record as a just, fair and impartial man, always performing his duties, efficiently and ably administering the duties of his office with justice to all and partiality to none.

"Due to the business-like administration of Judge Brooks, in good times and in bad," the resolution continues, "the county has at all times maintained its credit at a class A rating. During the depression the county has never defaulted its bonds nor gone upon a script basis. As members of the Commissioners Court it is gratifying to know that he has served the people of Brooks County so well, so faithfully, for so long a time." The court welcomed his appearance at any meeting and made him an honorary member.[14]

Brooks received many letters from colleagues and friends across the state following his retirement from the county bench. One from attorney Robert Lee Bobbitt is an example of the sentiments: "I have talked with many men in all sections of the State since your announcement and I know it would do your heart good to realize the very high esteem in which you are held, not only by all of us who have known you and appreciated you intimately during the past quarter of a century, but by all worthwhile people in our State who have known you by reputation.

"You hold a most enviable record in the public life of Texas," Bobbitt writes, concluding: "I dare say that no man in the long history of my native State has rendered finer public service than you have given in every position of public trust which you have filled through the years."[15]

On October 9, 1939, a remorseful, ailing Brooks sat down late at night and wrote this poignant testament: "I James Abijah Brooks of sound mind and body but old in age as well as experience address this to whom it may concern, especially my children, Good resolutions. Dreaming, lying awake at night will cause you to do a lot of serious thinking. June 27th, 1939, at about 6:30 a.m. I drank my last alcoholic beverage. It was done to please my two children Corrinne Kenny and John Morgan Brooks, they both being strict prohibitionists [who] abstain at any cost.

"Will power, I find that I am blessed with it. Old Bourbon whiskey has caused me many years of trouble, trouble that cannot be atoned for in this world or life. My only hope is that when I arrive at the end of life and arrive at the gate of my last heritage, the golden gate, the promised land, that I will find forgiveness for things that I would gladly give my life for if they could be corrected and be forgotten. I hope and pray that I may and will be forgiven, even at this late day when old age is overcoming me but not my good resolutions.

"For some reason," the old judge scribbled almost illegibly, "kind Providence has been good to me for which I am truly thankful, and my good Christian mother prayed, never ceased to follow me through my wild and reckless days for more than sixty years. Now that I have time to do some serious thinking, I look to make amends before it is too late, and hope and pray that all my sins will be erased before I have to face them, or I will see the writing on the board over Old Saint Peter's head, the guardian to the gate of my last heritage, I hope the promised land.

"It is my desire," Brooks writes in a last paragraph of what he intended to be his will, "that all my holdings and other things remain in the hands as they are now, in their possession my children to do as they wish to. I am truly glad that I have the [illegible] to give them a start with. I have no debts other than gratitude, and thankfulness. J. A. Brooks."[16]

On Friday morning, January 14, 1944, the eighty-eight-year-old Brooks dressed himself in the bedroom of his apartment adjoining his son's home in town where he had recently moved. The degenerative illness brought on by a lifetime of drinking and two strenuous careers made even the effort of dressing a painful one. But with an energy he conjured up from deep within, the old judge walked the four blocks from the corner of Miller and Center streets downtown to the Falfurrias square, greeting several friends on the sidewalk and in the stores as he passed by. He stepped inside the courthouse and spoke briefly with his son and a number of folks who paused to visit with the venerable Ranger captain: some believe he was saying goodbye.

That night after supper Brooks went to bed, and died peacefully in his sleep before dawn. He was buried in the Falfurrias Cemetery on Monday as an entire community paused to pay its respects.

Letters of condolence poured in from all over the Southwest. Robert Lee Bobbitt wrote to John Morgan: "We are all deeply grieved at the passing of our dear friend and one of the finest characters who ever served Texas. While, of course, his going is a matter of deep regret, there is much consolation in knowledge of the fact that he was one of the finest characters in the history of our State, and that he leaves a heritage to you and all his loved ones and friends that will last and be appreciated as long as the history of Texas is known." Added another: "He lived a long and useful life, leaving a rich heritage in noble deeds well performed to his family, to Brooks County and to the State of Texas."

Said a next-generation peace officer, "With his passing, Texas lost one of its best citizens, and I lost the man who inspired me to be a Texas Ranger."[17]

In 1969 an official Texas historical grave marker was placed at Brooks's grave. With only a couple of minor errors it reads: "Illustrious Texas Ranger for whom this county is named. Born in Kentucky–came to Texas 1876; became rancher and trail driver. Served in Texas Rangers 1882–1906. By order of the governor, aided in preventing Fitzsimmons-Maher world title prize fight, El Paso, 1896. Helped solve and halt South Texas cattle thefts. Served in Texas Legislature, 1909–1911; was county judge of Brooks County, 1911–1939. Married Virginia Wilborn."

★

To characterize someone as being enigmatic does little to distinguish that person from most anyone else who has lived a long and diverse life. Brooks presents a puzzle only in that he managed to keep the bitter aspects of his private life clearly out of the limelight–and out of the way–of his illustrious public service career. The plaudits for his Ranger service as well as his second career as a legislator and on the county bench allude to a man of immense popularity who garnered respect far beyond the norm. "A great citizen," he is called by one colleague; "one of the finest characters in the history of Texas," wrote another admirer. Fifty-six continuous and unblemished years as a public servant–Ranger, legislator, judge–speak to the integrity for which he was rightly acknowledged and appreciated.

On the private side of this man one sees a struggling, often lonely, frail human being. His family hardly knew him, and what they knew of him personally they did not much care for; his descendants acknowledge his public fame but admit "no one really liked him." He essentially ignored his wife of thirty-eight years, doted on his son to the serious emotional detriment of his daughter, and buried his most private miseries in a bottomless bottle of whiskey. When Virginia died in 1928, the captain lived alone out on his modest ranch for the next decade as his children moved into town and away from him. His last words in this life are confused and even desperate expressions of pride and penitence.

If there can be any summary statement about the life and career of Captain Brooks, it would be that whatever strengths and skills he possessed within him came to the fore with energy and zeal in his public life, leaving his personal life vapid and empty. The public persona of J. A. Brooks earned the accolades he received over five decades and even after his passing, while the private alter ego Bud Brooks struggled along finding solace in the only real companion he ever had, Bourbon whiskey. Here was a man who had greatness coursing through his veins, possessed with a human frailty that operated in unrelenting tension throughout his life. He deserves the glory he received, and perhaps was finally rewarded with the mercy he craved.

Life-size portrait of Brooks, taken from 1898 photograph, hangs in the Heritage Museum, Falfurrias, Texas.

Courtesy of Heritage Museum, Falfurrias, Texas.

ABBREVIATIONS

A–G Adjutant General of Texas, papers of, 1882–1907. Texas State Archives, Austin.

MoR Monthly Returns and Scout Reports of the Frontier Battalion, Texas Rangers, 1882–1901. Texas State Archives, Austin.

SR Captain's Reports and Scout Reports of the Texas Ranger Force, 1901–1907. Texas State Archives, Austin.

ENDNOTES

Introduction

1. "Brooks Surname of Bourbon County, Kentucky." The Shawhan Genealogy, p. 3, *www.shawhan.com*; Audry, "Early Bourbon Families," *Kentuckian Citizen*, June 20, 1944. The Brooks family was relatively well off throughout the ensuing generations, right up to the Civil War. Aside from the Kentucky Breckinridges to whom he was distantly related, Jim Brooks's best known kin was Rev. Phillips Brooks (1835–1893), a Bostonian Episcopal minister and composer of the Christmas hymn, "O Little Town of Bethlehem."
2. Dora N. Raymond, *Captain Lee Hall of Texas,* 197.
3. W. W. Sterling, *Trails and Trials of a Texas Ranger*, 316. Ranger and later legislative records, and the family, confirm the captain's name as James Abijah Brooks.
4. Richard Harding Davis, *The West From a Car-Window*, 11–13.
5. *San Antonio Daily Express* Austin Bureau, January 11, 1911.
6. November 22, 1935 interview, *Corpus Christi Caller Times.*
7. Sterling, 307. Sterling devotes an entire chapter to Brooks in addition to several references throughout his memoirs.
8. Walter Prescott Webb, *The Texas Rangers*, 460.

9. Ellis Davis and Edwin Grobe, eds., *The New Encyclopedia of Texas*, 2905: "[Brooks's] record as a county judge bespeaks work efficiently handled, in a spirit of cooperation, and has been stamped by the approval of the public, as is attested to by his consistent reelection to office."
10. Sterling, 367. In his last will and testament, written in 1939, Brooks again thanks his dearly departed mother for praying for him while she was alive.
11. Interview with Beverly Brewton, Captain Brooks's granddaughter, summer 2004. The family has no reservations in admitting that the captain was no family man, and cared little if at all for his daughter. Beverly Brewton recalls her grandfather peeling an orange for her when she was a child, but using a rusty pocket knife to do it! There are photographs of the old judge romping in the yard with Beverly, but it seems even to the family to be anachronistic.
12. Sterling, 333.
13. Family interview with Mrs. Brewton and her daughter Suzanne Montgomery, August, 2004. Corrinne condemned her father for his drinking, another cause for the permanent rift between the two.
14. Robert M. Utley, *Lone Star Justice: The First Century of the Texas Rangers*, 254.

Chapter One

1. Bourbon County, Kentucky, 1850 United States Census; "Bourbon County, Kentucky, Biographies, Hutchinson Precinct," 1–20; Bourbon County Clerk records; Langsam and Johnson, *Historical Architecture of Bourbon County, Kentucky*. There remain several buildings standing from that era, including the old Presbyterian church. The Brooks homestead would today be located on Harp-Innes Road just up from the main highway and at the edge of the county.
2. Brooks Memoirs, Brooks Family Papers, Pasadena, Texas. Throughout this book, Brooks's own words tell his story in an

especially personal way. During the year 1935 Brooks wrote several versions of his memoirs, some organized and others on scraps of old desk calendar sheets. They are all collected as his "Memoirs" for this biography and are quoted extensively here.

3. Bourbon County, Kentucky, United Sates Census, 1860; Bourbon County Clerk records. There is a reproduced photograph in the family papers, unsubstantiated, of two people who may have been Old Ned and Mary.
4. Interview in *Corpus Christi Caller Times*, Nov. 20, 1938.
5. "Historical Scrapbook; 175th Anniversary of Bourbon County, Kentucky" (1981); Hutchinson, *Bluegrass and Mountain Laurel: The Story of Kentucky in the Civil War.*
6. "The Battle of Cynthiana, Kentucky," *www.americancivilwar.com/ky*. Morgan was killed in 1864 but his legend lives on in central Kentucky.
7. *Estates Settled Book G*, Reference #2694, Bourbon County, Kentucky, dated Jan. 25, 1864, 104–7. James's mother was by all accounts a remarkably strong woman, able to rebuild her family's homestead to at least a comfortable level once more while fighting off the vagaries of Reconstruction.
8. Pitts and Champ, *Collin Co., Texas, Families,* 96–97, 524–25; Roy Hall, *Collin County, Texas: Pioneering in North Texas,* 93, 108; *Biographical Souvenir of the State of Texas,* 231.
9. Interview in *Corpus Christi Caller Times,* Nov. 20, 1938. The "pretty girls" were almost always first among his priorities.
10. Collin County, Texas, Tax Rolls of 1878, 26; Collin County and Wise County, United States Census, 1880. That land in Collin County is still open farm land, and the source of that spring can still be found. Looking south from that vantage point, one can see the roll of the land that was Brooks's first, and only, farm.
11. Memoirs; *The New Handbook of Texas* for information on Halsell, Barnett, C. V. Terrell, the 6666 Ranch; "6666: Portrait of a Texas Ranch," *Texas Highways* (June 2005), 34–41.

12. Terrell, *The Terrells: 85 Years-Texas from Indians to the Atomic Bomb,* 34–35; Mike Cox, *Texas Ranger Tales II,* 140–41.

Chapter Two

1. Memoirs; "Burkburnett, Texas." *The New Handbook of Texas*; Annette Ludeman, La Salle County, 186. The young Maltsberger was born in 1865, came to the area when he was twenty, and died in 1955.
2. Fisher and Dykes, "The Life and Times of King Fisher," *Southwestern Historical Quarterly* 64 (1961), 241–42, and their book, *King Fisher, His Life and Times,* 108–9; Paul Adams, "The Unsolved Murder of Ben Thompson," 326. King Fisher seemed to have been a Robin Hood character to some, intimidating to all.
3. Memoirs; Monthly Returns and Annual Company Reports (MoR), Adjutant General Records, 1877–1879.
4. *The New Handbook of Texas,* s.v. "San Diego, Texas."
5. *The New Handbook of Texas,* s.vv. "DuVal West" and "Burr Duval."
6. Paul Horgan, Great River: *The Rio Grande in North American History,* 434; *The New Handbook of Texas,* s.vv. "Shafter Mining District" and "Stonewall County"; Acker, "Development of Mineral Resources in Texas," Masters thesis, East Texas State University, 1939. See also Thomas J. Evans, *Gold and Silver in Texas,* Circular 56 (Austin: Bureau of Economic Geology, 1975).
7. Alexander C. Hunt was a prodigious character on the American mining frontier, delegate of the Territory of Colorado and later the state's governor.
8. The Brooks descendants tell the story of the gold nugget, and one version is that it is from an Alaskan gold mine. There is no indication that Brooks ever went to Alaska.
9. *The New Handbook of Texas,* s.v. "Los Mineras."
10. Janet Roy, "The Life and Times of Minera, Texas," *Southwestern Historical Quarterly* 49 (1946): 514–15.

11. Sterling, 305.
12. *The New Handbook of Texas*, s.v. "Cotulla."
13. Sterling, 306–7.
14. 1882 End of the Year Report, Company F, Frontier Battalion, Adjutant General Papers (A–G Papers).
15. Sterling, 307.
16. Memoirs; Frontier Battalion Monthly Report, March 1883, A–G Papers.
17. Memoirs; Frontier Battalion Monthly Report, April 1883, A–G Papers.
18. Memoirs; Frontier Battalion Monthly Reports, June–December 1883, A–G Papers.
19. Spellman, *Captain John H. Rogers, Texas Ranger*, x–xv.
20. Frontier Battalion Monthly Reports, November and December, 1884.
21. Frederick Wilkins, *The Law Comes to Texas: The Texas Rangers*, 1870–1901, 250.
22. Parsons and Fitterer, *Captain C. B. McKinney, The Law in South Texas*, 75–77, indicate that Scott and Shely arrived too late for the February 9 parlay, and that the Texas negotiators were McKinney, Rangers Lee and Frank Hall, and Brooks. Wilkins, 251.
23. The Dr. Pope that Brooks mentions was likely Benjamin Franklin Pope, an enigmatic army surgeon stationed at Ft. Clark and an irritant to his commanding officers; he often took extended leaves from the fort and would have been the kind of person to intervene in such a situation. Interview with Robert Utley, October 18, 2005; Parsons and Fitterer, 82–84; *The New Handbook of Texas*, s.v. "Dimmit County, Texas."
24. Memoirs; Frontier Battalion Monthly Reports, June and July, 1885.
25. Wilkins, 256; Spellman, 117–19; Adjutant General Annual Report, 1885.
26. Frontier Battalion Monthly Reports, February and March, 1886.

27. Oliver Knight, *Ft. Worth, Outpost on the Trinity*, 128–29.
28. Memoirs; Frontier Battalion Monthly Reports, April, 1886.
29. Memoirs; "Alex, Oklahoma," *Chickasaw Daily Express*, June 2, 1993. The towns of Alex, Erin Springs, and Pauls Valley are still there in central Oklahoma, although there is nothing left of the old general store where the gunfight took place.
30. Testimony, "United States v. Knight, Brooks, et al.," Western Arkansas District Court Proceedings, 1887.
31. Memoirs; Trial testimony. There is a hand-drawn map of the store, and the location of its occupants at the moment of the shoot out, in the trial papers.
32. Trial testimony as well as Brooks's own recollections years later.
33. Memoirs.

Chapter Three

1. Love to Sandels, May 26, 1886, Trial Records, Western Arkansas District, 1887, Ft. Worth.
2. Trial Records. Putz lived in Dallas at this time, and Knight returned to Ft. Sill.
3. Webb, 426–27: "What we want is about three good Rangers to come here and catch these law breakers," wrote Uvalde County judge John Nance Garner. "They can catch them within a week or ten days."
4. T. R. Havins, *Something About Brown: A History of Brown County*, 37–38. Baugh's fence was cut the next night after he left the note.
5. Frontier Battalion Monthly Reports, September 1886, A–G Papers; Ira Aten, *Six and One-half Years in the Ranger Service*, 17; Spellman, *Captain John H. Rogers, Texas Ranger*, 38–39.
6. Spellman, 40–42; Roy D. Holt, "Introduction of Barbed Wire into Texas and the Fence Cutting War," *West Texas Historical Association Yearbook* 6 (1930), 65–79; Ira Aten, 18–20.

7. Memoirs; Parsons and Fitterer, *Captain C. B. McKinney, The Law in South Texas*, 97–119.
8. Scott to Sieker, July 31, 1886, Adjutant General Official Correspondence; Memoirs; Frontier Battalion Monthly Reports, December, 1886 and January 1887; Wilkins, 273–74.
9. Spellman, 35; Sterling, 309.
10. Scott to Sieker, July 31, 1886. A–G Official Correspondence.
11. Newspaper interview by Sarah Ellen Davidge with J. Allen Newton, *Galveston Daily News*, unknown date, Brooks Family Papers.
12. Joe F. Combs, *Gunsmoke in the Redlands*, 111–12. Combs obtained some of his information from a local named Elmer Harper.
13. Spellman, 45–47.
14. Newton interview; Spellman, 47–50; Sterling, 309–11.
15. Newton interview; L. E. Daniell, *Texas: The Country and Its Men*, 484–88.
16. Scott to Sieker, July 31, 1887, Adjutant General Official Correspondence; Frontier Battalion Monthly Reports, March 1887.
17. Spellman, 51. James Polley to Dr. F. H. Tucker, March 31, 1887, Adjutant General Ranger correspondence. The small, torn note still exists in a file folder at the Texas State Archives in Austin.
18. Report of Dr. J. W. Smith to L. P. Sieker, May 19, 1887, A–G Correspondence.
19. Report of Dr. Frank Tucker to L. P. Sieker, April 4, 1887, A–G Correspondence; Spellman, 50–51. There seems to have been some contest for whatever compensation the "official" physician would receive.
20. Newton interview; Spellman, 53.
21. Combs, 114–15; W. S. Adair, "Rangers 40 Years Ago Had No Easy Life," 41–43.
22. Brooks memoirs and Newton interview.

23. Spellman, 52. It is interesting that Brooks never wrote about the Conner incident, although on the other hand that whole period of his life was little noted in the memoirs.
24. Newton interview. Martha Peddy was the daughter of the Baptist minister in Hemphill according to the 1880 U.S. Census for Sabine County and church records for the 1st Baptist Church of Hemphill, both of which can be found in the Genealogy Room of the Texas State Archives. Also, Blanche Toole's *Sabine County (Texas) Marriages*, 1875–1900, 13, gives additional information that helps identify Brooks's object of desire.
25. Frontier Battalion Monthly Reports, April–July 1887, A–G Papers.
26. Spellman, 54–55.
27 "Hangin' Judge Isaac C. Parker," *Ft. Smith Historical Society Journal* 3:1 (April 1979); Ft. Smith, Arkansas, Historical Collection. The judicial district itself has its origins as early as 1851.
28. Memoirs; Interview with Mickel Yantz at The Cherokee Heritage Center, Tahlequah, Oklahoma, Feb. 15, 2005.
29. Memoirs; Interview with Brooks in *Corpus Christi Caller Times,* Nov. 20, 1938; John Paul Pola, "Judge Parker," June, 1959, University of Arkansas Special Collections: Folklore MS F.16. A January 11, 1887, article in the Ft. Smith newspaper reported that "hangman deluxe George Maledon dispatched four more victims in a multiple hanging."
30. Transcript of trial testimony of Henry Putz, Western Arkansas District Court proceedings, NARA, Ft. Worth. The rash young Putz's cavalier attitude on the stand certainly did not help sway a jury made up of cowboys unsympathetic to two Rangers and an Indian police officer.
31. Transcript of trial testimony of James A. Brooks.
32. Transcript of trial testimony, Verdict.

Chapter Four

1. Transcript of Trial Records, "United States v. Knight, Brooks et al.," Western Arkansas District Court proceedings, NARA, Ft. Worth.
2. Scott to Sieker, Aug. 6, 1887, A–G. All of the information regarding the presidential pardon for Brooks, Knight, and Putz is housed in Record Group 60, File K–713, Box 99, at the National Archives (NARA), College Park, Maryland; for information on the congressmen who wrote letters of appeal, "The Biographical Directory of the U.S. Congress, 1774–Present." The original presidential pardon is in the Brooks Family Papers.
3. Frontier Battalion Co. F Monthly Report, August, 1887.
4. Frontier Battalion Co. F Monthly Report, September 1887; *Biennial Report of the Adjutant General of Texas, 1887–1888.*
5. Memoirs; Frontier Battalion Co. F Monthly Reports, November and December, 1887. Such a stunt took some moxie, of which the young Ranger Brooks seemed to have had plenty.
6. Frontier Battalion, Co. F Monthly Report, February, 1888.
7. Memoirs. In his papers Brooks had a notebook in which he wrote about thirty pages of notes on the early career of Scott and himself, sometimes confusing which person he was talking about but writing anecdotally about events otherwise missing from any official files.
8. *Biennial Report of the Adjutant General of Texas, 1887–1888*; Wilkins, 270, 278–79.
9. *Biennial Report of the Adjutant General of Texas, 1887–1888.*
10. Frontier Battalion Co. F Monthly Reports, September 1888, May 1889, October 1889, May 1890.
11. Gerald Witt, *History of eastern Kerr County; Kerr County Album* (1986), 458–59; Coldwell Family Records, Kerr County Library, Kerrville, Texas.

12. Texas Ranger Muster Rolls and Vertical Files on Neal and Vernon Coldwell, and Neal Willborn; *Kerr County Album,* 201.
13. Frontier Battalion Co. F Monthly Reports, June and July, 1888.
14. Frontier Battalion Co. F Monthly Reports, October 1888–June 1889; *Biennial Report of the Adjutant General of Texas, 1889–1890.*
15. Adjutant General Official Correspondence, Brooks and Gen. King: October 18, 1889; January 6, 1890. Isaac Terrell may have been an African-American stationed there with units of the "Buffalo Soldiers."
16. Adjutant General Official Correspondence, Brooks and King: Feb. 2, Feb. 8, and Feb. 20, 1890. The presence of the Rangers caused a disturbance all on its own among the local citizens and the Mexican officials across the river.
17. Frontier Battalion Co. F Monthly Report, March 1890; Spellman, 67–68.
18. Wilkins, *The Law Comes to Texas,* 295–96.
19. *Biennial Report of the Adjutant General of Texas, 1889–1890,* 30.
20. Harold Weiss, "Yours to Command: Captain William J. 'Bill' McDonald and the Panhandle Rangers of Texas"; *The New Handbook of Texas,* s.v. "William Jesse McDonald."
21. Company F Records of Scouts, September 26, 1891.
22. Frontier Battalion Co. F Monthly Report, June 1890; *The New Handbook of Texas,* s.v. "Catarino Erasmo Garza."
23. Gilbert M. Cuthbertson, "Catarino E. Garza and the Garza War." Texana 12 (1976), 338–39.
24. *Biennial Report of the Adjutant General of Texas, 1891–1892.*
25. Record of Scouts, Company F, September 26 and 27, 1891; Cuthbertson, 340; Wilkins, 303–4; Sterling, 373–75.
26. Uvalde *Leader News,* December 30, 1891.
27. Record of Scouts, Company F, December 16, 1891; Robert M. Utley, *Lone Star Justice,* 255–56.

28. Cuthbertson, 342–48; Wilkins, 303–5; Sterling, 314, 372–74. A *Chicago Herald* reporter published a story chronicling Garza's journey from Texas to New York City, to Venezuela and to France, and even a secret trip back to Laredo, "well disguised with a full beard which he had grown during his extended absence." Brooks kept that article in his personal papers.
29. Frontier Battalion Co. F Monthly Report, January 1892.
30. *Biennial Report of the Adjutant General*, 1891–1892; Wilkins, 305.
31. Frontier Battalion Co. F Muster Rolls, 1892, A–G Papers.
32. "Frederic Remington, 1861–1909," Sid Richardson Collection of Western Art, *www.sidrmuseum.org*.
33. Sterling, 315–17; "Richard Harding Davis," *The Columbia Encyclopedia*, Sixth Edition, 2001; see also the larger story by his son: C. B. Davis, ed., *Adventures and Letters of Richard Harding Davis*.
34. Richard Harding Davis, *The West From a Car-Window*, 6–15; "Pioneer Edition," Falfurrias Facts, June 15, 1934.

Chapter Five

1. Frontier Battalion Co. E Monthly Report, March, 1892; Wilkins, 306.
2. Wilkins, 306–7; Spellman, 69–71.
3. Frontier Battalion Co. F Monthly Report, April 1892.
4. Brooks to Mabry, June 3, 1892, A–G Official Correspondence.
5. Brooks to Mabry, January 7, 1893; Mabry to Brooks, January 11, 1893; Mabry to Brooks, January 28, 1893. Shely had been interviewed by a reporter from the *Houston Post*. Brooks kept that article and several others related to the Garza War in his personal files.
6. Brooks to Mabry, July 5, 1892; Mabry to Brooks, November 26, 1892, A–G Official Correspondence.
7. Frontier Battalion Co. F Muster Rolls, 1893, A–G Papers.
8. Frontier Battalion Co. F Monthly Report, January, 1893; Spellman, 72–73.

9. Monthly Returns for Co. F, April, May, June, and October, 1893; May and September, 1894. In February, 1895, a teamster named Castro was hired.
10. Webb, 457–59: "Of the four, Captain W. J. (Bill) McDonald is the most widely known, not because he was more deserving than the others, but because he had the ability to stage himself before the public; . . . Brooks, Hughes, and Rogers, though lacking McDonald's showmanship, were his equal in every respect as officers, and in the opinion of many, were superior."
11. Frontier Battalion Co. F Monthly Report, May, 1893; Memoirs.
12. Wilkins, 314–316; Frontier Battalion Co. F Monthly Report, July, 1893.
13. Mabry to Brooks, August 2, 1893; Mabry to Gov. Hogg, September 4, 1893; Brooks to Mabry, September 5, 1893, A–G Official Correspondence.
14. Sterling, 317.
15. Report of Scouts, Company F, November 17, 1892; Mabry to Brooks, November 26, 1892, A–G Official Correspondence.
16. Report of Scouts, Company F, November 17, 1892; Mabry to Brooks, November 26, 1892, A–G Official Correspondence; Brooks to Mabry, March 8 and 14, 1893.
17. Brooks to Mabry, March 8, 1893, A–G Official Correspondence.
18. Mabry to Brooks, November 16, 1893; Frontier Battalion Co. F Monthly Report, December 1893.
19. Webb, 441–44: "Jones straightened his broken leg out in front of him and fired two or three more shots when a Mexican ball struck him just over the heart. He said, 'Boys, I am killed,' and fell back dead."
20. Paine, *Captain Bill McDonald, Texas Ranger*, 154–64.
21. Wilkins, 316–17.
22. Frontier Battalion Co. F Monthly Report, September, 1894.

23. The Brooks family has a small lock of Mary Vernon's hair attached to a card where Brooks wrote in a rare poignant moment: "Mary Vernon Brooks, five months, 14 days, died Dec. 12, 1894, 5:35 p.m. This is all I have left of her."
24. Co. F Muster Rolls, 1895; Brooks to Mabry, February 22, 1895; Mabry to Brooks, March 26, 1895; Frontier Battalion Co. F Monthly Report, March 1895.
25. Frontier Battalion Co. F Monthly Reports, June–September, 1895.
26. Mabry to Brooks, November 14, 1895; Brooks to Mabry, November 15, 1895, A–G Official Correspondence.
27. Frontier Battalion Co. F Muster Rolls and Notes, 1896, 1898, and 1903. Livingston resigned from the Rangers on the last day of 1903.
28. Elmer Million, 156–57; Statute on "Prizefighting in Texas," *General Laws of Texas*, 1891.
29. Leo N. Miletich, *Dan Stuart's Fistic Carnival*, 11–14.
30. Miletich, 58–59, 220n; *General Laws of Texas*, 1895.
31. Spellman, *Captain John H. Rogers, Texas Ranger*, 78–79; Culberson to Mabry, October 1, 1895, Governors Official Correspondence.
32. Mabry to Brooks, October 4, 1895, A–G Official Correspondence.
33. Miletich, 89–90, 96–97.
34. Mabry to Brooks, January 18, 1896; Mabry to Brooks, February 1, 1896, A–G Official Correspondence.
35. Spellman, 79–80.
36. Miletich, 158–61.
37. Mabry to (Lt. Gov. and acting Governor) Jester, Feb. 27, 1896; Official Report from Capt. John H. Rogers, Feb. 28, 1896, A–G Papers.
38. Miletich, 177–79; Spellman, 85–86. Legend has it, thanks to Albert Bigelow Paine's sensationalized biography of McDonald, that the captain and Masterson came within a moment of a duel at an eat-

ing establishment along the way to Langtry. Masterson always testily denied it ever happened.

39. *Dallas Morning News*, February 22, 1896.
40. Miletich, 184–86.
41. O. Henry, "Hygeia at the Solito," *Heart of the West*, 71.

Chapter Six

1. O. Henry, *Heart of the West*, 71.
2. Mabry's Official Report to Lt. Gov. Jester, February 27, 1896.
3. Frontier Battalion Co. B Monthly Report, February, 1896; Spellman, 88.
4. Frontier Battalion Co. F Monthly Report, March and April, 1896.
5. Frontier Battalion Co. F Monthly Report, August, September, and October, 1896.
6. Brooks Family Papers. Fannie Brooks Morgan and over a dozen of the Brooks clan are buried in the sprawling Lexington Cemetery where the captain's father was buried during the Civil War. See *www.lexcem.org*.
7. Sterling, 410–11.
8. Frontier Battalion Co. F Monthly Report, January 26, 1897.
9. Frontier Battalion Co. F Monthly Report, December, 1896, January, 1897; Brooks to Mabry, February 21, 1897; Mabry to Brooks, September 19, 1897, A-G Official Correspondence.
10. *Biennial Report of the Adjutant General of Texas, 1897–1898.*
11. Frontier Battalion Co. F Monthly Reports, March and April, 1897. Ed Chandler owned a large spread southwest of San Antonio valued in 1897 at over $64,000. His neighbor John Meredith had died in 1896 and widow Mary K. Meredith operated their ranch thereafter (Bexar County Tax Rolls, 1896–1898). Brooks mistakenly reported his visit to Atascosa County rather than the Bexar County community just across the county line where Chandler lived.

12. A–G to the four captains, May 26, 1897, A–G Official Correspondence.
13. Frontier Battalion Co. F Monthly Reports, July and August, 1897; Spellman, *Captain John H. Rogers, Texas Ranger*, 101–3.
14. Frontier Battalion Co. F Monthly Report, July, 1897.
15. Frontier Battalion Co. F Monthly Report, August, 1897; Spellman, 92–94: "I looked in the door and saw him with his gun to his shoulder," Rogers reported. "There was but one thing to do and that was go in and get him right then and there. Praying, I walked in the door."
16. Frontier Battalion Co. F Monthly Report, October, 1897.
17. Frontier Battalion Co. F Monthly Reports, November 1897–March 1898.
18. Sterling, 409–11; Ludeman, *La Salle County*, 118–20.
19. Frontier Battalion Co. E and Co. F Monthly Reports, April and May 1898.
20. Adjutant General to the four captains, April 19, 1898; Mabry to Brooks, April 19, 1898, A–G Official Correspondence; Muster Rolls, Troop D (formerly Company H in the Texas Volunteer Guard), 1st Texas Cavalry Regiment, Texas State Archives. The regiment was commanded by Col. J. R. Waites and Lt. Col. (and later Texas Adjutant General) John Augustus Hulen. In his memoirs, Brooks makes only a passing remark about his service under Jake Wolters.
21. Wilkins, 333–34; *The New Handbook of Texas*, s.v. "Alfred Prior Wozencraft." Wozencraft grew up in Arkansas, made a legal career in Dallas, and served as attorney for Southwestern Telephone and Telegraph after his stint in the adjutant general's office; he died in 1917.
22. San Antonio Express, June 10, 1891. Brooks kept this article in his own papers where it still remains.
23. Annette M. Ludeman, *La Salle County*, 116.

24. Ludeman, 117; Stanley Casto, *Settlement of the Cibolo-Nueces Strip: A Partial History of La Salle County*, 14.
25. Ludeman, 118.
26. Brooks Family Papers. Corrinne's middle name is spelled differently from the family for which she was christened. Her injury, and her brother's subsequent premature birth, may have caused their father to dote on the boy while somehow blaming his daughter for Morgan's delicate start in life.
27. Interview with Capt. Brooks's great granddaughter Suzanne Montgomery, August 2004. Photographs of Corrinne in her later years verify the story, in addition to the sad frown that is almost always on her face.
28. Interview with Capt. Brooks's granddaughter Beverly Brewton, September 2004. Beverly and her daughter respect the captain and his exploits but have little affection for him or his memory.
29. *The New Handbook of Texas*, s.v. "Reds and Blues"; Anders, *Boss Rule in South Texas*, 43–44.
30. *The New Handbook of Texas*, s.v. "Stanley Welch."
31. Wozencraft to Brooks, December, 1899, A–G Papers; Frontier Battalion Co. F Monthly Report, December, 1899.
32. *The New Handbook of Texas*, s.vv. "Anderson Yancey Baker" and "John Closner."
33. Frontier Battalion Co. F Monthly Reports, June, July, and August, 1899. Brooks also took a leave of absence earlier that year, when the Brownsville *Herald* noted on April 20 that "Capt. Brooks had just returned after a month away in San Antonio and Cotulla."
34. Frontier Battalion Co. F Monthly Report, October 1899.
35. Frontier Battalion Co. F Monthly Report, December 1899. *The New Handbook of Texas*, s.v. "Thomas Scurry." Scurry was born in Waller County, Texas, and had careers in real estate and the railroad industry. He retired to Dallas and died in 1911.

Chapter Seven

1. *Colorado County Chronicles,* Vol. 1, 193; C. L. Sonnichsen, *I'll Die Before I Run: the Story of the Great Feuds of Texas,* 302–3.
2. *Colorado County Chronicles,* Vol. 1, 196; Sonnichsen, 304–5. Bill Stein, librarian and archivist of the Nesbitt Memorial Library in Columbus, helped demythologize the feud for me with valuable research he has done for more then twenty years on the subject. Stein claims that Sonnichsen and others built up a story that greatly exaggerates the connection of many of the incidents in this chapter; he provided me with important primary sources from the trials and newspaper accounts from that period.
3. *Colorado County Chronicles,* Vol. 1, 208.
4. Interview with Bill Stein, September 2005.
5. Frontier Battalion Co. B Monthly Reports, March and April, 1899; Wilkins, 335.
6. *Galveston News,* May 18, 1899.
7. Frontier Battalion Co. E Monthly Report, May, 1899; Sonnichsen, 312–13; Spellman, 104–5. Townsend claimed years later that he thought Rogers was an itinerant preacher when he first saw him in town, not the first time that the Ranger captain was mistaken for anyone but a peace officer.
8. Frontier Battalion Co. F Monthly Report, January, 1900; Scurry to Brooks, January 15, 1900, A–G Official Correspondence.
9. Interview with Bill Stein, September 2005; Sterling, 319.
10. Brooks to Scurry, Feb. 6, 1900, Feb. 19, 1900, March 1, 1900, A–G Official Correspondence.
11. Brooks to Scurry, March 6, 1900, A–G Official Correspondence.
12. Sonnichsen, 313–14, corrected by Bill Stein's records.
13. *Colorado County Chronicles,* Vol. 1, 210–11.
14. Interview with Bill Stein, September 2005.

15. December, 1899, Annual Report to the Adjutant General of Texas; Bates's poem appeared on the front page of the *Alice Echo,* January 7, 1900.
16. Scurry to the four Ranger captains, January 30, 1899, and January 31, 1899, A–G Official Correspondence.
17. Gov. Sayers to Gen. Scurry, March 9, 1900, June 14, 1900, Governors Correspondence.
18. Texas Legislature, April 10, 1874, *General Laws of the State of Texas* 1874, 88; Harold Weiss, "The Texas Rangers Revisited," *Southwestern Historical Quarterly,* 630–31.
19. Webb, 452–53: "The basis upon which active opposition to such a force was founded was the unfriendly attitude of the Anglo-American towards a centralized police power. The people of Texas were frequently reminded of the Reconstruction days when the state police exercised arbitrary powers."
20. J. H. King, "The Texas Ranger Service and History," in Wooten, *A Comprehensive History of Texas,* Vol. II, 345.
21. Webb, 452.
22. *General Laws of the State of Texas* 1874, 88.
23. Sayers to Scurry, May 22, 1900; Scurry to Attorney General Smith, May 23, 1900; Smith to Scurry, May 24, 1900, Governors Correspondence.
24. Sayers to Smith, May 24, 1900; Smith to Scurry, May 25, 1900, Governors Correspondence.
25. Brooks to Scurry, June 15, 1900; Scurry to Brooks, August 4, 1900, A–G Official Correspondence; Frontier Battalion Co. F Monthly Report, August, 1900.
26. Brooks to Scurry, March 25 and 30, 1900; Record of Scouts, Company F, March 19, 1900; *Biennial Report of the Adjutant General of the State of Texas, 1899–1900,* 24–25.
27. Report of Scouts, Co. F, June 6, 10, and 18, 1900; Scurry to Brooks, July 31, 1900, A–G Official Correspondence.

28. Sammy Tise, *Texas County Sheriffs*, 449–50.
29. Frontier Battalion Co. F Monthly Report, November, 1900.
30. *Biennial Report of the Adjutant General of the State of Texas*, 1899–1900, 25.
31. Scurry to Brooks, October 18, 1900, A–G Official Correspondence.
32. 1900 Annual Report by Capt. John H. Rogers, Company E; Sterling, 409–10.
33. Scurry to Brooks, October 25, 1900 and November 2, 1900; Webb, 461.

Chapter Eight

1. Gov. Sayers, "Message to Congress," January 10, 1901, 27th Texas Legislature, House Journal, 23–24.
2. House Journal, 122, 306.
3. Senate Journal, 37, 350.
4. Randy Roberts, "Galveston's Jack Johnson," *Southwestern Historical Quarterly*, 50.
5. Roberts, 51. The hurricane that struck Galveston on September 8, 1900, killed 6,000 people and destroyed over three-quarters of the island.
6. Sterling, 320–21; Roberts, 52.
7. Brooks to Scurry, February 19 and February 22, 1901, A–G Official Correspondence.
8. Roberts, 53. Reports corroborate the booing and jeering crowd, even though the fight was over before the Rangers took action.
9. Roberts, 54–55; Scurry to Co. F, February 27, 1901; Brooks to Scurry, March 5, 1901; Scurry to Brooks, April 29, 1901 and May 6, 1901, A–G Official Correspondence.
10. 24th Texas Legislature (1901), House Journal, 377.
11. House Journal, 377–78.

12. Senate Journal, 552.
13. Senate Journal, 1003.
14. 24th Texas Legislature, *General Laws of the State of Texas* 1901, 41–43.
15. Scurry to the four Ranger captains, April 1, 1901, A–G Official Correspondence.
16. Brooks Report to the Adjutant General of Texas for Ranger Force Company F, June, 1901, A–G Papers. Sterling, 523: "Those who cherish the organization always refer to it as 'the Service,' and never as a 'Force.'"
17. Webb, 457–58: "The Rangers were still mounted men, though they frequently traveled-often with their own horses-on the trains which now penetrated all parts of the state. They furnished their own horses and horse equipment; but they wore no uniform and carried no badge."
18. *Alice Echo,* April 20, 1900, and June 14, 1900.
19. Ranger Force Co. F Muster Rolls, 1901.
20. Scurry to Brooks, June 14, 1901; Ranger Force Co. F Monthly Report, June 1901.
21. Ranger Force Co. F Monthly Reports, May through July 1901.
22. Annual Report of Capt. John H. Rogers, Company A, January, 1902; Spellman, 111–14; *The New Handbook of Texas,* s.v. "Gregorio Cortez Lira."
23. Americo Paredes, *"With His Pistol in His Hand," A Border Ballad and Its Hero,* 171–72.
24. Memoirs.
25. Sterling, 139. Sterling tells many stories about A. Y. Baker throughout his autobiography.
26. Ranger Force Co. F Monthly Report, December 1901.
27. *Biennial Report of the Adjutant General of Texas, 1901–1902,* 30.
28. A–G Report, 30, 40.

Chapter Nine

1. Spellman, 96–102; Capt. J. H. Rogers Report to the Adjutant General, March 1899.
2. *Biennial Report of the State Health Officer of Texas, 1899–1900,* December 1, 1900, Governors Papers.
3. Ibid, 3–6.
4. Scurry to Brooks, January 6, 1902, A–G Official Correspondence.
5. Scurry to Brooks, January 7, 10, 22, February 3, and March 4, 1902, A–G Official Correspondence.
6. Sterling, 325.
7. Dora N. Raymond, *Captain Lee Hall of Texas,* 197. The setting for Brooks's comment in his interview was a story that occurred in Cotulla.
8. Sterling, 326; retold by Mike Cox, *Texas Ranger Tales II,* 231–32.
9. Brooks to Scurry, May 8, 1902, A–G Official Correspondence.
10. Tom Lea, *The King Ranch,* Vol. II, 94.
11. Brooks Report to the Adjutant General, May 16, 1902.
12. *The New Handbook of Texas,* s.v. "Alfredo de la Cerda."
13. Webb, 463; Catherine Baker, "The Man of the Hour," 13. Mrs. Henrietta King presented Baker with a beautiful white steed, and replaced it several times as each was shot out from under the peace officer. Stambaugh, *The Lower Rio Grande Valley of Texas,* 158; McAllen Amberson, *I Would Rather Sleep in Texas,* 442–44.
14. Lea, 482; Brooks Report to the Adjutant General, May 16, 1902.
15. Scurry to Sayers, November 11, 1902; *Biennial Report of the Adjutant General of Texas, 1901–1902,* 33–34.
16. Scurry to Brooks, June 5, 1902, A–G Official Correspondence.
17. Scurry to Brooks, June 24, 1902, A–G Official Correspondence.
18. Webb, *The Texas Rangers,* 455; Brooks to Scurry, August 25, 1902, A–G Official Correspondence. Judge Sam Woods had an illustrious

career in South Texas as judge and attorney before his death in 1929 at the age of sixty-nine.

19. Scurry to Sayers, November 11, 1902, Governors Papers.
20. Photo is in Sterling, 324. The 9mm semiautomatic pistol, known as the "broom handle" because of its peculiar shape when attached to the wooden stock, was the first in the 1896 series that bore the address on its barrel, in this case "New York" and its unique serial number 31793, identifying it as being manufactured in 1902. The Mauser was a six-shot pistol with an adjustable sight, its firing pin retained by a single lug to the solid bolt. *www.g6csy.net/c96/database.html.* The Mauser, along with Brooks's sawed-off 10-gauge shotgun and two other pistols, are housed at the Heritage Museum in Falfurrias.
21. Sterling, 323. Emmett Robuck's name is often misspelled Roebuck, for one in the official Ranger Service Records in Austin.
22. Scurry to Sayers, November 11, 1902; Brooks to Scurry, September 9, 1902.
23. Brooks to Scurry, August 31, 1902, A–G Official Correspondence.
24. Brooks to Scurry, September 9, 1902.
25. Scurry to Brooks, September 9, 10, and 11, 1902.
26. Webb, 464; Scurry to Sayers, November 11, 1902.
27. Sterling, 323–25; Scurry to Sayers, November 11, 1902; Catherine G. Baker, "The Man of the Hour," 14. Catherine was A. Y. Baker's granddaughter.
28. Brooks to Scurry, October 3, 1902, A–G Official Correspondence.
29. Scurry to Sayers, November 11, 1902; Baker, "The Man of the Hour," 14: One old version has Baker storming into the Fernandez store and shooting Alfredo in the back. The "El Cometa" newspaper article is in the Governors Papers for 1902.
30. Scurry to Brooks, October, 1902, A–G Official Correspondence; *Biennial Report of the Adjutant General of Texas, 1901–1902,* 33–34.

31. Judge Welch to Scurry, February 1903, A–G Official Correspondence.
32. *The New Handbook of Texas,* s.v. "George Washington West"; Ranger Force Co. F Monthly Report, March 1902.
33. *Biennial Report of the Adjutant General of Texas, 1901–1902,* 40.
34. Ranger Force Co. A Monthly Reports, February and March, 1903.
35. *The New Handbook of Texas,* s.v. "Anderson Yancey Baker"; Sterling, 136–38: "A. Y. Baker had been one of the most outstanding Rangers who ever served his native state . . . It is a pity that [he] should be remembered for his participation in these affairs rather than for the many good deeds he performed." His years as "boss" in Hidalgo County certainly led to dissension among many and cast a dark shadow over his Ranger career. Writes one historian: "Baker kept the Anglo settlers at bay for twelve years through a combination of voter manipulation, election fraud, and large-scale graft" (Anders, 239). Taxes rose disproportionately during his "reign," and over 2,000 telegrams stacked up on President Calvin Coolidge's desk in 1928 demanding a federal investigation of Baker's practices. McAllen Amberson, 609n32. But see also the family's perspective, in Baker, "The Man of the Hour," 28: "To his children, A. Y. was a fine father and perhaps because of his own bleak childhood, he seemed to love them especially."

Chapter Ten

1. Ranger Force Co. F Monthly Report, March 18, 1903.
2. Spellman, *Captain John H. Rogers, Texas Ranger,* 115, from the J. H. Rogers Family Papers in San Antonio. Rogers had retired from the Ranger Force and was serving in Austin as United States Marshal at the time he spotted Gregorio while on a family visit to San Antonio.
3. Scurry to Brooks, May 20, 1903, A–G Official Correspondence; Lott and Martinez, *The Kingdom of Zapata,* 63–64.

4. *The New Handbook of Texas*, s.v. "John Augustus Hulen."
5. Brooks to Hulen, June 3, 1903, A–G Official Correspondence; *The New Handbook of Texas*, s.v. "Zavala County."
6. Brooks Family Papers. There is a map of the land tracts purchased in what would become Crystal City.
7. Ranger Force Muster Rolls 1903, Company A.
8. Brooks to Hulen, January 7, 1904, A–G Official Correspondence.
9. Ranger Force Co. A Monthly Report, January and July, 1904.
10. *Biennial Report of the Adjutant General of Texas, 1903–1904*, 164.
11. *New Handbook of Texas*, s.v. "Edward Cunningham Lasater."
12. Mike Cox, Texas Ranger Tales II, 144; Dale Lasater, *Falfurrias: Ed C. Lasater and the Development of South Texas*, 76. An early Brooks County map shows the captain's name on tracts of 324, 306, 267, 213, 160, and 140 acres, all within three miles of one another.
13. Spellman, *Spindletop Boom Days*, 187–88.
14. Sterling, 326–27.
15. Sterling, 328: "A seething mass of humanity moved restlessly on the rough board sidewalks, with frequent fights breaking out among those rowdy men. Any fancied act of hostility such as a slight jostling was ample provocation for a pair to square off and go to it."
16. Hogg to Cullinan, December 19, 1903, Governors Papers.
17. Brooks to Hulen, February 8, 1904, A–G Official Correspondence. Webb, 465: "The sheriff has not asked for Rangers and I don't think he will."
18. Sterling, 328–30: "It was common knowledge that the deputy was taking bribes by the wholesale. The only respect he could command was the fear of his six-shooter."
19. Brooks to Hulen, February 15, 1904, A–G Official Correspondence.

20. Brooks to Hulen, February 20, 1904; Hulen to Brooks, February 24, 1904, A–G Official Correspondence. Webb, 465–66: "There is no record that Captain Brooks called for additional help."
21. Texas Pioneers of Oil Collection, Center for American History, Austin; Spellman, *Spindletop Boom Days*, 193. The collection comprises nearly 200 interviews of eyewitnesses to the Spindletop oil boom, done in the 1950s following the fiftieth anniversary celebration.
22. Ranger Force Co. A, various monthly reports throughout 1904.
23. Brooks to Hulen, February 8, 1904, A–G Official Correspondence.
24. Spellman, *Spindletop Boom Days*, 205–7.
25. Sterling, 330–31.
26. *The Alice Echo*, June 21, 1904. There is a display of one of the mescal bottles at the Heritage Museum's Texas Ranger Room in Falfurrias.
27. Sterling, 295–96. W. W. Sterling provides an entire chapter on Ross Sterling-no relation-in his autobiography: "His native ability, keen intellect and thirst for knowledge, made it possible for him to become a man well versed in business, political and cultural subjects. By dint of copious reading, he compensated for the lack of what is known as formal education."
28. Spellman, 206, from the Pioneers of Oil Collection.
29. Spellman, 207–8.

Chapter Eleven

1. *Biennial Report of the Adjutant General of Texas, 1903–1904*, 155.
2. *The New Handbook of Texas*, s.v. "Minera, Texas."
3. *The New Handbook of Texas*, s.v. "Morris Sheppard."
4. Calendar of the 1904 St. Louis World's Fair and Exposition, *www.worldsfairstlouis.org*. Also see *www.tlaupp.com*.

5. "Geronimo: His Own Story," Chapter 19, *http://odur.let.rug.nl/-usa/B/geronimo.*
6. *The New Handbook of Texas,* s.v. "Humble, Texas"; Spellman, *Spindletop Boom Days,* 208–10.
7. Ranger Force Co. A Monthly Report, January 1905.
8. Ranger Force Co. A Monthly Reports, February through April, 1905.
9. Falfurrias Facts, January 11, 1911.
10. *Biennial Report of the Adjutant General of Texas* 1905–1906, 32.
11. *Biennial Report,* 1905–1906, 30.
12. Company A Muster Rolls 1904, 1905.
13. Ranger Force Co. A Monthly Report, June 1905.
14. *The New Handbook of Texas,* s.v. "Tom Green County"; Ranger Force Co. A Monthly Report, July 1905.
15. *The New Handbook of Texas,* s.v. "San Angelo, Texas."
16. *The New Handbook of Texas,* s.v. "William Thomas Eldridge"; Brooks to Hulen, June 9, 1905, A–G Official Correspondence.
17. Ranger Force Co. A Monthly Report, July 1905.
18. Ranger Service Records, J. A. Brooks, July 10, 1905.
19. Ranger Force Co. A Monthly Report, November 1905.
20. Interview with the Brooks Family, May 2005. "The Place," as they called it over the years, was located eight miles south of Falfurrias in a small rolling valley. Brooks sold off the remaining tracts of land during his years on the bench to mitigate the expenses left unattended by his public servant's paycheck. The family sold the homestead in the 1970s.
21. Ranger Force Co. A, various monthly reports throughout 1906.
22. Company A Muster Rolls, 1906, Ranger Service Records.
23. Weaver, *The Brownsville Raid,* 19; Sterling, 348–52; *The New Handbook of Texas,* s.v. "Brownsville Raid of 1906."
24. *Ector County Democrat,* June 18, 1906; Hulen to Brooks, June 18, 1906; Brooks to Hulen, June 25, 1906, A–G Official Correspondence.

25. Company A Muster Rolls, 1906.
26. Weaver, 34–42, 81–91: When Judge Welch was murdered, Judge Jim Wells sent a telegram to the governor asking for an immediate investigation, with this plea: "'Do not think of sending anyone but Captain Hughes or Captain Brooks. You will understand why it should be either Captain Hughes or Captain Brooks.' Brownsville, in short, wanted nothing to do with Captain McDonald"; Webb, 466–69: "The citizens of Brownsville do not accord to Captain McDonald much credit for his action in the negro riot." See also Ann J. Lane, *The Brownsville Affair: National Crisis and Black Reaction* (Port Washington, New York: Kenni-kat Press, 1971).
27. Dunaway et al. to Hulen, November, 1906 A–G Official Correspondence.
28. Ranger Force Co. A Monthly Report, November 1906; copy of the notes in Brooks Family Papers.

Chapter Twelve

1. Brooks's letter of resignation in the A–G Papers, and a copy in family papers.
2. Hulen to Brooks, November 16, 1906; Webb, 466.
3. *The New Handbook of Texas*, s.v. "John Augustus Hulen." Hulen served as a director at Texas Tech, on the Texas Centennial Commission in 1935–36, and was a delegate to the Democratic national convention in 1932. Besides the Silver Star for bravery during the uprising in the Philippines in 1900, he was awarded three more medals for his efforts in World War I. He retired as a lieutenant general of the army.
4. Sterling, 523: "Imported efficiency experts who know nothing of our traditions endeavor to turn the Rangers into State police," writes Sterling. "They would lose over one hundred years of prestige by scrapping the name of 'Texas Rangers.' Their next step will probably be to streamline the Alamo."

5. Sterling, 332–33.
6. Interview with P. H. Chilton, in Dyer, "The History of Brooks County," 14; Sterling, 332: "Obviously, another county was badly needed, and the citizens of Falfurrias worked toward that end."
7. Lasater, *Falfurrias*, 99.
8. Anders, Boss Rule, 45–47; John E. Clark, 24: "The state attorney can order the Texas Rangers to investigate crimes, but he has no authority to go into a county to prosecute anyone without a specific invitation from the locally elected district attorney. Therefore, a political boss who controls the elected officials in his home county is virtually immune from prosecution under the laws of Texas. So long as he violates no federal laws, he is free to do whatever his political machine is strong enough to let him get away with."
9. Lasater, 101–2. Ed Lasater's son Tom remembered vividly as his father and entourage set out from Falfurrias that day.
10. Lasater, 102; Anders, 47–48.
11. Lasater, 103.
12. Anders, 49. A later report indicated that nothing in the room had been disturbed, the door lock still intact and the windows closed. The coroner's report said that the murderer of Judge Welch had stood over him and shot at close range.
13. Anders, 51.
14. Anders, 53–54. The assault seemed premeditated, as Duffy stood in the shadows of an alley relieving himself at the time he was gunned down.
15. Anders, 58–59: "Brooks participated in the negotiations and agreed to support Lasater's scheme to organize a new county centered at Falfurrias . . . In making his commitment to the formation of Falfurrias County, Brooks acted on his own initiative and misrepresented the intentions of his fellow Democrats." This author finds no substantiation of Brooks being accused of such, but it is

reasonable to assume that local Democrats would not have appreciated the captain's political mate.

16. 31st Texas Legislature, House Journal, March 15, 1909, 1144. Newspaper accounts indicated that Speaker Kennedy had allegedly used taxpayer money to furnish his office beyond the customary style of legislators; also, House Journal, 151. By virtue of this office, of course, Brooks's bill would be directed to his own committee: This did not prove to be as successful as he had hoped.
17. House Journal, 155, 384, 491, 954.
18. *Daily Express* Austin Bureau, February 3, 1909, and *San Antonio Express*, February 4. Apparently this "debate" took place in some Austin forum other than the House floor, but the newspaper accounts do not say where or when; also, Dale Lasater, 113.
19. House Journal, 683–84, 1144.
20. Interview with the Brooks Family, August 2004.
21. 32nd Texas Legislature, Called Session, House Journal, 175. The one special session was held from July 31 to August 29, 1911.
22. Brooks memoir written Dec. 22, 1935, Brooks Family Papers. John Nance Garner served in Congress from 1903 until 1932 when he was elected Vice-President of the United States. He served as party whip, minority floor leader, and was elected Speaker of the House in 1931. Joe Bailey was a U.S. congressman from 1887 to 1901, and served two terms as U.S. senator beginning in 1901, the latter years under various clouds of controversy. See relevant entries in *The New Handbook of Texas*. The citizens' petition is framed on the wall in the Texas Ranger Room of the Heritage Museum in Falfurrias.
23. 32nd Texas Legislature, House Journal, 147, 433–38, 1222, 1251.
24. *Falfurrias Facts*, March 16, 1911.
25. "Brooks County Elected Officials, 1911–1978," 3. There is also information in the *Diamond Jubilee* brochure that was published in Brooks County in 1978. That brochure was dedicated to Judge J. A. Brooks and his son Morgan.

26. Mrs. E. R. Jenson to Gov. Colquitt, August 17, 1911; Adjutant General to Sergeant Levi Davis, August 30, 1911, A–G Official Correspondence. E. R. Jenson, a former "private Ranger" for Captain Richard King, was elected county commissioner. Harris and Sadler, *The Texas Rangers and the Mexican Revolution*,74–75.
27. Anders, 256–66; Hailey, "Founding the Dukedom," 15–22. Glasscock, who moved to Hidalgo County in 1912 and became a voice of reform, ran and apparently won the state senate seat in a heated campaign against Archie Parr in 1918. But the hard work of Parr's chief counsel Marshall Hicks, and the aid of payrolled judges, unveiled apparent corruption in Glasscock's own camp, and an intimidated legislative committee gave the victory to Parr in the end.

Chapter Thirteen

1. "Brooks County Elected Officials, 1911–1978," 4; Florence Schuetz, "A County for Falfurrias," 2–4.
2. See the various articles on the named counties in *The Handbook of Texas*; Montejano, 109–10, 133–40; Anders, 139–46; John E. Clark, 23: "The South Texas formula for successful boss rule was simple and effective: (1) control the election of every local public official; (2) use local government to provide jobs and handouts for your friends and to punish your enemies; (3) help yourself to as much tax money as you wish." Brooks's letter to the state legislature is filed in the records of the 33rd Legislature; Dale Lasater, *Falfurrias: Ed C. Lasater and the Development of South Texas*, 194–95; Anders, *Boss Rule in South Texas*, 179–85.
3. *Falfurrias Facts*, August 1, 1913. The 1932 petition is on the front page, *Brooks County Texan*, July 1, 1932, the voting results in the July 23 edition; also, *Falfurrias Facts*, July 23 and September 2, 1938. Bennett was part of a concentrated faction opposing Lasater on all fronts, and included Frank Rachal, J. R. Scott, Jr., and H. W. Oberwetter. Dale Lasater, 195.

4. Sterling, 316, 333. Billy McBride was foreman of the Encino division of the King Ranch at the time Sterling interviewed him. Writes Sterling: "Some Western historians deny that the old single action Peacemakers were ever fired by 'fanning the hammer.' Captain Brooks used this method repeatedly, and it especially suited his game left hand. He gave me a personal demonstration of how it was done."
5. Lasater, *Falfurrias: Ed C. Lasater and the Development of South Texas,* 132–37, 194–96, 265. Florence Schuetz was invited back to teach the next year by Lasater; in 1922 she was again ousted, this time by a school board dominated by Ku Klux Klan members, a group she, a Catholic, had vigorously opposed. In 1913 Ed Lasater's assets totaled \$3.77 million, \$1.5 million of which were his real estate holdings. Dale Lasater, 272–73.
6. *Falfurrias Facts,* January 28, May 7, October 16, and November 24, 1926
7. *The New Handbook of Texas,* s.v. "Brooks County"; *Falfurrias Facts,* March 29, 1929.
8. Brooks's mother lived on Fayette Park Road when she died, which is today located within the city limits of Lexington. *Brooks County Texan,* March 29, 1929; Brooks Family Papers. The marker over Virginia's grave in the Alice City Cemetery is a large gray, rough-hewn stone with only her name etched at an angle across the front. It is located in the back portion of the cemetery.
9. "Brooks County Elected Officials," 8; Brooks Family Papers, including the invitation and tickets to the two inaugural events. "The Lone Ranger" radio series began its remarkable run in 1933, eighteen years after-and not related to-Brooks's drawing.
10. Pioneer Edition, *Falfurrias Facts,* June 15, 1934.
11. Brooks Family Papers; "Brooks County Elected Officials, 1911–1978," 10–21.
12. Lake Newell Porter, Brooks County sheriff from 1919 to 1922, "fiddled" (unknowingly) over the years with a rare Stradivarius

violin he had picked up on the cattle trail back in 1873. A Jewish family from Europe had been massacred by Indians, and Porter was one of the first cowboys to arrive at the tragic scene. It wasn't until after his own death years later that the violin was identified. *Corpus Christi Caller Times*, December 1, 1938.

13. *Falfurrias Facts*, February 10, 1939, also printed in the *Dallas Morning News*, February 9, 1939. The Brooks family indicated that President Lyndon B. Johnson recognized the longevity of the two Brooks judges in Texas some years later in a letter, since lost, written to John Morgan Brooks.
14. "Resolution of Gratitude," Brooks County Commissioners Court Records, Falfurrias. The original resolution is in the Brooks Family Papers.
15. Robert Lee Bobbitt to J. A. Brooks, Feb. 12, 1939, Brooks Family Papers.
16. Handwritten will and testament of J. A. Brooks, October 9, 1939, in the Brooks Family Papers.
17. The death certificate signed by Dr. C. H. Otken indicates that Brooks died of "acute cardiac dilation" as a result of "nephritis chronic servility": The captain died of heart and kidney failure. Robert Lee Bobbitt to Judge John Morgan Brooks, Jan. 17, 1944; Lon A. Smith to Judge John Morgan Brooks, Jan. 25, 1944, Brooks Family Papers; Sterling, 333.

BIBLIOGRAPHY

The official records of the Texas Rangers are housed primarily among the Papers of the Adjutant General of Texas in the Texas State Archives in Austin. These include the monthly returns filed by the company commanders of the Frontier Battalion (through 1901), the reports and files from the Ranger Force (after 1901), the correspondence files of the Adjutant General, and the files that include company Muster Rolls and individual Ranger Service Records. Also included are the annual and biennial reports of the Adjutant General to the Governor, 1890–1908. Other primary sources for this biography include:

Brooks Family Papers, including the unpublished memoirs of J. A. Brooks, and various correspondence, newspaper clippings, and photographs, in possession of Mrs. Beverly Brewton of Pasadena, Texas, granddaughter of Captain Brooks.

Brooks County Clerk's office files, Courthouse, Falfurrias, Texas.

Brooks County Heritage Museum Collection, Texas Ranger Room, Falfurrias, Texas.

Census Records of the United States for Bourbon County, Kentucky (1850, 1860, 1870) and various counties of Texas (1870, 1880, 1890, and 1900).

Collin County, Texas, Tax Rolls, 1878, County Clerk's Office, Plano.

Estates Settled Book G, Dower and Division Records, Reference #2694, Bourbon County Courthouse, Paris, Kentucky.

Gammel, H. P. N. (ed). *The Laws of Texas, 1897–1902.* Vol. XI. Austin: Gammel Book Company, 1902.

Government Documents: "Proceedings of the 31st Texas Legislature (1909–1910) and its called sessions, House and Senate Journals;" "Proceedings of the 32nd Texas Legislature (1911) and its called session, House and Senate Journals."

Governor of Texas Papers: John Ireland (1883–1887); L. S. Ross (1887–1891); James S. Hogg (1891–1895); Charles A. Culberson (1895–1899); Joseph D. Sayers (1899–1903); S. W. T. Lanham (1903–1907); Thomas M. Campbell (1907–1911); and Oscar B. Colquitt (1911–1915), Texas State Archives, Austin.

National Archives and Records Administration, Ft. Worth: Records of the Western Arkansas District Court, 1887, Files #15, 112, and T16; and NARA in College Park, Maryland: Records of the office of the pardon attorney and its predecessors, 1887, Record Group 60, File K-713, Box 199.

Newspaper accounts from the *Alice Echo, Chickasaw Daily Express, Corpus Christi Caller Times, Brooks County Texan, Ector County Democrat, Falfurrias Facts, Galveston Daily News, San Antonio Daily Express,* and *Uvalde Leader News.*

Tabor, George R. "Biennial Report of the State Health Officer of Texas to the Governor, from November 1, 1900, to August 31, 1902." Papers of Texas Governor Joseph D. Sayers.

Vertical Files, J. A. Brooks, Texas Rangers Hall of Fame and Museum, Waco.

Published Primary Sources

Aten, Ira. *Six and One-Half Years in the Ranger Service: The Memoirs of Sergeant Ira Aten, Company D, Texas Rangers.* Bandera: Frontier Times, 1945.

Davis, Charles Belmont, ed., *Adventures and Letters of Richard Harding Davis,* New York: Scribner's, 1917.

Davis, Richard Harding. *The West From a Car-Window.* New York: Harper, 1892.

Lasater, Dale. *Falfurrias: Ed C. Lasater and the Development of South Texas.* College Station: Texas A & M Press, 1985.

These next two writers knew Captain Brooks personally, interviewed him for their research, and considered themselves friends of his:

Sterling, William Warren. *Trails and Trials of a Texas Ranger.* Norman: University of Oklahoma Press, 1959.

Webb, Walter Prescott. *The Texas Rangers: A Century of Frontier Defense.* Austin: University of Texas Press, 1935.

Secondary Sources

Adair, W. S. "Rangers 40 years Ago Had No Easy Life." *Frontier Times* 4 (1927): 41–43.

Adams, Paul. "The Unsolved Murder of Ben Thompson." *Southwestern Historical Quarterly* 48 (1945): 321–29.

Amberson, Mary Margaret McAllen, James A. McAllen and Margaret H. McAllen. *I Would Rather Sleep in Texas: A History of the Lower Rio Grande Valley and the People of the Santa Anita Land Grant.* Austin: Texas State Historical Association, 2003.

Anders, Evan. *Boss Rule in South Texas: The Progressive Era.* Austin: University of Texas Press, 1982.

Audry, Mrs. William Breckenridge. "Early Bourbon Families." *Kentuckian Citizen,* June 20, 1944.

Baker, Catherine G. "The Man of the Hour." *The Junior Historian* 26:1 (September, 1965): 13–16, 27–29.

Biographical Souvenir of the State of Texas. Chicago: F. A. Battey & Company, 1889.

Brooks County Historical Commission. *Brooks County Elected Officials, 1911–1978.* Falfurrias, 1979.

Casdorph, Paul. *A History of the Republican Party in Texas, 1865–1965.* Austin: Pemberton Press, 1965.

Casto, Stanley D. *Settlement of the Cibolo-Nueces Strip: A Partial History of La Salle County.* Hillsboro: Hill Junior College Press, 1969.

Clark, John E. *The Fall of the Duke of Duval.* Austin: Eakin Press, 1995.

Clarke, Mary Whatley. *A Century of Cow Business: A History of the Texas and Southwestern Cattle Raisers Association.* Ft. Worth: Evans Press, 1976.

Coerver, Don, and Linda Hall. *Texas and the Mexican Revolution: A Study in State and National Border Policy, 1910–1920.* San Antonio: Trinity University Press, 1984.

Colorado County, Texas, Historical Commission. *Colorado County Chronicles, From the beginning to 1923.* 2 vols. Columbus, Texas: County Historical Commission, nd.

Combs, Joe F. *Gunsmoke in the Redlands.* San Antonio: Naylor Company, 1968.

Cox, Mike. *Texas Ranger Tales II.* Plano: Republic of Texas Press, 1999.

Cuthbertson, Gilbert M. "Catarino E. Garza and the Garza War." *Texana* 12 (1976): 335–48.

Daniell, L. E. *Texas: The Country and Its Men.* Austin: np, 1916.

Davis, Ellis, and Edwin Grobe, eds. *The New Encyclopedia of Texas.* Dallas: Texas Development Bureau, 1930.

Debo, Angie. *Geronimo.* Norman: University of Oklahoma Press, 1976.

De Leon, Arnoldo. *They Call Them Greasers: Anglo Attitudes Toward Mexicans in Texas, 1821–1900.* Austin: University of Texas Press, 1983.

Dyer, Lloyd. "History of Brooks County." Masters thesis, Texas A & I University, 1938.

Fisher, O. C. and J. C. Dykes. "The Life and Times of King Fisher." *Southwestern Historical Quarterly* 61 (1961): 232–47.

———. *King Fisher, His Life and Times.* Norman: University of Oklahoma Press, 1966.

Fulmore, Z. T. *The History and Geography of Texas (as seen through its counties and towns).* Austin: E. L. Steck Company, 1915.

Gard, Wayne. "The Fence-Cutters." *Southwestern Historical Quarterly* 51 (1947): 1–15.

Hailey, James L. "Founding the Dukedom: The 1918 Election of Archie Parr." *The Journal of South Texas* 2:1 (Spring, 1989): 13–27.

Hall, Roy F., and Helen Gibbard Hall. *Collin County: Pioneering in North Texas.* Quanah: Nortex Press, 1975.

Halsell, H. H. *Cowboys and Cattleland: Memories of a Frontier Cowboy.* Ft. Worth: Texas Christian University Press, 1983.

Hardin, Stephen. *The Texas Rangers.* London: Osprey Press, 1991.

Harris, Charles H. III, and Louis R. Sadler, *The Texas Rangers and the Mexican Revolution: The Bloodiest Decade, 1910–1920.* Albuquerque: University of New Mexico Press, 2004.

Havins, T. R. *Something About Brown: A History of Brooks County.* Brownwood: Banner Press, 1958.

Henry, O. *Heart of the West.* Montreal: Readers Digest Association, 1993.

"Historical Scrapbook, 175th Anniversary of Bourbon County, Kentucky." Brochure. Paris, Kentucky: np, 1961.

Holden, W. C. "Law and Lawlessness on the Texas Frontier, 1875–1900." *Southwestern Historical Quarterly* 44 (1940): 199–200.

Holt, Roy D. "The Introduction of Barbed Wire into Texas and the Fence Cutting War." *West Texas Historical Association Yearbook* 6 (1930): 72–88.

Horgan, Paul. *Great River: The Rio Grande in North American History.* New York: Rhinehart, 1954.

Hutchinson, Jack T. *Bluegrass and Mountain Laurel: The Story of Kentucky in the Civil War.* Cincinnati: Civil War Round Table, 2000.

Kerr County (Texas) Album. Kerr County Historical Commission, 1986.

Kildare, Maurice. "The Rangers Got Their Man; Gregorio Cortez." *The New Mexico Lawman* 4 (1978): 6–15.

King, W. H. "The Texas Ranger Service and History of the Rangers, with Observations on their Value as a Police Protection." In *A Comprehensive History of Texas, 1685 to 1897*, edited by Dudley G. Wooten, 2 vols. Dallas: Scharff Company: 329–67.

Knight, Oliver. *Ft. Worth: Outpost on the Trinity*. Norman: University of Oklahoma Press, 1953.

Langsam, Walter and William G. Johnson. *Historic Architecture of Bourbon County, Kentucky*. Paris: Kentucky Heritage Council, n.d.

Lea, Tom. *The King Ranch*. 2 vols. Boston: Little, Brown Company, 1957.

Lott, Virgil, and Mercurio Martinez. *The Kingdom of Zapata*. San Antonio: Naylor Company, 1953.

Ludeman, Annette M. *La Salle County*. Quanah: Nortex Press, 1975.

Lynch, Dudley. *The Duke of Duval: The Life and Times of George B. Parr*. Waco: Texian Press, 1976.

Martin, Jack. *Border Boss: Captain John R. Hughes, Texas Ranger*. San Antonio: Naylor, 1942.

McCallum, Henry D. "Barbed Wire in Texas." *Southwestern Historical Quarterly* 61 (1957): 207–19.

McCallum, Henry D., and Frances T. McCallum. *The Wire That Fenced the West*. Norman: University of Oklahoma Press, 1965.

McDaniel, Robert C. *Sabine County, Texas: The First 150 Years, 1836–1986*. Waco, Texas: Texian Press, 1987.

McMinus, J. *Kerr County, Texas, Marriage Records*, 1856–1956. Austin: Ingmire Press, 1985.

Mertz, Richard J. "'No One Can Arrest Me': The Story of Gregorio Cortez." *Journal of South Texas* 1 (1974): 1–17.

Miletich, Leo. *Dan Stuart's Fistic Carnival*. College Station: Texas A & M University Press, 1994.

Million, Elmer M. "History of the Texas Prize Fight Statute." *Texas Law Review* 17 (1939): 152–59.

Montejano, David. *Anglos and Mexicans in the Making of Texas, 1836–1986.* Austin: University of Texas Press, 1987.

The New Handbook of Texas. 6 vols. Austin: Texas State Historical Association, 1995.

Paine, Albert Bigelow. *Captain Bill McDonald, Texas Ranger: A Story of Frontier Reform.* New York: Little & Ives, 1909.

Paredes, Americo. *"With His Pistol in His Hand": A Border Ballad and Its Hero.* Austin: University of Texas Press, 1958.

Parsons, Chuck, and Gary P. Fitterer. *Captain C. B. McKinney, The Law In South Texas.* Wolfe City, Texas: Henington Press, 1993.

Perrin, William Henry. *History of Bourbon, Scott, Harrison and Nicholas County, Kentucky.* 3 vols. Chicago: O. L. Baskin & Company, 1882.

Pierce, Frank Cushman. *A Brief History of the Lower Rio Grande Valley.* Menasha, Wisconsin: n.p., 1917.

Pitts, Alice, and Minnie P. Champ. *Collin County, Texas, Families.* Santa Maria, California: Janaway Books, 1994.

Pollard, Neva V. "History of Jim Wells County." Masters thesis, Texas A & I University, Kingsville, 1945.

Procter, Ben. *Just One Riot; Episodes of the Texas Rangers in the 20th Century.* Austin: Eakin Press, 1991.

Raymond, Dora N. *Captain Lee Hall of Texas.* Norman: University of Oklahoma Press, 1940.

Reese, Walter, and Lillian Reese. *Flaming Feuds of Colorado County.* Salado: Anson Jones Press, 1962.

Roberts, Randy. "Galveston's Jack Johnson." *Southwestern Historical Quarterly* 87 (1983): 37–56.

Robinson, Charles M. III. *The Men Who Wear the Star: The Story of the Texas Rangers.* New York: Random House, 2000.

Roy, Janet. "The Life and Times of Minera, Texas." *Southwestern Historical Quarterly* 49 (1946): 510–17.

Samora, Julian, Joe Bernal and Albert Pena. *Gunpowder Justice: A Reassessment of the Texas Rangers.* Notre Dame: University of Notre Dame Press, 1979.

Schuetz, Florence. "A County for Falfurrias." *Brooks County Diamond Jubilee, 1911–1978,* 1–4. Brooks County Historical Commission, 1978.

Smith, Thomas T. *The Old Army in Texas: A Research Guide to the U. S. Army in Nineteenth-Century Texas.* Austin: Texas State Historical Association, 2000.

Sonnichsen, C. L. *I'll Die Before I Run: The Story of the Great Feuds of Texas.* New York: Devon Adair, 1962.

Spellman, Paul N. *Captain John H. Rogers, Texas Ranger.* Denton: University of North Texas Press, 2003.

———. *Spindletop Boom Days.* College Station: Texas A&M University Press, 2001.

Stambaugh, J. Lee, and Lillian J. *The Lower Rio Grande Valley of Texa*s. San Antonio: Naylor Company, 1954.

———. *A History of Collin County, Texas.* Austin: Texas State Historical Association, 1958.

Terrell, C. V. *The Terrells: 85 Years–Texas From Indians to Atomic Bombs.* Austin: np, 1948.

Tise, Sammy. *Texas County Sheriffs.* Albuquerque: Oakwood Printing, 1989.

Toole, Blanche. *Sabine County (Texas) Marriages, 1875–1900.* St. Louis: Ingmire Press, 1983.

Utley, Robert M. *Lone Star Justice: The First Century of the Texas Rangers.* New York: Oxford University Press, 2002.

Watkins, Clara. *Kerr County, Texas, 1856–1956.* Kerrville: Hill Country Press, 1975.

Weaver, John D. *The Brownsville Raid.* New York: W. W. Norton, 1970.

Weiss, Harold J. Jr. "The Texas Rangers Revisited: Old Themes and New Viewpoints." *Southwestern Historical Quarterly* 97 (1994): 621–40.

———. "Yours to Command: Captain William J. 'Bill' McDonald and the Panhandle Rangers of Texas." PhD dissertation, Indiana University, 1980.

Wilcox, Seb. "The Laredo City Election and Riot of April, 1886." *Southwestern Historical Quarterly* 45 (1941): 1–23.

Wilkins, Frederick. *The Law Comes to Texas: The Texas Rangers, 1870–1901.* Austin: State House Press, 1999.

Witt, Gerald. *The History of Eastern Kerr County.* Austin: Nortex Press, 1986.

Woolford, Sam, ed. "The Burr G. Duval Diary." *Southwestern Historical Quarterly* 65 (1962): 487–511.

Young, Elliott. *Catarino Garza's Revolution on the Texas-Mexico Border.* Chapel Hill: Duke University Press, 2004.

Index

D

N

O

S

Y

Z